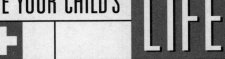

HOW TO SAVE YOUR CHILD'S LIFE

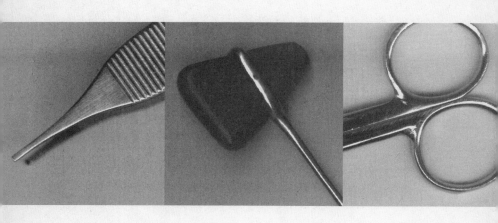

ST. MARTIN'S GRIFFIN ≈ NEW YORK

HOW TO SAVE YOUR CHILD'S LIFE

WHAT TO DO AFTER YOU CALL 911

DEBRA A. BRADY, EMT-P

Foreword by **WILLIAM ZAJDEL, D.O., FACOEP**

Illustrations by **JUDITH PRAY**

www.stmartins.com

BOOK DESIGN BY JUDITH STAGNITTO ABBATE/ABBATE DESIGN

Library of Congress Cataloging-in-Publication Data

Brady, Debra A.
    How to save your child's life : after you call 911 / Debra A. Brady ;
    illustrations by Judith Pray.—1st ed.
          p. cm.
       Includes bibliographical references (page 251) and index (page 261).
       ISBN 0-312-28176-5
  1. Pediatric emergencies. 2. Children's accidents—Prevention. 3. Traffic
  safety and children. 4. School accidents—Prevention. 5. Home
  accidents—Prevention. I. Title.

  RJ370 .B735 2003
  618.92'0025—dc21

                                                          2002036886

First Edition: March 2003

10 9 8 7 6 5 4 3 2 1

FOR LARRY

CONTENTS

ACKNOWLEDGMENTS

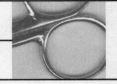

Thanks go to my editor, Heather Jackson-Silverman, for her expertise, her perspective as a parent, her insight as a writer, and for standing by a bereaved mom during the worst of times. Without her courage, without her encouragement, and without her stubborn refusal to give up on me, this book would never have happened. Thanks to Dr. William Zajdel for demanding excellence from all of us who work with him and for him. Thanks to the veteran paramedics who taught me the skills necessary to save a child's life and gave me the courage to perform those skills under the most horrific stress imaginable. Thanks, finally, to my husband—for his love and support and faith through everything.

FOREWORD

A s I read this book, written by a talented paramedic, I asked myself why she had gone to such extraordinary measures to tell parents what we already know. Every caring parent realizes how quickly an accident can happen. Every loving caregiver realizes how precious and vulnerable are our children. Why, then, I asked myself, had she taken so much time and effort to emphasize again the dangers, the perils, the potential for heartache? And then I remembered that not all fathers are physicians. Not all mothers know pediatric cardiopulmonary resuscitation and advanced first aid. Not all baby-sitters understand the risk of a lack of supervision that, even for a brief moment, can result in tragedy.

I am not just an emergency physician at a level-one trauma center. I am not just the husband of an experienced nurse. I am more than a medical command physician. When Deb called in medical command reports from her ambulance I was frequently the physician on the other end of the radio. I learned to trust her judgment. I learned to read the level of anxiety in her voice. I learned that if she claimed she was treating a critical pediatric patient, she was working hard to save a child's life and to prepare for her arrival—with her little patient—with every tool and resource available.

But while working with this author, I also became the proud father of two exceptionally beautiful daughters. My wife and I know firsthand about the dangers Deb describes and about the prevention techniques and first-aid skills to keep our daughters safe. It dawned on me only as I read this book that not all parents have this knowledge or these skills. I realized that not all parents know that if children bounce unsupervised on a backyard trampoline they are likely to break a bone, a spine, or fracture a skull. I realized that not all parents know when a sudden illness requires emergency intervention. And I realized, with regret, that the health-care industry has only begun to emphasize the importance of training in how to clear a choking child's airway, to perform rescue breathing, and to stop external bleeding.

I believe Deb has done an outstanding job of educating parents about the dangers and perils of raising a child and an excellent job of describing first-aid techniques that can save a child's life. I believe she has worked hard to share her skills as a prehospital emergency medical provider and to describe how to respond to an emergency. And she has been diligent and comprehensive in offering accident and illness prevention information.

What, then, of risk? Is risk not advantageous? If we restrain our children from every risk, do we not inhibit their development? Shall I stand on the stairway at each attempt and cry to my toddler, "Stop! You could be injured!" Shall I stop my daughters from trying new skills from attempting new endeavors? If I could, I would not shelter my little girls from all possible risk. I do not want to stop them from enjoying the triumph of mastering a new skill or the pain of defining a new limit.

Children need and want excitement and adventure. They deserve an opportunity to learn about the world in which they live in a care-free environment. Parents are not obligated to stifle children, to harness or restrain. Yet, every day, we *are* obligated to make judgment calls about a child's level of skill and ability, and about an appropriate level of supervision. The best way to make these judgments is with the assistance of experts. If we rely entirely on our own experience, we offer our children less than the best. There simply was not the volume of information available when we were children that exists today. We must constantly seek updates on issues like safety standards, first aid, and risk prevention.

Most of the skills Deb offers in this book include tired, old stuff from a doctor's perspective. Pediatric CPR, the Heimlich maneuver, and direct pressure to stop the bleeding seem stale. As a medical professional I say, "Yes? So?" But then I remember that most young parents have never attempted to resuscitate a dying child. Too many young parents do not realize that an appropriately sized and secured child safety seat can save their child's life in an accident. Many new parents may not realize how fast an accident can occur or how innocent their children can be when it happens. And many do not know what to do until help arrives.

I found myself reading these chapters and reviewing the proper steps in Pediatric Advanced Life Support and Advanced Pediatric Life Support, excellent practice classes for medical providers. And the more I reviewed the appropriate steps from a physician's perspective, the more I appreciated this caring paramedic's attempt to share these skills with nonmedical parents and caregivers. Read. Practice. Learn. Protect. Love.

—WILLIAM ZAJDEL, D.O., FACOEP
Attending Physician
Department of Emergency Medicine
Lehigh Valley Hospital Center

PROLOGUE:
ALICE STILL LIVES HERE

 *It was an otherwise idyllic summer afternoon. A warm breeze tempered the sun's heat and offered up the aromas of flowering plants, barbecues, and freshly cut grass. Children were everywhere, kicking balls, riding bikes, and playing. At Alice's house on this quiet street, Mom was in the kitchen preparing for a late afternoon barbecue. Dad was mowing the lawn. Five-year-old Alice had tired of her bicycle and opted for the swing set. She hadn't bothered to remove her new bicycle helmet. Why should she? And who would think it necessary to ask a child to remove a piece of protective equipment?*

But Alice wasn't interested in just swinging. She was testing her developing agility and climbing on the apparatus. When she slipped, her helmet caught on a piece of the swing set, and she hung by her neck. Mom was still in the kitchen. Dad was still mowing. We do not know how much time elapsed before Dad glanced up and noticed his little daughter's dangling, apparently lifeless body.

When a child is in danger, a unique set of skills is required, and a similarly unique plethora of obstacles are thrown in our way. It is almost impossible to remain clearheaded, calm, and logical when a little one you love can't breathe, or they are bleeding, or they won't wake up. Some, most of them well-intentioned and caring, add to the dilemma by reacting hysterically. Others freeze and cannot speak, much less make a decision or take action. Oddly, the same adrenaline rush we have all experienced causes both extremes, as the well-known "fight or flight" reaction erupts in our bodies.

Alice's dad was an exception to this rule. He yelled for Mom to call 911 and gently lifted his daughter to the ground. He then carefully removed her helmet and began mouth-to-mouth resuscitation. At this time Alice was unresponsive and blue. While there are numerous caveats and rules about removing protective helmets—the simple action of removing a helmet can cause irreversible damage from a fractured cervical spine—he had no choice. Alice was not breathing.

By the time I arrived in my ambulance, Alice was still lying on the ground but awake and breathing on her own. While Mom and Dad were relieved by this improvement, I was enormously concerned and knew the trauma could still be life threatening. An ugly abrasion traversed the front of her neck. Broken capillaries spread tiny red starbursts called petechiae across her cheeks and the bridge of her nose. We took care to ensure that Alice's airway was open, fully immobilized her to protect her spine, and placed an oxygen mask over her mouth and nose. We then loaded her into the ambulance for transport to a trauma center.

It is not always advisable for a parent to accompany a child in the back of an ambulance. When Alice's mom followed me into the truck, I decided to allow her to stay. As I assessed Alice, Mom held her hand and spoke calmly and soothingly to her daughter. I was concerned that Alice's neck could be broken, that her airway would swell shut, that the back pressure of blood may have caused bleeding into her brain, that there could be significant damage to her trachea, esophagus, or the blood vessels, nerve bundles, and other organs in her neck. I also checked for signs of other injuries, in case she had slammed into the metal swing set when she fell. I reported my findings to an emergency physician at the hospital by radio and prepared to start an intravenous line (IV) on Alice as a precaution.

In order to accomplish this, Mom had to sit on the floor next to her daughter's head while I moved around at Alice's side. I explained to both Alice and Mom what I was about to do and that it would sting a little. Obtaining IV access in a small child in a moving ambulance is never easy.

It wasn't until I had successfully started the IV and secured the line that I realized something unusual was happening and looked up to witness a scene that will stay with me forever.

Alice and her mom were staring deeply into each other's eyes. And they were singing. It was a silly child's song about a school bus. Alice was only able to whisper along. Mom's quiet voice was clear and lilting. This child had just suffered a major trauma, was immobilized and restrained—trapped from a child's perspective—with a strange-smelling mask on her face. She was in a huge moving vehicle with scary-looking equipment all around her. Sirens were screaming in the background, and a stranger was sticking a needle into her arm. Her lips were forming the words along with her mother as though nothing else on earth existed. In her reality, nothing else did.

I could try to use words to describe what I saw and felt between mother and daughter that day. Love. Faith. Trust. But they are inadequate. No words I have ever learned can approximate the strength of that bond revealed or the courage of that mom.

As parents, it is necessary for us to know more than pediatric first aid. While it is critical that we take the time to learn pediatric CPR and the ABCs of emergency medicine, it is equally important to battle the effects of adrenaline at the scene of an emergency and to give our children the means of coping by setting an example.

The most horrifying part of any emergency involving a child is the unknown. What should you do first? When should you call 911? How long will it take for rescuers to arrive? What should you do while you wait? What will happen when emergency personnel take over? What will happen to your child in the back of the ambulance? What will happen to them in the emergency department at the hospital? How can you best help these emergency medical providers care for your child?

This book, written by a paramedic, is intended to remove some of those unknowns. It is written for anyone who loves and cares for a child and offers realistic expectations from your local Emergency Medical Services (EMS). It also offers sound first-aid advice.

But this is *not* a first-aid primer. There is absolutely no substitute for training from an accredited institution, especially when a child is not breathing. Take an American Heart Association or American Red Cross class on pediatric CPR (Cardiopulmonary Resuscitation). While it is preferable to have these skills before your child is born, it is never too late to learn. Such a classroom environment will give you the hands-on training, experience, and confidence you will need to effectively handle a life-threatening pediatric emergency.

No amount of training is too much. Tragically, at times, no amount of training is enough. Children die every day in a variety of ways. In 1996, over 2.3 million people died in the United States. Over 1.7 million were over the age of sixty-five, dying primarily from heart disease and cancer. But 3,050 babies died from sudden infant death syndrome (SIDS). Over 5,500 children ages one through fifteen were killed in accidents. Over 400 children under the age of four were murdered. Homicide and suicide took the lives of almost 12,000 between the ages of five and twenty-four. In 1966, injuries were the leading cause of death of all Americans ages one through thirty-seven.[1] Over thirty years later, injuries remain the leading cause of death for all of our children.[2]

The death statistics are tragic. The injury statistics are horrifying. According to the National Health Interview Survey conducted by the U.S. Public Health Service in 1994, almost 20 million children under the age of eighteen sustained injuries that required medical attention. Over 6 million of those injuries occurred in the home. In 1997, almost 83,000 injuries occurred on backyard trampolines![3]

It does not matter if you are a doctor, a pediatric intensive care nurse, or an engineer who faints at the site of blood. It does not matter if you never graduated from high school or have multiple Ph.D.s. It does not matter if this is your first child or you have a dozen. When your child is in trouble, struggling to breathe or bleeding, you will still benefit from the information in this book. This is an effort to provide you with a sense of what will happen *after* you call 911. The only true cure for a sick or injured child is prevention. But once a tragedy begins to unfold, you will be best equipped to handle the situation if you know what to expect.

PART

EMERGENCY BASICS

ONE

PREPARING FOR AN EMERGENCY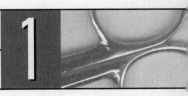

1

- ✚ **What Are Your Options?**
- ✚ **A Medical Home Versus the Hospital Emergency Department**
- ✚ **Doctors and Hospitals**
- ✚ **Insurance Coverage**

✚ *At four o'clock on a Saturday morning, my partner and I are dispatched to help a toddler having trouble breathing. We find an anxious mom holding a two year old in her arms. The child, she explains, was seen by a pediatrician Friday afternoon, diagnosed with a respiratory infection, and sent home with prescriptions for an antibiotic and a decongestant. Mom had the prescriptions filled and has given the child appropriate doses of the medications, but the child is no better. She tried to contact the doctor, but was told by his answering service that he would not call her back until after 9:00 A.M. The mom begins to cry.*

As I assess the child, I ask the mother, "Why did you call for help now?" This question is not intended to challenge the mom's decision to call 911 or her assertion that the child needs emergent care. I have never seen this child before. I have no idea how serious the illness was when the physician evaluated the child twelve hours earlier. I need to understand what has changed. What is different now? The mom explains that she can no longer wake the child easily. Instead of working hard to breathe and wheezing with each breath, the babe now seems exhausted, his color is worse, and he is making a grunting noise.

This situation represented a true emergency. This child was deteriorating from respiratory distress to respiratory failure. Without supplemental oxygen and intensive support, this child may have died. While the mom knew this intuitively, she had difficulty being specific. Fortunately, we had sufficient training in pediatric emergency care to recognize the impending failure and were able to take prompt, appropriate action to stabilize the child while transporting him to the hospital.

Oftentimes the need for an ambulance is obvious. A car crashes into a tree. A child falls from a roof and is unconscious. A power tool accidentally slips. No special training is necessary to recognize the need for emergency assistance. But the decision to call for help is not always so easy to make. When your child comes in crying and holding an arm or limping after a fall, do you need an ambulance? Does that bump on the head represent a possible concussion? Is that cut bad enough to need stitches? Your child has suffered from vomiting and diarrhea for two days. But now, in the middle of the night, his fever has suddenly risen, his lips are dry and caked, his eyes are sunken, and he pushes you away. Should you call the pediatrician first? Should you just drive your child to the emergency room yourself?

Once we accept the possibility that an accident or acute illness may happen, there are actions we can take to prepare for any emergency. Planning to cope when things go wrong is not tempting fate. Preparing for the worst is not the same as wishing for the worst. If we trust our instincts and remember that nobody knows our children as we do, we can be our children's champions and greatest advocates. We are the leading experts on our children; we will be the first to know when something is not right. But knowing help is needed is only the first step; knowing how and where to go for that help requires planning and preparation.

WHAT ARE YOUR OPTIONS?

When you realize you need help, you will be in the best position to make sound decisions if you fully understand your options. You need to be familiar, not just with your doctor's strengths and areas of expertise, but with his limitations as well. The middle of the night is not the time to learn that your doctor is not available outside of normal office hours. Similarly, you need to be aware of the capabilities and limitations of local Emergency Medical Services (EMS). And you need to know about restrictions to your medical insurance coverage, which will allow you to make choices promptly, without wasting precious time on bureaucratic detail. Only by planning ahead can you prevent an emergency from becoming a tragedy.

Handling an emergency well requires dialogue with your child's doctor. Continuity of care, having a physician who knows your child, his history, and his idiosyncrasies is optimal for care in an emergency, but it is not always possible or appropriate. Circumstances sometimes warrant care somewhere other than your doctor's office. But the conversation necessary to determine what those circumstances are can be difficult. We can hardly enter the doctor's office with a six-page list of all possible childhood emergencies and make notes about each one. This conversation must therefore be general in nature and specific only when dealing with a new illness or injury.

A recent survey of pediatricians in one state documented significant limitations in both training and on-scene equipment necessary to deal with a life-threatening pediatric emergency in office settings. Less than three-quarters of the pediatricians surveyed were trained in Pediatric Advanced Life Support (PALS), and less than half of the support staff in their offices knew how to perform pediatric CPR.[1] Should this surprise us? Not really. One estimate of the frequency of serious medical emergencies in a pediatric office setting was less than once per office per year.[2] Office care is often very different from emergency hospital care. Evaluation of earaches and sore throats, tummy aches and sprained ankles is a huge departure from making the split-second decisions and performing the invasive skills necessary to resuscitate a dying child. While physicians may have the experience and skill, they may not have the necessary equipment and medications sitting around in their offices.

Should this concern us? Probably. While the frequency with which office-based physicians deal with life-threatening emergencies is low, the nature of those emergencies requires preparation and preparedness. In a survey of 119 primary care physicians studied by researchers at the University of Rochester, children were brought to the doctors' offices suffering from epiglottitis, asthma, foreign body airway obstruction, severe dehydration, suspected meningitis, and active seizures.[3] All of these illnesses can threaten a child's life; all require not just medical training but adequate equipment and supplies.

- True emergencies are not always obvious.
- Planning and preparation are important.
- Is your child's doctor prepared for an office emergency?

A MEDICAL HOME VERSUS THE EMERGENCY DEPARTMENT

According to the American Academy of Pediatrics (AAP), each child in America should have a "medical home."[4] This may be a single pediatrician (a doctor who specializes in the care of children), a pediatric group, a family physician, a general practitioner, or even a clinic where your child is seen regularly. This is where your child's complete medical records can be found easily and quickly. This is where your child will receive appropriate immunizations, screenings, growth and development assessments, and regular medical care. It is where most of your child's illnesses and minor injuries will be diagnosed and treated, and where a decision and referral may be made for your child to be seen by a pediatric specialist when necessary. Hopefully, your child will never see the inside of a hospital emergency department.

Emergency departments, like Emergency Medical Services (EMS), were created to care for people with acute illness or injury. The emergency department, like EMS, is open around the clock, all day, every day. Most primary care physicians, including pediatricians, are not available all of the time. In addition, emergency departments are required by law to provide care regardless of a patient's ability to pay for that service. They cannot turn you away. Americans make over 95 million visits to hospital emergency departments each year. In a study published by *The Journal of the American Medical Association (JAMA)* patients seen in fifty-six different emergency departments nationwide during a single, twenty-four-hour period were evaluated:[5]

- Twenty-one percent arrived by ambulance.
- Twenty-four percent were children.
- Forty-nine percent had nonurgent conditions more appropriately treated in a doctor's office
- Of those with nonurgent conditions, many could not afford care elsewhere, but half denied that their reasons for going to the emergency department were financial. Most claimed they could not see a primary care physician during office hours due to job or school responsibilities, sibling care issues, or lack of transportation.

Unfortunately, for millions of children across the country, the emergency department has become their medical home. For a variety of reasons, some involving money and lack of insurance, many of them involving the convenience of the parents, children are brought to the hospital emergency department for nonemergency care. They are evaluated for earaches and sinus infections, for stomachaches and fevers and bruises that could and should appropriately be handled in an office setting. Care in the emergency department is expensive. One news article suggested that American families using the emergency department in this manner represent excess health-care spending of approximately $7 billion each year.[6] Unfortunately, emergency medical services are similarly misused and abused, with patients citing lack of alternative transportation as a common reason for calling 911.

Using the emergency department for routine care is not the best that we can give our children. Continuity of care is important. According to several studies, children who are seen regularly by a primary care physician have lower rates of hospitalization, surgery, and illness. This is illustrated nowhere as clearly or as sadly as within a population of homeless children in New York. Children appear regularly and frequently in hospital emergency departments suffering from asthma. In EMS, these children are referred to as "frequent flyers." Just over 6 percent of children nationwide have asthma (a scary number and one that is growing annually). But this subset of children in New York, without insurance, without regular roofs over their heads, and with no single doctor or clinic directing their care had an asthma rate of 38 percent![7]

UNDERSTANDING ASTHMA

Asthma can be controlled, and asthma deaths can be prevented. With appropriate, consistent treatment these children do not have to suffer and die. Without that appropriate, consistent treatment even those who do not die can develop chronic lung disease that may be disabling throughout their lives. As these children are dragged from emergency room to emergency room, the time and resources to initiate proper family-centered care are not available. Less than half of these little ones with asthma found in New York had a written treatment plan. While many had inhalers and nebulizers to administer bronchodilators during acute attacks, few had the anti-inflammatory drugs to prevent the attacks, and family members had not been instructed to anticipate and prevent recurrences.

- All of our children deserve a medical home.
- Hospital emergency department care and EMS are designed to treat acutely ill and critically injured patients. Most of our children's minor illnesses and injuries should not be treated in the hospital emergency department.
- EMS is not a fancy taxi service.

DOCTORS AND HOSPITALS

The number of children in America rose 5.4 percent between 1982 and 1992, while the number of pediatricians rose by over 46 percent. But the distribution of those doctors was not even. These physicians tended to work in clusters in high-income areas like New England, Maryland, and Washington, D.C. The lowest ratios of pediatricians to children were found in rural states like Wyoming and Idaho. The mean ratio of pediatrician to child population nationwide was 48.6 per one hundred thousand kids. Working with the numbers, this means that each pediatrician would be responsible for the care of over two thousand children. In Idaho, each pediatrician would be responsible for the care of over five thousand children.[8]

In addition to pediatricians, we have general practitioners, family physicians, a variety of pediatric specialists and nonphysician providers like nurse practitioners and physician assistants to help our children. Still, you may have difficulty finding a provider who will remember your child's name, or that his favorite flavor is strawberry, or that he is allergic to penicillin. I recall my pediatrician fondly as a man with big, warm hands and gentle, blue eyes. My son referred to his pediatrician as "that guy with the weird baggy pants who was always in a hurry." A huge portion of the responsibility for obtaining quality care for our children is in our laps. In a time when pediatricians are seeing so many children, talking to our primary care provider requires prior planning, a list of questions, and a sound recollection of our child's allergies and history.

If your insurance carrier allows you a choice of primary provider for your child, you should try to find a medical home where both you and your child will be comfortable. Keep in mind that really nice people do not necessarily make really good doctors. Just because a physician doesn't have big, warm hands or gentle blue eyes doesn't mean he or she is not a dedicated, talented, and conscientious provider. Sometimes technical skills and attention to detail are more important than compassionate bedside manners. As you conduct your search, you should investigate the following:

- Does the physician have office hours that will allow you access for appointments after work and after school?
- Can you reach the provider during nonoffice hours when needed?
- If the provider has a telephone triage service in place, does a registered nurse, nurse practitioner, or physician assistant handle that service? Or will a clerk answer?
- Can you find friends, acquaintances, or parents of neighborhood children who use this physician or group who are happy with the service?
- Is the provider certified in Pediatric Advanced Life Support (PALS)?
- Are office staff members trained in pediatric CPR?
- Does the office have the equipment and medications necessary to deal with a life-threatening illness? While this is especially important in rural areas, physicians may not maintain stocks of these medications and equipment if they are familiar with the fast response and advanced capabilities of local EMS.
- Is the pediatrician familiar with local emergency medical services? Is he involved in the system administration and the training of paramedics and EMTs?
- Is the physician in frequent contact with emergency physicians and pediatric emergency medicine specialists at the emergency department of a nearby hospital? Which hospital? Does the provider know where the nearest regional pediatric facility is located?

URGENT-CARE CENTERS

These freestanding clinics are useful for minor injuries or illnesses during nonoffice hours if you are unable to contact your primary physician. They are certainly less expensive than acute care centers like hospital emergency departments. But I have transported patients from these centers when there was **no physician on the premises.** There is no consistent nationwide regulation of these centers, and they are sometimes incapable of handling life-threatening conditions. If you are on vacation and your child has a sore throat or ear infection an "urgent care" facility may suffice. If your spouse has chest pain, or your child has a seizure, find the nearest hospital emergency department.

- In what kinds of emergencies does the doctor recommend use of EMS and/or the hospital emergency department? Trouble breathing? Seizures? Possible fractures? High fevers? Allergic reactions? Cuts that require stitches?

It is important to differentiate between hospital facilities as they have varying abilities to treat our children. Paramedics are trained to transport patients to the closest *appropriate* hospital for care. EMS providers can make this recommendation but cannot make this decision for you. EMS providers cannot do anything to patients or take patients anywhere against their will unless the patients are not competent to make decisions for themselves. This caveat extends to a patient's parent or legal guardian if the patient is a minor. While this issue is addressed in greater detail below, the choice of hospital can be the difference between the life and death of a child. Significant differences exist between facilities.

If you live in a rural area and there is only one emergency facility within a two-hundred-mile radius, you have little choice. If a child is critically ill, the closest hospital is best. If a child is injured, air medical services may be available to transport the child to a trauma center. Trauma care differs substantially from the care of a child who is simply sick. Any hospital should have emergency physicians who can identify a life-threatening condition and attempt to stabilize a seriously ill child. Transport can be arranged later, if necessary, to a more comprehensive-care center. *Regional trauma centers* have highly specialized capabilities for patients who have been seriously injured, including immediate access to an operating room, if required. Because timing and speed are so important, injured children may be transported by ambulance or flown to a trauma center (usually by helicopter) directly from the scene of an accident. Additional descriptions of trauma services are provided in chapter 5.

Alternatively, a *stand-by pediatric emergency facility* will not necessarily have a physician on-scene when the patient arrives, but registered nurses, nurse practitioners, or physician assistants will be available for initial care and a physician will be accessible when needed. These facilities are so designated because they are intended to have the equipment and in-house training to identify a life-threatening illness or injury and provide specific stabilizing treatment while transfer is arranged to an appropriate facility. Not all "urgent care" centers live up to this standard.

A *basic pediatric emergency facility* describes a typical community hospital emergency department. A physician will always be immediately available with the training to identify a life-threatening pediatric emergency and attempt to provide stabilizing treatment until transfer to an appropriate facility can be arranged. These hospitals may also have beds to admit children as patients, but only for minor illnesses or procedures. This "stabilizing treatment" may not be successful. Sometimes children die before reaching a facility with more comprehensive capabilities. But any emergency physician is capable of providing this "stabilizing treatment," involving standard pediatric resuscitative care and focusing on airway, breathing, and circulation.

A *general pediatric emergency facility* will have a separate pediatric in-patient service (a separate pediatric floor or unit) and a Department of Pediatrics within the hospital organization. These hospitals will have emergency physicians or specialists in pediatric emergency medicine to rapidly identify and treat life-threatening illnesses or

TEACHING FACILITIES

When children are in a teaching facility, they and their parents may be approached by a large and diverse number of students. Whole flocks of white-coated providers of all descriptions and backgrounds may want to poke, prod, and examine your child. You may say, "No!" There are times when a child's level of discomfort or fear makes these examinations inappropriate. You have the right to refuse. But try to remember that these young students are the attending physicians, nurses, and paramedics of the future. They must learn "on the job" if their training is to be of value. If your child's condition permits, and if your emotional state allows, let them in. Let them learn. And if you have the heart, help to teach them what your situation is like from a parent's perspective. It will make them better providers in the future.

injuries and the ability to admit a child to a separate pediatric unit within the hospital for continued treatment.

A *comprehensive pediatric center* or *regional pediatric center* will similarly identify and rapidly treat life-threatening emergencies but will also provide specialized care for children. These are also teaching facilities. They are centers that conduct research, discover new cures and treatments for pediatric illnesses, and provide the best care available for our children. When a child who is critically ill or injured is delivered to a stand-by, basic, or general pediatric facility, they will be treated, stabilized, and eventually transferred to a regional center if more comprehensive care is needed.

- Find out about the differences that exist between individual doctors and individual hospitals in your area.
- Conduct a little research before you choose your child's medical home. Ask for opinions from other parents and caregivers; question the doctor and his staff about after-hours' care and office capabilities.

- An EMS provider will know which hospital is the closest and most appropriate facility for your child in an emergency.

INSURANCE COVERAGE

Does your insurance company require a referral prior to any emergency room visit? What is the insurance company's definition of of an "emergency"? It may be quite different from yours or even your child's doctor. This need for prior approval can result in non-payment of certain bills, including the ambulance transport. It can also, however, cause you to inappropriately delay your call for help.

There is a nationwide effort being made to mandate that all insurance carriers utilize as a basis for payment a definition of "emergency" that is realistic. This definition would ensure payment for services for "a medical condition, with a sudden onset, that manifests itself by symptoms of sufficient severity, such that a prudent layperson, possessing an average knowledge of health and medicine, could reasonably expect the absence of immediate medical attention to result in placing the person's health in serious jeopardy."[9]

According to the Miriam-Webster dictionary, an emergency is "an unforeseen event or condition requiring prompt action." My definition is more practical: You have an emergency if your child's condition is beyond your ability to treat, and you know in your heart that action must be taken quickly. In reality, a decision to call for an ambulance can be one of the most anxious, agonizing, difficult decisions a parent or caretaker can make.

The government has enacted legislation to attempt to provide more of our children access to a primary health-care provider and a medical home. Along with Medicaid, which pays the cost of health care for children who live at or below the poverty level, Congress authorized $39 billion over ten years to subsidize insurance coverage for another 5 million children who do not qualify for Medicaid but remain uninsured. The Child Health Insurance Plan (CHIP) provides funds, but many states have been slow to locate and provide coverage for these children.[10]

CHIP was created in 1997 because 11 million American children were reportedly uninsured and therefore at increased risk for preventable health problems. By October 2000, over 3.3 million children were insured through Medicaid, CHIP, or state coverage that combined the two programs (not including Title XIX Medicaid enrollment).[11] These children are primarily from working families that make too much money to qualify for Medicaid but too little to afford insurance on their own. Some states will cover children under this program from homes with incomes as high as 3.5 times the federal poverty level. A complimentary presidential campaign called Insure Kids Now attempts to facilitate state efforts to increase coverage of children by both CHIP and Medicaid. Successes with this program, as in South Carolina, have been greatly enhanced by grassroots, civilian efforts. In many other states children remain uninsured and the money unused.

Find your child a good medical home. If your primary care physician cannot provide guidance for dealing with an emergency, find a different doctor. If your insurance company does not have a layperson's definition of emergency, or penalizes consumers for calling 911 in an emergency without prior approval, find a new insurance company. If your family is insured through your employer, complain to the Human Resources Department about the carrier, survey fellow employees about their emergency needs, and start a petition to have your employer change carriers. If your child has no medical home due to lack of insurance, investigate assistance through either CHIP or Medicaid.

Our children have a right to sound care. But as parents making demands on the health-care system, we have responsibilities to balance those rights. Question your primary care physician about general office capabilities and after-hours care in an emergency. Telephone triage techniques frequently allow a nurse or other non-physician to screen calls and offer home treatment of minor problems when appropriate. Because this service can save expensive trips to after-hours clinics and emergency departments, it should be used efficiently. If you believe your child needs assistance emergently, call 911 and worry about gatekeepers and insurance approvals later. But if your child's symptoms do not involve potentially life-threatening signs or symptoms, call the doctor's office for help in making this decision.

If employees at your insurance company deny benefits, challenge them, repeatedly and often. There are sometimes internal policies in place that incline adjusters or claims clerks to automatically and repeatedly deny benefits. Write letters. Refer to your policy. Keep copies of everything. Ask for a supervisor's name and address your next letter to that person. If you don't get a response, try the manager's name for your next letter, then the director's name, the chief executive officer's name, etc. Enlist the assistance and support of your physician. Be sure you make copies of correspondence for providers who are sending you bills. If they know you are making this effort, they may wait before involving a collection agency.

If benefits are still denied, do not hesitate to enlist the assistance of your state's insurance commissioner. The names and addresses of each state's insurance commissioner are available on the Internet through the U.S. Health Care Financing Administration (HCFA) Web site (cms.hhs.gov) or at your local library. Compare the exact wording of the definition of "emergency" from your policy to the circumstances surrounding your child's illness or injury. State in clear language that you believed your child was in jeopardy. Do not give up or give in. Sometimes protection of our rights requires perseverance. How unfortunate that this need sometimes arises in the aftermath of a pediatric crisis.

- Insurance coverage for children is critically important—and available.
- Know your insurance company's definition of "emergency," but never hesitate to call for help when needed.
- We must sometimes challenge insurance carriers for appropriate coverage.

After you conduct the research necessary to find your child a good medical home, identify any limitations to care in that doctor's office. You will avoid unnecessary trips to the hospital emergency department. You will also know when that level of emergency care is appropriate. Knowing your insurance company's definition of "emergency" will prevent you from wasting time on gatekeepers and unnecessary referrals. The next step is to learn how to recognize an evolving emergency so your call for help can be made in time to save a child's life.

RECOGNIZING AN EMERGENCY

2

- ✚ We Know Our Children Best
- ✚ Age-Dependent Differences
- ✚ When Is a Child Critically Ill?
- ✚ When Is a Child Seriously Injured?
- ✚ When to Call for Help
- ✚ When to Call the Ambulance

✚ *Dad was moving at fifty-five miles per hour on a congested highway when the front tire blew. He was using all of the strength in his arms to control the steering wheel when the car rolled. His right arm snapped from the force of the impact. The shattered windshield sprayed shards of glass into Mom's face. Their infant son, strapped carefully into a car seat in the back, was completely uninjured. Their four-year-old son, also riding in the backseat, had been restrained with only a lap belt. The family insisted that they wanted to stay together and be taken to a nearby community hospital. While my first choice would have been the trauma center based strictly on the violent nature of the crash, the entire family was alert, stable, and showing no signs of severe injury. Dad was admitted to the hospital as a patient to allow an orthope-*

dic surgeon to set his fractured arm. Mom's lacerations were sutured, the children were evaluated, and a friend of the family took them home. Three hours later I was dispatched for an emergency transport from the community hospital to the trauma center.

*After arriving home, even with her body aching and her stitches stinging, Mom realized something was wrong with her preschooler. She knew that it was more than just stress from having been in an accident and concern for his dad. It was almost as though an alien had abducted her child and left this strange, listless creature in his place. She immediately returned with him to the emergency room. She had to demand that they reevaluate her son, claiming, "He's just not right." Based strictly on this mom's concern, doctors ordered her son's transfer to the trauma center for a more comprehensive evaluation. Her son underwent surgery to repair his damaged small bowel that evening. Without the surgery he may have died during the night. Emergency medical providers have learned the hard way that the persistent concern of a parent can be an invaluable diagnostic tool. **You are your child's expert.***

WE KNOW OUR CHILDREN BEST

Each of our children is unique. Each will act and react differently to a given illness and to various levels of discomfort and pain. While one child may howl for twenty minutes after stubbing his toe, another may yelp, walk it off, and continue playing. While one child will simply lie down and become listless when he is ill, another may whine and become cranky and need a great deal of our attention. Children are very aware of their bodies and know when something is wrong, but they may be unable to communicate this very well. Knowing your child and how he reacts to less acute stressors will help you to recognize an evolving emergency. This intimate familiarity with your child's normal behavior may be critical in helping medical providers determine the level of urgency needed and the extent of appropriate evaluation and treatment.

• We must trust our instincts. If we think something is very wrong, something is probably *very* wrong.

AGE-DEPENDENT DIFFERENCES

Children are considered infants if they are less than one year old. Under one month of age, a child may be referred to as a neonate. Babies less than six months are in early infancy, those older than six months are in late infancy. From one to two years of age, children are referred to as toddlers. Preschool children are aged three to six years, school-aged children from seven to thirteen, and teenagers are generally referred to as adolescents.

NEONATES *(Under One Month)*   Neonates can be very difficult to assess until you develop a familiarity with their normal patterns of behavior. They sleep, sometimes very deeply. They eat. They pee and poop. They cry, sometimes incessantly and with no indication of why. Frequent difficulties with breast-feeding, formula feeding, colic, and early weight loss make a solid relationship with your doctor or health-care provider invaluable in preventing both anxiety and unnecessary trips to the hospital.

Neonates are particularly vulnerable to changes in temperature and should always be kept comfortably warm. They should never be placed on their bellies to sleep. Their breaths can be very noisy and wet sounding, and hiccups can interfere with a normal breathing pattern. Neonates sometimes stop breathing for short periods (a couple of seconds) as these patterns change. If their breathing becomes noisier than usual, call your doctor. Similarly, if diapers turn up empty over several hours, this should be reported to your doctor early. Learn the normal feel of your baby's *fontanel*, the soft spot at the front of the top of the head. A bulging or sunken fontanel can be a sign of serious illness. Neonates should not run fevers. Elevations in temperature should be reported to the doctor early.

EARLY INFANCY *(One to Six Months)* At this age babies will begin to focus on bright, shiny objects. They will begin to gaze into your face and learn to smile. Their crying will begin to change based on need, and you will begin to recognize and differentiate between cries that indicate hunger, a wet diaper, and a sleepy babe. As with neonates, infants should not be put to bed on their bellies. Children in early infancy who develop fevers should be seen by a doctor immediately. Children younger than three months with a fever above 101° Fahrenheit are usually suspected of having meningitis until proven otherwise.

LATE INFANCY *(Six to Twelve Months)* As children find their own voice, they will also discover their unique personality. They will be alert and curious about the world around them while awake, and will reach for those shiny objects that they could only track with their eyes when they were younger. They will also inevitably try to put everything into their little mouths. They will know when they leave Mom's arms to be held by a stranger, and this may distress them. Their immune systems will be developing rapidly and allow for healthy fevers to help them fight occasional infections.

As they begin to crawl and become both mobile and more independent, children are at very high risk. Choking incidents are common. Since they are no longer stationary and predictable, this is the beginning of an important time of child care when vigilance and constant attention are required. And this is a time when socialization and exposure to communicable illnesses increases. These babies will giggle and babble and wail when they are unhappy. They may also inadvertently inhale pieces of balloon, plastic wrap, potato chips, and peanuts. They will reach for objects that fascinate them, and they may fall from high chairs, shopping carts, and windows. They will try to eat anything, from grandpa's heart medicine to lead-based paint chips.

TODDLERS *(One to Two Years)* Toddlers are entertaining, funny, cagey individuals. They can communicate in their way with adults and other children. They know Mom, Dad, grandparents, and other regular caregivers compared to strangers, although they may not automatically associate a stranger with danger. In fact, they lack the experience to associate much of anything with danger and frequently overestimate their abilities. Toddlers out of sight for mere minutes may run into traffic, enter the swimming pool alone, climb out of windows, and shave with Daddy's straight razor. Like younger infants, they will try to eat everything from Mom's lipstick to Dad's hair-replacement medicine.

They will lay their heads quietly in your lap for hours when ill or whine incessantly. And they find illness everywhere as their immune systems develop and exposures are frequent. They face viral infections, bacterial infections, parasites, and fungi. The cleanest, best-groomed children at this age can still manage to find everything from intestinal worms to head lice. They may be hit by chicken pox, streptococcal and staphylococcal infections, influenza, and the common cold.

Children tend to run higher fevers than adults during illness. While we, as adults, may feel like we've been hit by a truck with a temperature of 101°, our children may run fevers as high as 105° and still not show signs of acute illness. Do not hesitate to take a child's temperature. In fact, during illness, fevers should be tracked and recorded. If elevated, do not hesitate to administer appropriate doses of antipyretics like acetaminophen (Tylenol) or ibuprofen (Advil). If you begin to feel uncomfortable or anxious about your child's condition, involve your doctor early and keep him advised of changes.

It is important for families to understand that a healthy child can fight most of these infections with symptomatic care alone. Antibiotic intervention is only useful to battle bacterial infections and is usually unnecessary. The misuse and abuse of antibiotics begins in these years, and the inappropriate treatment of viral illness with antibiotics places all children at higher risk. An anxious parent can pressure a doctor to "do something." We learned this fear of fever from our own parents and from their parents before them, when a variety of deadly illnesses could not be prevented through immunization and vaccination. Physicians can and sometimes do prescribe antibiotics simply to placate parents. But the administration of unnecessary medication is not a trivial matter.

This is the beginning of the age of febrile (fever-related) seizures. Seizures, for parents who have never witnessed one, can be very frightening. It is rarely the number on the thermometer that matters, but rather how fast the fever rose. (The subject of seizures and fevers are addressed more thoroughly in chapter 13.) The first time any child has a seizure should trigger an automatic call for help.

PRESCHOOLERS *(Three to Six Years)* Preschoolers, like toddlers, are mobile and verbal. Like toddlers, they may overestimate their own abilities. These children are still too young to be expected to cross streets alone. They still have a level of curiosity that overwhelms good judgment, and they can wander away and become easily lost. When you hear that PA announcement for little Joey's mom to please see the store manager, you can bet little Joey is probably between three and six years of age.

This age group is also at higher risk of developing seizures associated with fevers as their immune systems fight to find some balance in the world of microbes. As with toddlers, seizures associated with fevers are horrifying for parents, but are usually self-limiting and last for only a couple of minutes. And as with toddlers, the problem with a seizure in any child who does not have a seizure history is that we cannot be sure that the fever triggered the event. A physician must always evaluate a child who seizes for the first time.

SCHOOL-AGED CHILDREN *(Seven to Thirteen)* Fevers and illness are common and normal for school-aged children as they grow and develop. Illnesses are frequently viral in nature and not responsive to antibiotic treatment. While the risk of febrile seizure is lower, the risk of dehydration during illness remains high. School-aged children can converse freely with adults and are better able to describe an illness or injury. However, these children are also developing protective inhibitions and may be hesitant or embarrassed to expose parts of their bodies for medical evaluation and treatment.

Providers must do their best to respect and protect the privacy and modesty of school-aged children.

ADOLESCENTS In the scope of this book, adolescents can be considered similar to adults. While their activities become high risk and they are frequently involved in preventable accidents, their injuries are less closely correlated with a lack of direct supervision as with toddlers and preschoolers. An adolescent who is critically ill may present with the same signs and symptoms as a critically ill adult.

- Age-dependent differences in children can complicate medical evaluation.
- We know what "normal" is for our children. We will be the first to know when something is not "normal."
- Not all illnesses respond to antibiotics. A trip to the doctor should not necessarily result in a prescription of some kind.

WHEN IS A CHILD CRITICALLY ILL?

Mom brought her son to the clinic for a regularly scheduled checkup when he was six weeks old. As she sat in the waiting room, he stopped breathing. Again. She knew that babies sometimes stopped breathing for short periods and intended to ask the doctor about the episodes. She had first noticed them the previous evening, and they appeared to be happening more and more frequently. This time he didn't start breathing again right away, and his color started to change. She carried him to the doorway where a nurse could see him, and she was quickly escorted into an examining room.

When I arrived at the clinic I found a sweetheart in the nurse's arms. His color was excellent. He was alert and squirming. His heart rate and breathing rate were normal. A sensor, called a pulse oximeter, was taped to his toe and told us his bloodstream was saturated with oxygen. He was cute as a button and showed no sign of illness. The doctor wanted him admitted for evaluation at the hospital.

Mom rode in the back of the ambulance with me. I continued to monitor the pulse oximeter, and his color, level of consciousness, breathing, and heart rates. Just minutes from the hospital he stopped breathing. His color changed dramatically and rapidly. I flicked the soles of his feet sharply with my fingers to stimulate him. He remained lifeless. I quickly removed the straps of the child safety seat and pulled him onto my lap. He was still not breathing. I grabbed a bag valve mask device and was about to begin breathing for him when he took a big breath on his own. His color returned quickly. Now he seemed okay again. I kept the face mask with oxygen blowing near his mouth and nose and kept him on my lap. When he stopped breathing a second time, I didn't wait for his color to change. When he did not respond to stimuli, I placed the mask over his mouth and nose and began delivering gentle breaths. As my partner opened the back door of the ambulance, he began breathing again. Carrying the child wrapped in a blanket and the bag valve mask in my arms, and my partner carrying the oxygen tank behind me, we hurried into the emergency department instead of upstairs to the pediatric floor.

The staff in the emergency department was not expecting me. The nurse was annoyed that I had not given them advance warning of my arrival and began complaining that there were no open beds. Standing there in the hallway, the baby in my arms stopped breathing again. I laid the babe down on the unit clerk's desk and began bagging again, raising my voice to the doctor across the room that I had a six-week-old child in respiratory arrest. Within seconds a bed, three nurses, and two physicians were available. A respiratory therapist took over ventilating the child, and I explained what was happening to the doctors. Within half an hour the child was intubated, and a helicopter was ordered to fly him to a specialized children's hospital.

While this child showed absolutely no other signs or symptoms of illness, he was suffering from a life-threatening viral infection that was causing him to stop breathing for extended periods of time. He recovered completely and was released after two weeks in a pediatric intensive care unit.

All children will become ill, usually two or three times during each year as bacterial and viral infections rocket through our homes, schools, and day-care centers. This should not cause alarm and is actually a good sign that our children are developing strong immune systems. It is not unusual for the onset of a given illness to be mild, escalating rapidly, and then slowly ebbing until your child returns to a state of good health. It is a paradox that the rapid escalation of an illness will frequently occur in the middle of the night or on a weekend when the doctor's office is closed. And this stage of illness can be frightening, especially for new parents. Occasionally, an infection will overwhelm a child's defenses and require intervention. Sometimes an illness is not associated with infection and requires a diagnostic workup from a qualified physician. Rarely, a previously undiagnosed illness or infection will threaten a child's life. Recognizing that rare event can be difficult but not impossible for most parents.

Assessing the extent of a child's illness requires that you look at your child and remember that you are your child's expert. In the past, critically ill children were described as "toxic." A toxic child was described using words like "lethargic," "obtunded," and "shocky."

WHAT IS NORMAL?

It is crucial to properly interpret the term *abnormal,* especially as it relates to level of consciousness. To determine that one of these signs is *not* normal, you must know what *is* normal for your child. What is your child's normal level of consciousness? This can be age dependent. An infant may be unable to recognize his name, but his facial expression will normally change when he sees Mom. A child too young to talk will usually cry when taken by a stranger from Mom's arms. "Normal" may also be a reflection of existing illnesses or conditions. If your child is autistic, he may not turn his head and look when his name is called. What is considered abnormal in a healthy child may not be considered abnormal in your child. Again, your input based on your intimate familiarity with your child's normal appearance and behavior can be critically important.

These are words even doctors cannot define easily. Recognizing that a child has crossed the line from simply sick to critically ill involves assessment of three specific signs:

- Level of consciousness
- Skin color and tone
- Respiratory effort

In a critically ill child, one, two, or all three of these signs will be abnormal. All three are indications of how well blood is circulating and/or supplying needed oxygen to a child's organs. Regardless of the reason for poor oxygen delivery, when this inadequacy reaches a dangerous level, your child's appearance will change dramatically. A trained provider can usually recognize a child in trouble as soon as he walks in the door. You can learn this, too.

LEVEL OF CONSCIOUSNESS This is a term used to describe how awake a child is. A child may be awake and alert and capable of interacting with you. Or he may be drowsy and sleepy and acting strangely. Sometimes a child will be asleep but will awaken when stimulated, either by a loud noise or a pinch. When a child will not awaken at all, he is considered unresponsive. A scale is used to describe these varying levels of consciousness, represented by the acronym AVPU.

- Alert
- Verbal stimulus response
- Painful stimulus response
- Unresponsive

A child is either alert or not alert. An alert child's eyes will be open, and he will be aware of, and react spontaneously to, his surroundings. If a child is alert, he may be further described as oriented or disoriented based on the age-dependent criteria described above (an infant will recognize Mom, a toddler will become fretful when handed to a stranger, an older child should know if it is morning or after dinner). If he is not alert, he may respond to a verbal command. If a child will not respond to a loud verbal or auditory stimulus (like hand clapping), he may move or respond to a painful stimulus (like a pinch). If he does not respond to pain, he is considered unresponsive. If your child becomes confused or disoriented, if he is initially alert and becomes responsive only to loud auditory stimuli or pain, or if he becomes unresponsive, these are called mental status changes. Notice that the word "unconscious" is not used. Unconscious is a poor description of a child's mental status.

Many children are assessed as "not alert" simply because they are very sleepy. If a provider is attempting to assess your child and this is his normal nap time, a finding that a child is not alert is not necessarily abnormal. Mental status changes in conjunction with illness, difficulty in breathing, and changes in skin color and tone constitute emergencies and you should not hesitate to call for help.

Initially, a child whose body is not capable of delivering enough oxygen to his brain cells may become agitated, upset, or even combatant. He may become restless. He may begin to panic. He may push you away. When that oxygen deprivation, called *hypoxia*, becomes severe, or when the level of waste carbon dioxide in a child's bloodstream becomes dangerously elevated, he may become increasingly less alert and eventually unresponsive. Breathing and heart rates that drop precipitously and become far too slow are warning signs of impending cardiac arrest. Be prepared to begin mouth-to-mouth or mouth-to-mouth-and-nose breathing until help arrives with supplemental oxygen.

SKIN COLOR AND TONE   These refer to a child's color, but also to changes in moisture and temperature. As he battles an infection, a child may be hot and dry, or cool and clammy. He may be pale (lighter in color with an absence of pink in lips, mucous membranes, lower eyelids, or nail beds) or flushed (like a sunburn). Paleness, or a grayish color, can be referred to as pallor. Sometimes a child's color is described as dusky, which is a darkened color. These changes are indicative of illness, but, alone, are not necessarily signs of critical illness.

Cyanosis means blue. Cyanosis in a child refers to the bluish tint that can begin at the child's lips or nail beds and spread. The presence of cyanosis is ominous, but a child can be critically ill in the absence of cyanosis. A child's skin can become mottled, showing different color blotches. Where this mottling originates (the arms or legs versus the belly) can be an important clue to providers in diagnosing a child's problem and should be noted. Dry skin is not, by itself, indicative of acute illness. But unusually dry skin combined with consistently dry diapers, a lack of tears, and/or a sunken fontanel are important warning signs of dehydration. Again, a critically ill child may have changes in skin color and tone, he may not be alert and oriented, and/or he may be having trouble breathing.

RESPIRATORY EFFORT   This refers to both breathing rate and breathing difficulty. If a child is breathing too fast or too slow, or is working hard to breathe, he is in respiratory distress. Respiratory distress can result from a wide spectrum of illnesses. When a child becomes so fatigued or weak during illness that he can no longer breathe fast enough or deeply enough, he needs emergency help. Rapid breathing is a sign of distress, slow and shallow breaths may signal impending respiratory failure. If the child's heart rate also begins to drop below normal ranges, you must be prepared to begin rescue breathing until EMS arrives. You may also need to be prepared to do pediatric CPR if the heart rate drops away completely. This change in your child's condition can occur very, very rapidly.

There are many reasons for a child to have difficulty breathing. Emergency breathing problems can begin with mild symptoms that become worse over time. This insidious progression of illness from mild to acute can make it difficult for parents and caregivers to know when to seek help. No bells ring. No lights flash. Sometimes no single sign or symptom makes the need for assistance apparent until a child's life is already at stake.

The level of a child's respiratory distress can be classified as mild, moderate, or severe. A child's condition can change from mild to moderate or severe rapidly, or over hours and even days. The hallmark of mild respiratory distress is an increase in breathing rate. A child's normal, resting breathing rate can increase for many reasons not related to illness, like anger, excitement, frustration, anxiety, and fear. Similarly, illness can begin in many different ways, from simple fatigue to fever, nausea, vomiting, diarrhea, sore throat, earache, or headache. Whenever symptoms of illness combine with a rapid breathing rate, it is time to call the doctor for guidance. It is therefore essential that you know your child's normal, resting breathing rate.

(NORMAL RESPIRATORY RATE BY AGE)

Newborn	30–60 breaths per minute
1–6 weeks	30–60 breaths per minute
6 months	25–40 breaths per minute
1 year	20–30 breaths per minute
3 years	20–30 breaths per minute
6 years	18–25 breaths per minute
10 years and older	15–20 breaths per minute

Normal respiratory rates decrease as children grow. In addition, the rates noted above are ranges only. Different children may exhibit different rates that are entirely normal for them. It is important to know your own child's normal breathing rate and pattern. As he sleeps, or rests comfortably in your lap, watch an infant or very young child's belly as it moves with each breath. Watch for chest rise in an older child. Use a watch or clock with a second hand and count breaths for one whole minute. When a significant increase in rate is noted during illness, call the child's doctor.

A child in moderate respiratory distress will breathe at a higher than normal rate, but will also be working hard to take each breath. The child may have to use chest and abdominal muscles not normally needed for breathing and may be straining to move the air in and out. The child's color may change if he cannot breathe easily, and he may become pale or even gray. Cyanosis can spread from a child's lips and nail beds to the face and torso if the child is not getting enough oxygen for an extended period of time. And a child's breathing can become noisy, including a high-pitched stridor, musical-sounding wheezes, or wet slurpy sounds. A child in moderate respiratory distress may need supplemental oxygen.

Severe respiratory distress is actually the onset of respiratory failure. The child becomes exhausted and no longer has the strength to breathe. The breathing rate will become too slow, instead of too fast. The child's heart rate will eventually slow down as well. The child will become increasingly drowsy, sleepy, and difficult to arouse. A child's color will become even worse, and cyanosis may spread. Breathing that was previously very noisy may become quiet and even silent. Moderate respiratory distress can become severe respiratory distress very fast and without warning. The result of untreated severe respiratory distress is respiratory arrest. After a child stops breathing, his heart will eventually stop beating and he will die. These children not only need supplemental oxygen; they need assistance moving the air in and out as well. At this point they are no longer able to breathe on their own. They need air delivered, mouth-to-mouth if necessary, until help arrives.

Breathing rate is only one sign of distress. Other abnormal respiratory findings include nasal flaring, when a child's nostrils flare with each labored breath. Take off your child's shirt and look at his chest. If he is working hard to breathe, he may be using more than just his abdominal muscles. He may be using many other accessory muscles, and this may be causing *retractions,* or the sinking of skin and tissue in certain areas as the muscles contract. These sunken areas will occur as the child tries to breathe air in (during inhalation) and may be found above the collarbones, at the top of the breastbone, and/or between his ribs. Grunting is caused when breaths out (exhalations) are forced against a partially closed upper airway. This action helps a child maintain sufficient pressure inside his lungs and may be indicative of lower airway illness.

There are also a variety of breathing noises, outside the normal realm of sloppy, slurpy baby sounds, that indicate illness:

Snoring. While snoring is normal in both sleeping adults and sleeping children, it is abnormal when a child is awake. Snoring occurs when air movement is necessary to displace the tongue from the back of the throat. In a conscious child, it can be a sign of upper airway swelling or obstruction.

Stridor. A high-pitched noise as a child breathes in, breathes out, or both. It is similar to the high-pitched noise that will issue from your own throat as you inhale sharply when you see an accident about to happen or realize that dinner is on fire. If stridor is heard on inhalation only it may be indicative of a blockage in the upper airway. If stridor is heard on both inhalation and exhalation it may be a sign of a lower obstruction, possibly in the trachea. Stridor may be heard in children with croup or epiglottitis, but may also indicate the presence of a foreign body blocking the airway.

Wheezing. A high-pitched musical sound that all parents of asthmatics know well. It is usually heard first during exhalation and is a sign of lower airway illness. This includes asthma and bronchiolitis, but may also indicate a bronchial foreign body. Imagine a distant accordion player pulling his instrument apart with no keys held down (that is a quiet inhalation), and then pushing his instrument together with many keys held down (a noisy exhalation). Whether your child has been diagnosed with asthma or not, wheezing needs to be treated and should be assessed by a physician rapidly.

Rales. Fine crackles that actually sound like the movement of little bubbles, due to fluid in the lower airway. This can occur during illnesses like pneumonia. Take a piece of plastic wrap from the kitchen and crinkle it in your hands. This sounds like an amplified version of what you may hear when you place your ear against the back of your child's chest when he is ill.

Body language. This can be an important indication of your child's condition. Observe your child's position. A child in trouble may want to sit up, lean forward, and place one or both hands in front to form a tripod. This tripod position allows a child to maximize use of those accessory muscles. A child may also lift his head and thrust his jaw forward into a sniffing position. A child will do this to naturally open their airways as much as possible. If he is also drooling or having difficulty swallowing, his upper airways may already be dangerously swollen or partially blocked.

Heartbeats. Heartbeats are evaluated by feeling a pulse and counting beats for one full minute. The rate of a child's heartbeat is a less valuable indicator of acute illness than the triad of level of consciousness, skin color and tone, and respiratory effort. A rapid heart rate, called *tachycardia,* is a sign of distress, but is also a child's natural, normal reaction to stress. A child's heart rate will go up when he is upset, frightened, angry, or excited. Alone, an elevated or decreased heart rate is not necessarily a sign of illness. When a changed heart rate combines with an altered mental status, poor color or skin tone, and respiratory difficulty, a child is sick. Again, it is when that heart rate and breathing rate begin to drop rapidly that a sick child is in dire trouble and may go into cardiac arrest.

- When a child's illness becomes dangerous and requires emergency care, his appearance and/or behavior will change dramatically.
- A critically ill child will show changes in level of consciousness, respiratory effort, and/or skin color and tone.
- When a child develops this triad, including changes in mental status, trouble breathing, and/or poor skin color and tone, the diagnosis does not matter. Giving the illness a name will not make it better. Call for help.
- Changes in level of consciousness can be dependent on both the child's age and existing illness. Remember that you are your child's expert.

WHEN IS A CHILD
SERIOUSLY INJURED?

His arms were cradling bottles of soda pop and he worried that he might drop them as he glanced at the traffic. The light turned and he ran into the roadway gripping the bottles tightly to his chest. The van that struck him had just accelerated, hoping to pass the intersection with the light still yellow. He was thrown through the air, landing on his head. When I arrived he was awake, alert, and capable of recognizing his dad at the scene, but screaming. He complained of pain along his right flank. A single, tiny drop of blood was drying to one side of his nose, and abrasions covered his right side and hip. We immobilized him to protect his spine, placed an oxygen mask over his mouth and nose, and loaded him into the ambulance. His head and neck looked and felt normal. There was no blood or fluid in his ears, his pupils were equal and reactive to light. I was concerned about the possibility of internal bleeding.

Dad rode up front with my driver. I kept telling his father that as long as his son was screaming, we were okay. A screaming child is a live child. I established an IV and my partner talked to the hospital on the radio, mobilizing the trauma team. As we approached the driveway to the hospital, the little boy suddenly became stone quiet. His eyes were open but now unfocused. His mouth was open. His airway was clear, and he was still breathing well. But this sudden change in his mental status was ominous. We rushed inside. Five minutes after his care was transferred to the waiting trauma team, he was intubated, supported by a ventilator, and actively seizing. The CT scan revealed a circumferential skull fracture. Fortunately, I had delivered this child to a level-one trauma center where the team included neurosurgeons who were able to save his life.

Children are not just small adults. They respond to injury differently than adults. Their strong, healthy little bodies are capable of compensating for insults longer. But when they begin to decompensate, they crash hard and they crash very fast. This child had none of the normal indications of a severe head injury. There was no observed loss of consciousness, no obvious injury or deformity to his scalp or

skull, no neurological signs of an acute insult in the minutes immediately after the impact.

Major injuries are not always obvious. It is extremely important
to assess, not just the way the child appears, but the manner in which
the child was hurt. This is referred to as the mechanism of injury. If
we evaluate the force and direction of an impact and compare these
forces to the tissue in a child's body, we can project a potential for
injury. A child struck by a car will almost certainly sustain serious
injury. Sometimes these impacts are glancing and may throw a child
to the ground but not cause serious trauma. Sometimes the worst of
a child's injuries are caused by the impact with the ground and not
the initial glancing blow by the vehicle. In the case above, the child
was struck hard enough to throw him through the air. While this
impact probably caused the abrasions and pain in his side, and the
potential for injury to internal organs and internal bleeding, it was
surely when he landed on his head that the skull fracture occurred.

We can also assess obvious injuries and extrapolate the force necessary to cause those injuries to other areas of the child's body. If a
fall involved sufficient force to break a child's arm, it may also have
caused a head injury, a spinal injury, or trauma to the child's chest
that will not always be as obvious. By recreating the event in your
mind, you can begin to anticipate trauma to areas of the body where
signs and symptoms of injury may not become apparent until later.
Medical providers are taught to make assumptions that are in the
best interest of the child. If a head injury has occurred, for example,
we will assume that the child's neck may also be injured, and take
action to immobilize the entire spine until the child is evaluated by a
physician and X rays can rule out spinal damage. If a force was powerful enough to cause abrasions and bruising to the flank or
abdomen, injury may have occurred to the underlying organs such
as the kidney, liver, or spleen as well.

There are two broad types of trauma that can be inflicted on a
child's body. *Blunt trauma,* as described above, requires that some
force impact the child. This doesn't have to be a car. It can be the
ground as the child lands after a nasty fall from a height or off a
bicycle or skateboard. Or it can be the impact of a bicycle's handle-

bars against a child's pelvis and belly as they are thrown forward, or the supports of a backyard trampoline when the child misses the soft, flexible center. Blunt traumas occur frequently during motor vehicle accidents, as an unbelted child is thrown into the dashboard or windshield, the seat in front of him, or against the window and door during a side impact. Even the force of a child being thrown against a lap belt without the additional safety of a shoulder harness can be a very harmful blunt force.

The other broad type of trauma involves sharp objects that may penetrate a child's skin. *Penetrating injuries* do not have to be caused by knives or bullets. Less obvious penetrating injuries may occur when glass shards fly or when a dog's incisors bite down. Because penetrating injuries by definition involve holes in the child, they are easier to find. But even tiny, seemingly minor penetrating injuries can be deadly depending on what internal organs may be injured beneath the skin. Air-powered "toy" guns may seem harmless. But children have died from the penetrating injuries the guns can inflict. Any penetrating injury to the head, neck, chest, or abdomen must be considered a potentially life-threatening event, even if the hole appears tiny or external bleeding is minimal. And penetrating injuries to the eyes, ears, sinuses, rectum, and genitals can be severely disabling if not treated promptly.

- Always consider the manner in which a child was hurt and look for hidden injuries.
- Blunt traumas can cause internal bleeding that may not be apparent right away.
- Even minor-looking penetrating wounds can threaten a child's life.

WHEN TO CALL FOR HELP

Triage guidelines have been established to assist providers in deciding when adults need to be evaluated at a trauma center immediately. These guidelines are based on both mechanism of injury and physical findings. Generally, because they are capable of compensating so well after a trauma, a physician should evaluate children regardless of physical findings like bleeding and bruising if the mechanism of injury suggests the possibility of hidden injuries. Such mechanisms include the following:

FALLS   For adults, guidelines suggest a fall from a height of twenty feet or more warrants rapid, professional trauma evaluation. Children are killed and severely injured in falls from much lower heights. Infants have been killed falling from couches, beds, and high chairs. Forget height. Review how the child landed (on their head, for example) and the type of surface they landed on (padded carpet versus ceramic tile). Any fall that results in a change in mental status, or disability, requires emergency care.

MOTOR VEHICLE ACCIDENTS   Even if children are not complaining of any discomfort or pain and showing no signs of injury after a crash, they should be evaluated at a hospital emergency department if another vehicle occupant was seriously injured, if the vehicle was badly deformed, if the vehicle rolled over, or if the child was ejected from the vehicle during the crash. Children can be seriously injured in such accidents even if they were properly restrained.

BURNS   Burn injuries are immediately life threatening if they cover enough body surface area or involve the respiratory tract, but easily become life threatening later, even if small areas are involved, if infection sets in. Small burn areas should be evaluated early, but may be treated appropriately in an office setting. Check with your doctor. Burn injuries should be handled as an emergency if they involve the face (including the ears), multiple fingers, genitals, rectum, if they involve large areas of skin, or if the child may have suffered an inhalation injury. Inhalation injuries involve damage to airways and lungs from flames, hot gases, and/or smoke, and are not always obvious. Look in the child's mouth and nose for soot or ash, any indication of damaged or swollen mucous membranes, or singed nasal hairs. A simple but important sign of a possible inhalation injury is a hoarse voice. A child's airway can swell shut rapidly and completely. Inhalation injuries are life-threatening emergencies.

PENETRATING WOUNDS   All injuries involving firearms and knives require emergent evaluation. Even when guns and knives are not involved, penetrating injuries to the head, neck, chest, abdomen, or those that involve the eyes, ears, nose, rectum, or genitals require emergency transfer to a hospital. A dog bite to an arm, a leg, or a fanny may not be life threatening, but proper exploration, cleansing, and closing of such wounds may result in a trip to the emergency room anyway if your doctor does not stock the necessary equipment and supplies in his office. Call 911 immediately for penetrating wounds that involve the torso, neck, head, or any time bleeding cannot be controlled with direct pressure.

ASSAULT   Victims of assaults need to be evaluated as early as possible. If the injuries are not severe (cuts and bruises only), it may be appropriate to have the child evaluated at the doctor's office. But this evaluation should be conducted as soon after any attack as possible and in a manner that will allow the details of the attack, as well as the physical condition of the child, to be fully documented. Look for bruising to the abdomen and flanks, which may indicate the threat of internal bleeding, or bleeding inside the mouth or nose that could block a child's airway.

NEAR DROWNING   A child pulled from the water who may have inhaled fluid into his lungs should be seen by a doctor promptly, preferably at the emergency room. Even if the child is no longer having difficulty breathing, if he may have aspirated water (sucked the fluid into their lungs) he needs to be evaluated by a physician. An emergency physician should immediately evaluate any child having trouble breathing after a near drowning.

BEHAVIOR A physician should see any child immediately, regardless of age, who attempts or threatens suicide or violence against others. Whether the child has succeeded in injuring himself or others or not, an emergency physician will be capable of checking his physical health as well as arranging for psychiatric evaluation, involuntarily if necessary, to ensure his well-being. Children do not need to have reached their teens to require emergency psychiatric care.

- Triage guidelines for adults are not good enough for children.
- Talk to your doctor about these types of emergencies and know where to go for appropriate care.

TIME TO CALL THE AMBULANCE!

Pedestrian accidents, bicycles, tricycles, skates, scooters, skateboards, all-terrain vehicles, ride-on mowers, fireworks, trampolines, falls from horses, bites from animals, and even infant walkers can kill or injure our children. In the absence of one of the obvious hazards noted above, an ambulance should be summoned if, following any injury:

- A child loses consciousness
- He stops breathing
- He has trouble breathing
- He becomes confused or combatant
- Bleeding is uncontrollable
- He has a tender or sore abdomen
- If you suspect a head, neck, or back injury
- If he has a severely deformed or open fracture

As noted earlier, you know your child better than anyone else. Sometimes the only early indication of a serious injury is too subtle for others to note. If your child becomes listless or weak, if he becomes pale or his skin becomes clammy, or if you feel he is simply not "acting right," it is best to have him evaluated. If changes are subtle and you are not sure, your doctor should guide you to an appropriate facility for evaluation. An emergency physician should

FIRST-AID TRAINING

The farther you live from emergency services, including ambulance and hospital facilities, the more critical it is to have advanced first-aid training. If you live in a rural area, you probably own lots of candles and extra food in a pantry somewhere. Your child's health deserves at least as much planning. If you know help will not arrive in ten minutes, taking a first-aid class may save your child's life. The American Red Cross offers these courses, as well as many community hospitals, community colleges, and ambulance corps. If you are unable to locate a convenient class, talk to your doctor.

evaluate the child immediately if these changes are sudden or dramatic and they follow an injury.

- Always call for an ambulance if a child is seriously injured.
- If changes in your child's appearance or behavior are subtle and you are not sure, call your doctor. If changes are sudden or dramatic, call for emergency help.
- A simple first-aid class can teach you how to save a child's life.

When you decide an emergency has occurred and you need emergency help, you need to know how to get that help as rapidly as possible. Learning about any limitations to care at the doctor's office, and understanding differences between hospitals and insurance companies, is an important first step. Learning about emergency medical services in your community is just as important. How do you call? Who will respond? What are they capable of? What will they do to your child? What are your rights? You may have to research these questions, as well. Each community in America is different. Now that you know how to recognize an emergency, how will you respond?

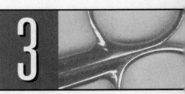

RESPONDING TO AN EMERGENCY

3

- ✚ Are You Ready?
- ✚ Protect Yourself First
- ✚ How to Call for Help
- ✚ What to Expect
- ✚ Prehospital Care
- ✚ Who Will Respond to Your Call for Help?
- ✚ Who Pays for EMS?

ARE YOU READY?

I was in the kitchen cooking dinner in our rural Pennsylvania home one autumn evening several years ago. The butter was just hot enough to add my minced garlic and chopped onions when—as always seems to happen at that moment—the phone rang. "Hello," I answered, hoping to promise a return call and hang up quickly. A woman's hysterical voice initially made no sense to me. She was screaming something about a baby down the street and CPR. She was out of control, and I worried that she would hang up before actually communicating with me. I asked for her name. Her name was irrelevant. But I needed her to calm down long enough to make sense. Finally, after the third time I asked for her name, she

45

told me. To retrieve that simple piece of data, she had to go to a part of her brain where information was stored. The process of finding and delivering her own name allowed her to start functioning on an intellectual level again. "Where's the baby you're talking about?" Breathlessly, she described a house nearby on my street. "Where are you calling from?" California?

Her sister lived on my street. Her sister's baby had stopped breathing, and her sister did not know how to do CPR. She also did not realize that we did not have 911 service at the time (it has since been added in my area). After struggling with the operator, she finally hung up and called the only number that came automatically to her mind, her sister in California. She told her sister my name, that I lived nearby, and that I worked as a paramedic. The California sister had obtained my phone number from information and called me. How long had this child now been without air? I told her to write down our number for emergency medical services, including area code, to hang up and to call that number immediately. I then grabbed my portable radio and ran out the door, calling in the request for an ambulance by radio myself, just in case.

When I arrived I found a distraught mom with her toddler in her arms. The little guy had suffered a febrile seizure, scaring his mom half to death, but was now breathing normally. He was not alert, but his airway was open, he was taking in adequate volumes of air with each breath, and his color was good. By the time the ambulance arrived, he was beginning to open his eyes when I called his name. The duty crew assessed him, administered oxygen, and loaded both him and his mom into the ambulance for evaluation at the hospital. When I returned home, I found my husband glowering at me with his hands on his hips, a house full of smoke, and the aroma of burned butter. Oh, well.

Not all communities have 911 service. You may need to dial a seven-digit number for help. You need to know this number and have it posted next to each phone in your home. Some communities even require that you dial a different seven-digit number for fire, police, or EMS. Post them all, along with your doctor's number and the closest poison control center, where they can be dialed quickly and easily. The following phone numbers should be taped next to every telephone in your home:

Police	Emergency department
Fire	Insurance company (or gatekeeper)
Ambulance	Insurance policy number
Poison Control	Relative (grandma/ grandpa/Aunt Millie)
Pediatrician	Nearby neighbor

I'd include the emergency department of a nearby hospital on this list in case your child's doctor does not have an after-hours telephone triage service in place. If you are agonizing over whether or not your child needs emergency care, and the doctor's answering service cannot help, a nurse at the emergency department may be able to assist you.

- Do you know how to call for help?
- Not all communities have 911 service.

PROTECT YOURSELF

Coping with a life-threatening emergency requires specific steps taken in sequence.

- Recognizing that an emergency has occurred
- Ensuring the scene is safe
- Calling for help
- Initiating care
- Continuing care until help arrives

Once you realize an emergency has occurred, you must stop and ask yourself if the scene is safe. This first step is not trivial and, if ignored, can cost both you and the child your lives. Look around. Try to determine what caused the emergency. Make sure you are not also in danger. This point is best illustrated through examples:

- Your neighbor bangs on your door screaming for help. You find her child on their basement floor, and he is not breathing. Why did the child stop breathing? Is it because he fell down the steps and broke his neck? Or is it because your neighbor's heating system is malfunctioning and the basement is full of carbon monoxide gas? It may not take long for you to lose consciousness and perhaps die, also.

- You find a child lying in the road. That car crashed into the tree nearby, with power lines down and puddles in the road should tell you something. It should tell you that you could be electrocuted trying to help.

- A car strikes a child. No matter how much you want to help the child, the same traffic dangers that caused this accident could kill you. Approaching vehicles do not automatically know that there are people in the roadway around the next bend.

- If swiftly running water can carry away a child, it may carry away an adult as well. Never go into the water intent on rescuing anyone without appropriate training. Scene safety requires your well-being. Emergency providers are taught early, and repeatedly, that a dead rescuer cannot help anyone. Furthermore, a dead or injured rescuer will dilute the rescue resources at the scene. If you are hurt, anyone sent initially to help the child will also be required to assist you. Instead of helping the child, you just diminished the response team's ability to save that life. Instead of *all* providers concentrating on resuscitating a child, they will have a Good Samaritan adult to treat as well.

- Protect yourself first—it could save a child's life.

HOW TO CALL FOR HELP

Once you reach an emergency dispatcher, assume that he does not have an enhanced system and does not have a computer in front of him showing your location. Not all emergency dispatch centers in America have this advanced capability. Usually, trained dispatchers will ask you first for the nature of your emergency and the number you are calling from. This way, if another call comes in or several other callers are already on hold, they will know whether they should continue their conversation with you or place you on hold as well. And they can call you back if you are disconnected. This is the beginning of a system called *triage* that can be extremely upsetting to parents in an emergency. Your child is having a seizure. There is nothing else in the world more important than this, you think. But what you may not know is that your neighbor's child has drowned, and they are doing pediatric CPR down the street. Priorities in emergency medical care are difficult to manage. Dispatchers are guided by specific protocols. The worst thing you can do is lie about the nature or extent of your emergency. This will NOT get help to you sooner, and may endanger someone else. If you have a true emergency, the closest appropriate help in your community will be sent.

The dispatcher will require the following information immediately:

- What is the nature of your emergency?
- What is your name, location, and the number of the phone you are calling from?
- What is your child's age?
- Is your child breathing?
- Is your child conscious?

The dispatcher may or may not be able to assist you. If you are fortunate enough to live in an area served by trained medical dispatchers, he will provide instructions and assistance for you until the ambulance arrives. These instructions will be clear and easy to follow. Listen to him and do exactly as he says. Emergency Medical Dispatching (EMD) certification is not required nationwide though. Not all dispatchers are trained to assist. Find out if dispatchers have this training in your community before an emergency occurs. If your local dispatchers do not have EMD, ask why not! And be prepared to handle the emergency yourself.

The paramedics will need to know immediately if your child is breathing. Even as they approach the scene they will be asking, "What happened?" Do not assume that they have the same information that you already provided to the dispatcher. They will be looking around as they approach, to ensure their own safety, as they have been trained, but will quickly focus on your child. An understanding of the events leading to the emergency will tell them whether or not they need to worry about protecting your child's spine. It will also allow them to develop a high degree of suspicion regarding injuries that may not be initially obvious. They will immediately determine a chief complaint and a history of present illness to guide them in developing a treatment plan for your child.

They will also need the following information. Family members of patients who are chronically ill and make frequent trips to the hospital learn to keep this information available and up-to-date. They frequently write this information down for providers on a piece of paper or index card that they know may not be returned to them. It is helpful, particularly if your child has a significant medical history or takes multiple medications or has numerous allergies to medications, to have this information readily available. Your child may not become ill at home. You should keep copies of this information in your purse or wallet, and data provided to school officials, day-care providers, baby-sitters, and extended family members who care for your child should be updated regularly.

- Your child's name
- Age and date of birth
- Address
- Phone number
- Social security number
- Doctor's name
- Insurance company name and subscriber information
- Medical history
- Medications
- Allergies to medications

The process of obtaining all this information while simultaneously initiating treatment for your child can be difficult. Parents sometimes feel as though they are being interrogated and frequently insist that the medic stop asking questions and just help their child. EMS providers are trained to do both at the same time, and they absolutely need most of this information. If a child is not breathing, they may not need a social security number or even the child's name. But the last three items—information regarding pertinent medical history, medications the child is taking, and any allergies to medications—are crucial to the development of an appropriate treatment plan.

The hospital will need all of the same information. EMS providers do not always have the opportunity to share this informa-

KNOW YOUR RIGHTS

Most people dial 911 and then forfeit all their rights. They do not realize they are still in control. A patient may refuse to go to the hospital. A patient may refuse offered treatment. A patient may refuse some treatments and not others. A patient has rights in an ambulance just as they have rights in a hospital to make their own decisions about care. Similarly, parents have the right to make those decisions for their children. While it is important to understand that training for care in a prehospital environment focuses on life-saving treatment and that usually the prehospital provider will know what is best and which hospital is most appropriate, a parent can and should be involved in these decisions.

Unfortunately, in an emergency, a screaming, hysterical, belligerent parent cannot always be considered a competent guardian. Your rights, including your right to make decisions for your child, will almost always be honored if you can remain calm, make sense, provide credible information to the provider, and request resources or destinations that are logical and practicable.

tion with admitting clerks before leaving on another call. At the hospital, you will also be asked for copies of your insurance cards and additional information about religion, next of kin, etc.

- Not all emergency dispatchers are trained to assist you.
- Be prepared to answer many, many questions that may seem unimportant at the moment. At the very least, know what medications your child takes, the names of any medications your child is allergic to, and your child's medical history.
- Do not assume the EMS providers have the information you provided to the emergency dispatcher. You may have to repeat the information over and over.

WHAT TO EXPECT

She was slumped over in a chair when I arrived at the doctor's office. She was forty years old, pale, wet, dizzy, and nauseous. The nurse explained that the doctor wanted her evaluated at the emergency department at the hospital and handed me a copy of her insurance information. "What's her blood pressure?" I asked. I was told not to worry about it, just transport her quickly. It became rapidly apparent that the staff in this office had no clue what a paramedic is capable of and didn't care. We were just a fancy taxi service. Instead of arguing, we quickly loaded the patient onto a stretcher and moved her to the ambulance. Along the way we slipped an oxygen mask over her face.

Once in the ambulance, I began to do my job. Her blood pressure was extremely low, her heart rate excessively fast. She was alert and oriented but nauseous, dizzy, and weak. She complained of breathlessness. The cardiac monitor showed a potentially dangerous rhythm called supraventricular tachycardia. *Her heart was beating so fast that the chambers weren't filling with enough blood to maintain her blood pressure. As we moved toward the hospital, I completed my evaluation, obtained IV access, tested her blood sugar level, and administered a powerful drug to correct the heart dysrhythmia. By the time we arrived at the emergency department, her heart rate and blood pressure were within normal ranges, she no longer felt breathless or dizzy or nauseous. She had stopped perspiring, and her color was good. "Next time this happens," she whispered, "I'm just calling 911."*

Paramedics are not physicians. We do not go to medical school and endure the comprehensive training requirements of internship and residency in a hospital. We do not diagnose illness or treat injuries, exactly. We do not prescribe medications or offer opinions. We act as the eyes and ears and hands of a physician at the hospital. We act promptly to correct very specific life-threatening situations to keep a patient from dying on the way to the hospital, and we try very hard to resuscitate patients already in respiratory and cardiac arrest. We do this by initiating specific treatment protocols that fit very concise patient conditions.

If a patient does not have an open airway, we will open and secure it for them. If a patient is not breathing, we will breathe for them and provide supplemental oxygen. If a patient is bleeding to death, we will take appropriate actions to stop the bleeding, and may provide intravenous fluids in an effort to replace volume and maintain a normal blood pressure. If a patient's heart is not beating, we will initiate very specific treatment designed to resuscitate him. Sometimes this treatment involves powerful drugs. Sometimes we perform invasive procedures. Occasionally, our actions are dangerous and require advanced skills.

If the patient's condition doesn't fit a specific protocol, or we have any doubt regarding an appropriate treatment plan, we call the doctor at the hospital by radio or telephone, report our findings and impressions, and receive treatment orders directly. This isn't always possible. The very nature of our work requires split-second judgment and independent decision-making skills. If an asthmatic child is already unresponsive and blue, we cannot take the time to solicit advice and guidance. We must act. Once the child's airway is secured, once oxygen and bronchodilators are being delivered to his lungs, once he is brought back from the brink of death, we can relax and chat about his condition.

In the case above, I did not diagnose my patient's problem. I do not know why she was suffering from supraventricular tachycardia. My actions did nothing to prevent a recurrence. Her evaluation at the hospital was crucial, regardless of the improvement in her condition. I simply kept her alive until a qualified physician could diagnose the cause of her condition and develop a long-term treatment plan. My job was to keep her alive until that could happen.

If a child trapped inside a crashed car is having difficulty breathing, my hands and eyes and ears may remain focused on treatment during the entire extrication and transport period, and I may never speak to a doctor on the radio. If your child's condition does not fit neatly into a specific protocol, I may ask you dozens of questions and spend many precious minutes conversing with a physician during the transport. I use my senses to evaluate for a distant physician, and then use my skills to initiate his treatment plan.

- Paramedics are not doctors.
- EMS training is focused on life-saving treatment.

PRE-HOSPITAL CARE

Emergency medical technicians (EMTs) are taught to administer advanced first aid and may provide oxygen. Most EMTs will have immediate access to an Automatic External Defibrillator (AED). They may also assist a patient in taking his own prescribed medications, like nitroglycerine and asthma inhalers. Paramedics are EMTs with advanced training and skills, and carry with them a supply of powerful drugs and additional equipment. Some nurses take extra classes to allow them to function outside a hospital or doctor's office in an Advanced Life Support (ALS) capacity. All levels of emergency care providers are also taught about scene safety, extrication, and defibrillation for patients in cardiac arrest. What will they do for your child?

They will follow the same rules regarding airway, breathing, and circulation that you will read about in chapter 4. They will safeguard their own safety diligently. They will work closely with law-enforcement and fire-fighting personnel as well as doctors and nurses in the hospital. They will treat your child with dignity and respect. Above all, they will do everything in their power to prevent your child from further harm.

If a child is alert and breathing on his own, they may provide supplementary oxygen with a mask or nasal prongs. If a child is not alert, they may secure his airway with an adjunct, either a nasopharyngeal or oropharyngeal device. A *nasopharyngeal airway* is a small, flexible rubber or plastic tube that slides into one of a child's nostrils, which will bypass the tongue as it may block the back of a child's throat. This tube will be lubricated, and it will not hurt the child. An *oropharyngeal airway* is a hard plastic device that is shaped and sized specifically to fit into a child's mouth, keeping the tongue off the back of a child's throat and maintaining access to the airway for suctioning in case the child bites down.

If a child is in respiratory arrest, instead of mouth-to-mouth breathing, rescuers will use a device called a bag-valve mask, which not only covers the child's nose and mouth but is also attached to tubing to allow providers to administer pure oxygen from a tank to the child's lungs. A paramedic will be capable of using an instrument called a laryngoscope to place a clear plastic device, called an endotracheal tube, deep into a child's airway. The bag-valve unit can then be attached directly to this tube. This is referred to as *"intubation"* and is the most efficient and secure means of breathing for an unresponsive child.

If a foreign body is blocking a child's airway, that same laryngoscope can be used to see within a child's upper airway, and long, curved prongs—or forceps—can be used to remove the object. If the blockage is too low, or if damage or swelling to the upper airway prevents providers from opening a child's airway and/or inserting an endotracheal tube, a specially designed large bore needle can be inserted into a child's trachea through the front of the neck. This is called a *cricothyroidotomy*. It is not a good airway; it is strictly a temporary fix and requires specialized training and equipment. A much better treatment would involve even more specialized equipment that allows a qualified physician at the hospital to visualize the child's entire airway, or a surgeon to place a hole in the child's neck, called a *tracheotomy.* But until that child and that doctor and that specialized equipment are together, the child has to breathe. While a similar procedure used to be taught in ancient first-aid classes, NEVER attempt this on your own. A child's little neck is packed tight with huge blood vessels, nerve bundles, and organs that can be easily and permanently damaged. A paramedic's cricothyroidotomy can keep a child breathing until arrival at the hospital. But a paramedic will take this step only as a last resort, and he has both the appropriate equipment and the advanced training necessary.

If you are administering CPR, do not stop the minute you see emergency personnel arrive at the scene. They will need a moment to unpack their equipment and will be grateful for your continued assistance. Along with securing an open airway, providers will need to know quickly what the child's heart is doing. Paramedics will attach electrodes to the child's chest to determine what electrical activity can be detected in the child's heart. Regardless of what electrical activity shows on the cardiac monitor, as long as no pulse can be felt, chest compressions will continue. If that electrical activity represents one of two rhythms, either *ventricular fibrillation* or *ventricular tachycardia,* an electrical jolt called *defibrillation* will be administered rapidly. For adults, and in rare cases children, this electrical stimulation can resuscitate a patient quickly. If the rhythm on the monitor will not respond to defibrillation, or it is a rhythm not responsive to an electrical jolt, drugs will be needed.

If a child's airway can be quickly secured with an endotracheal tube, several drugs can be administered directly through that tube and absorbed through the child's lungs. Some drugs cannot be administered this way and need to be injected directly into a vein by first obtaining intravenous (IV) access. Sometimes it is necessary for a paramedic to access a larger vessel in a child's neck, rather than a smaller vessel in the child's arm or leg. Occasionally, IV access is simply not possible, and a paramedic must obtain access to the marrow in a child's lower leg bone to administer the drugs. This is called *intraosseous access* and can be difficult for parents to watch. The medic is not hurting the child. If this step is being taken, the child may die without the medication the paramedic is trying to administer.

Once IV access is achieved, a paramedic can administer fluids to treat dehydration or blood loss, a sugar solution to treat a diabetic, powerful drugs to open air passages, alter blood pressure, stimulate or calm a heart, reverse the effects of a severe allergic reaction, or stop a seizure. Sometimes no medication is needed immediately, but

AUTOMATIC EXTERNAL DEFIBRILLATION

Patients in cardiac arrest sometimes suffer from heart rhythms that will respond to an electrical shock, called defibrillation. These heart rhythms include ventricular tachycardia and ventricular fibrillation. These potentially fatal heart rhythms are frequently caused by heart disease, which is only rarely the cause of pediatric cardiac arrest. Rapid access to a defibrillator is crucial for an adult patient and may be helpful for some children. Machines are available for use on adults that require very little training to provide the needed electrical stimulus, called Automatic External Defibrillators (AEDs). Simple and safe to use, AEDs are being purchased for use in a wide variety of settings. These automated machines are programmed to deliver shocks only when certain heart rhythms are detected, and only in doses of electric shock for patients over age eight and over ninety pounds. AEDs cannot yet be calibrated easily for use in children under age eight or who weigh less than ninety pounds. Because the amount of electrical shock administered through the use of an AED is calibrated for an adult, these otherwise invaluable machines should not be used on young children. Paramedics use far more complex and far more expensive cardiac monitoring and treatment equipment that *can* be calibrated based on a child's weight. If a young child needs defibrillation, it must wait until paramedics arrive.

that access is still important in the event your child's condition deteriorates before arrival at the hospital. While paramedics can test a diabetic child's blood for sugar levels, very few prehospital providers take blood samples for other reasons—like blood alcohol tests, drug tests, or microbial cultures. These tests will usually be run later at the hospital. Paramedics can administer Syrup of Ipecac or activated charcoal to a child who has been poisoned, and may be capable of reversing the effects of some medication overdoses.

Paramedics can administer nebulizer (breathing) treatments to children having trouble breathing, to help open swollen breathing passages. If evidence exists that a child's lung has collapsed, called a *pneumothorax,* and if this condition becomes life threatening, paramedics can perform a *needle thoracotomy,* providing a tiny hole so that air inside the chest but outside the lungs can escape—allowing a child to breathe easier.

Usually, paramedics will not attempt to reduce or manipulate fractures. But it may become necessary if no evidence of adequate blood flow exists below the fracture. As long as signs of blood flow exist, fractures will simply be immobilized, and the child will be kept as comfortable as possible. One exception is for fractures of the upper leg bone, called the *femur.* A fractured femur is extremely painful when unstable and can result in significant blood loss inside the leg. A traction device may be used to pull the fractured bone ends apart. While this can cause intense pain for just a moment while it is attached, it provides for an incredible amount of pain relief and stability for the leg during transport, and prevents further damage.

Direct pressure and pressure points will be used to stop external bleeding, exactly as you can do yourself at the scene prior to EMS arrival. Sterile bandaging material will be used, and providers will be wearing protective gloves. When necessary, paramedics can also obtain IV access and administer fluids, usually a simple salt solution, to combat the effects of blood loss. Paramedics do not carry blood products. The IV solution they use is not the same as the blood being lost, it does not contain red blood cells and cannot carry oxygen the way blood does. While fluids can keep blood pressure from falling too low, care must be taken regarding the rate and volume administered to keep from simply diluting a child's blood-stream too much.

- EMTs provide advanced first aid, oxygen, and usually have AEDs.
- Paramedics are EMTs with advanced training and equipment.
- EMTs and paramedics are trained to save lives.

WHO WILL RESPOND TO YOUR CALL FOR HELP?

I was a paramedic intern with an urban service. My preceptor was big, mean, tough, and irreverent. I was terrified. We responded to a call for a patient having trouble breathing and dragged our equipment up three flights of stairs. He pushed open the apartment door without knocking and bellowed, "Did somebody here call for help?" A whole flock of family members appeared, all talking at once, and herded us into a back bedroom where a frail, elderly woman lay clutching her nightgown to her chest, obviously in respiratory distress. My preceptor's partner murmured something about obtaining medical history and a medication list and pushed the family out of the room. I fumbled with the oxygen mask and blood pressure cuff. As I watched, openmouthed, this big, mean, tough medic crouched on the floor next to our patient's bed, reached with one hand to her wrist to feel for quality and rate of her pulse, and reached with the other to tenderly caress her cheek. "Hi," he said, in a voice I did not even recognize, so gentle and calm, "What's your name?" As I slipped an oxygen mask over her head and took her blood pressure, I watched him rapidly assess our patient. He cared for her with the kind of compassion and respect I would want for my own grandmother. Her broken English didn't matter to him. Neither did her color, gender, race, or creed. It didn't matter if she was rich or poor, able to pay for his service or not. He didn't seem to notice the cluttered, filthy apartment or urine-soaked sheets. It didn't matter if she suffered from AIDS or hepatitis or tuberculosis. It didn't matter that she couldn't walk, and after assessing her, that big, mean, tough medic bundled her into his arms like he was lifting his own little sister and carried her to the stretcher waiting outside.

In most large American cities, these medics wear firefighter uniforms. If you live in a rural area, the local ambulance squad roster may be filled with retirees, housewives, off-duty nurses and teachers, construction workers and mechanics. They may not look particularly big or tough. But all of these people share certain attributes and traits. These are risk takers, people who will go anywhere, do anything, and face any challenge to access and help your toddler having an asthma attack. They are skilled, intuitive, and perceptive. They are natural leaders and need to be in control. They are obsessive and strive to do a perfect job. They are compulsive and traditional. Their laughter can be boisterous and sometimes bawdy. They are street smart and antsy, easily bored and action oriented. They are highly motivated and highly dedicated. Ask any applicant why they want to be a paramedic and you will inevitably be told, "I want to help people."

In most urban areas, EMS is provided as part of the fire service. These providers may be cross trained to respond to either a fire or a medical emergency, they may be dedicated to EMS, or they may be simply physically located in fire department facilities, functioning as a "third service" for the community, complimenting law enforcement, and fire fighting. These providers may be EMTs or paramedics, and they will locate the patient and provide initial treatment. Sometimes this service is provided under the direction of the health department or other government agency, with municipally owned vehicles and equipment and civil service employees. The patient is sometimes turned over to a different service for transport to the hospital. The acting transport service may be similarly municipally operated or may be a private company.

In many rural areas, EMTs will respond to all emergencies supported by a regional paramedic service offering support and assistance only for critically ill patients. Regional air medical services frequently provide helicopter transport for critically injured patients to regional trauma centers. Because the EMTs are local, they will usually arrive at the scene first. In many rural and suburban areas, these services are the remnants of nonprofit, volunteer organizations founded to serve our communities in the 1960s and 1970s. This is where many of the last remaining volunteer providers can be found struggling to survive, trying to keep up with expensive and time-consuming training requirements, and fund the purchase of two-hundred-thousand-dollar ambulances with bake sales and bingo parties. As money has become scarce and volunteer ranks have suffered from attrition, many of these organizations have consolidated with other services or given up their "territories" to private, for-profit companies.

BECOME INVOLVED IN EMS

ozens of variations on this theme exist nationwide as community leaders, EMTs, and paramedics struggle to offer what has become an expected part of emergency medicine. The American public has been led to believe that "911" service, as seen on television, is available everywhere. The public rarely takes part in the planning for the administration of these services. The first time members of a community realize that the television version is not a reality in their neighborhood can be when a family member dies in their arms waiting for Captain Kirk to appear without his Star Trek uniform.

While the U.S. Department of Transportation has established training and certification standards, states are not obligated to require that training for EMTs and paramedics. There are currently almost forty different certification programs for EMTs required by different states. Depending on where you live, the first rescuer arriving at the scene of an emergency may have anywhere from twenty-five to two thousand hours of didactic, practical, prehospital, in-hospital, and internship training and education. This huge disparity in training levels is usually lost to patients who have no idea what the different color patches signify. I stopped introducing myself as a paramedic and learned to simply tell patients that I was "with the ambulance."

Because the rural paramedic service is regional, it may be physically located farther from the scene and arrive later, or rendezvous with the EMTs on the way to the hospital. If the paramedics are committed on other calls in the region, there may be no advanced intervention for patients until the ambulance arrives at the hospital. This can result in significant delays in life-saving treatment. Paramedic units are expensive, with heart-monitoring equipment, sophisticated communication equipment to converse with physicians at the hospital, and stocks of powerful drugs. There are precious few volunteers left with the resources to commit to the extensive training necessary to function in an advanced capacity. Most paramedic units are staffed by paid professionals.

Other medical professionals rarely treat EMS providers like members of a health-care team. This lack of respect within the medical community has been euphemistically referred to as "suboptimal recognition." They are poorly compensated, almost never thanked, and frequently exposed to high-risk environments. Back injuries are common. They work in closely confined environments with patients who have communicable illnesses. They are subject to assault by patients, family members, or bystanders while attempting to administer care. They have limited career options and cannot move easily from state to state without repeating much of their training. And every year their compassion, skill, and generosity touch the lives of over twenty million vulnerable and frightened Americans. About two million of those are our children.

- Is your local service staffed by EMTs or paramedics?
- Is the service adequately funded and managed?
- Find out how you can help.

WHO PAYS FOR EMS?

Different sources of money are used to fund emergency medical services. Some states, counties, and/or individual municipalities dedicate tax money to support ambulance services, in the same manner that they use tax money to fund police, fire, rescue services, schools, and roadway maintenance. These tax subsidies rarely cover the entire cost.

Many fee-for-service EMS send bills either directly to the patient or to the patient's insurance company. Insurance coverage may be through Medicare, Medicaid, a private insurance carrier like Blue Cross/Blue Shield, or an HMO. Medicare and Medicaid reimbursement rates are calculated based on what is considered reasonable and customary. These reimbursement rates, combined with call volumes, are rarely adequate to appropriately fund the service.

EMS may also be funded through subscription enrollment plans. Subscription services are controversial but popular. A family may pay a single subscription fee for emergency services, nonemergency services, or both. One fee may cover an entire extended family living under the same roof or may involve a separate fee for each family member. If the service is used, your insurance company is billed, but any bill amount in excess of what the insurance carrier will pay is forgiven and not collected. This allows services to maintain consistent budgets and prevents additional medical expenses for the patient. Occasionally, ambulance services are based at a hospital. The fee for EMS may therefore be incorporated into your hospital bill or be billed separately. There are almost as many different combinations of these methods used to finance EMS, as there are services in the country.

Private ambulance services sometimes offer more than just emergency response. In order to supplement budgets, they may also offer nonemergency ambulance and wheelchair van transportation. Sometimes the same ambulances used to respond to emergencies are used to ferry nonambulatory patients to and from doctors' offices, nursing homes, hospitals, rehabilitation centers, dialysis centers, and for chemotherapy and radiation services. Some services also offer public education, CPR classes, and injury-prevention training.

Emergency services are expensive, and equipment and personnel utilization is often less than optimal. It is not unusual for ambulances and paramedics normally dedicated to emergency response to be "taken off the street" to perform nonemergency transports, occasionally leaving the community with fewer ambulances and providers than needed. There is little oversight or regulation of this dangerous practice, and patients are not told the reasons for longer-than-appropriate response times when this occurs. Lives can be lost or endangered by this practice with no penalties for poor service management.

Tax-subsidized (public) services are used almost exclusively for emergencies. These providers are sometimes capable only of first responding to initiate life-saving treatment and rely on private companies to transport the patients. Tax-subsidized services rarely provide nonemergency transportation. These providers are usually part of the fire service or health department.

Imagine the benefits if Medicare, Medicaid, and private insurance carriers covering members of a community would get together and fund EMS with or without a local tax subsidy. The cost of providing adequate emergency and nonemergency services to a specific community or region could be estimated and divided by the covered population. A per-capita payment by each carrier for covered members of the community could then be applied to the service's annual budget and nobody would receive a bill. Expensive billing and collection bureaucracies could be eliminated. EMS would serve as a subcontractor to commercial health-care programs.

If managed care organizations that disdain inappropriate use of the emergency department provided for an appropriate level of home care, many unnecessary trips to the hospital could be eliminated. But paramedics are not nurses, and not all nurses have the additional training necessary to provide emergency care in an ambulance. Paramedic training is very limited in scope at this time. Paramedics function with standing orders and protocols that provide them with an enormous amount of autonomy. They make many treatment decisions in advance of direct contact with a physician in order to save lives. But a paramedic's normal scope of practice is limited specifically to life-threatening or potentially life-threatening situations. A great deal of additional training and education would be necessary to allow EMS providers to administer nonemergency home-nursing care.

When sufficient funds are not available for high-quality EMS, the community protected by these services suffers. Fewer emergency vehicles may be available when needed. And cost-cutting practices also limit continuing education and training of providers, force services to hire less capable managers and supervisors; and limit equipment, supply, and vehicle-maintenance budgets. All American children deserve access to and provision of high-quality EMS. The system in place to provide that service was built and designed for adults. Without sufficient funding, specialized pediatric training and equipment needs are frequently the first victims of budget cuts.

Even if you've prepared for an emergency, even if you know how to recognize an evolving emergency and know how to call for help, there will still be a gap between the time you make that call and the time emergency providers arrive to assist. When a child is critically ill or injured we may panic. We will not have time to grab a first-aid manual and look up appropriate treatment methods. Minutes can seem like hours when a child is bleeding or cannot breathe, and we may have trouble thinking clearly because we are scared and upset. Knowing what to do to help a child until the ambulance arrives does not require a medical degree or a paramedic certification. All we need to do to remain calm and care for a critically ill or injured child until help arrives is to remember the ABCs of emergency medical care. While chapter 4 describes the ABCs of emergency medical care, you will always benefit from classes in pediatric cardiopulmonary resuscitation and first aid. No amount of training is too much.

CARING UNTIL
HELP ARRIVES

4

- ✚ Airway—the "A" in the ABCs
- ✚ If a Child's Neck or Back Are Injured
- ✚ Practice Makes Perfect
- ✚ Clearing a Blocked Airway
- ✚ Heimlich Maneuver for Children
- ✚ Hemlich Maneuver for Infants
- ✚ Breathing—the "B" of the ABCs
- ✚ Circulation—the "C" of the ABCs
- ✚ Stop the Bleeding
- ✚ When in Doubt—Remember the ABCs

✚ *She was born with clubfeet. This was the only anomaly the doctors could find, and she was sent home with casts on both lower legs to repair the deformity. At the age of one week her mom buckled her into her infant car seat and headed for a routine checkup with the orthopedist. When they arrived, Mom discovered her child was blue and not breathing. Bloody froth covered her lips. Mom rushed with her into the building screaming for help. The average orthopedist does not anticipate a life-threatening pediatric emergency in the office setting. There was no equipment available to help this little girl. When I arrived, two physicians were working on the child. One was performing chest compressions with two fingers; the other was gently puffing air into her mouth and nose.*

I brought with me all the equipment necessary to secure her airway and help her to breathe. I also had IV equipment, powerful drugs, and the means to transport her to the hospital with cardiopulmonary resuscitation (CPR) in progress, where an emergency physician and his team awaited our arrival. She was successfully resuscitated in the emergency department and later transferred by ambulance to a specialized children's hospital. The child suffered from a previously undiagnosed congenital heart defect.

Your level of training is irrelevant. These two physicians were gifted, highly educated professionals. They did not have the needed equipment at the time this emergency occurred, and they could do no more than the average bus driver could. But what they did, what you or any bus driver can also do, was exactly correct. This child was not breathing. They opened her airway and did that for her. This child's heart was not beating. They performed chest compressions correctly, to circulate the oxygenated blood for her. They ensured that help was on the way, and continued pumping and blowing until we arrived.

Open the airway. Start the breathing. Circulate the blood. Anything more requires special equipment as well as specialized training. These simple actions alone can save a child's life. The alphabet helps us to remember the steps in the correct sequence. The ABCs of emergency medical care allow us to remember what to do and when to do it, even when we are upset and scared. "A" stands for Airway, "B" stands for Breathing, "C" stands for Circulation. Faced with an emergency, whether we are helping an adult or a child, all we have to do is follow the ABCs.

The American Heart Association (AHA) and the American Red Cross teach that if you are concerned about infectious diseases or communicable illness you may perform compressions without ventilating a patient by performing mouth to mouth breathing. Unprotected mouth-to-mouth breathing may place us at risk of contracting some illness. There are no reported cases of AIDS or HIV or hepatitis being transmitted during CPR. However, illness can be transmitted during mouth-to-mouth breathing, and it would be inappropriate to discount this danger entirely. It would be great if we all carried pocket masks to perform this skill with a protective barrier in place. You must make a decision based on your familiarity with the child and their condition, your understanding of disease transmission, and any fear you may have of contracting some illness. I would never hesitate to perform mouth-to-mouth ventilations on a child who was not breathing. I will always be willing to take this risk if a child's life is in danger. You must make your own decision.

This book is no substitute for learning these skills in a classroom environment. When you take a class in pediatric CPR you will be given an opportunity to practice these skills on baby-and child-sized mannequins with trained professionals guiding you. Taking this class requires several hours of your time and can be very scary. While teaching pediatric CPR, I have watched young parents stand and leave the classroom. It can be upsetting to talk of babies not breathing and children with hearts that are not beating. But nothing can match the horror of finding a child who is not breathing and not knowing what to do. Anyone can, and everyone should, *learn this skill.*

- The ABCs of emergency medical care help us to remember what to do when tragedy strikes.
- Unprotected mouth-to-mouth rescue breathing may pose a risk of disease transmission.
- You can practice the ABCs of emergency medical care by taking a class in CPR.

AIRWAY—THE "A" OF THE ABCS

If a child does not have an open airway, air containing oxygen cannot get into his lungs. If oxygen cannot get into his lungs, it cannot be transferred to his bloodstream and circulated to the cells that require oxygen to survive—like his brain cells and heart muscle cells. You can perform chest compressions until you collapse. But if all you are doing by performing those compressions is circulating blood that does not contain oxygen, it will do the child no good. Chest compressions without an open airway and adequate ventilations are not enough to save a child's life. While recent changes to CPR standards for adults suggest that chest compressions alone are sometimes sufficient, *children need air*.

Before attempting to give a breath, make sure the child's airway is in an open position. No air can be transferred to a child's lungs if something is blocking his airway. Two things may get in the way and prevent you from moving air into a child's lungs. Either the child's own tongue is in the way, or a foreign body is blocking it. Children do not "swallow" their tongues as the old wife's tale claims. But a flaccid tongue can fall back and cover the entrance to the lower airway. Simply tipping the child's head back

Head-tilt chin-lift maneuver

and lifting the chin, or gently thrusting the lower jaw forward, should be sufficient to move the tongue away from the back of the throat. Moving the child so the airway is in an open position is always your first step. If the child's airway is swollen shut, due to injury, infection, or an allergic reaction, no amount of tipping will help. This is a life-threatening emergency requiring advanced skills and advanced life-support providers with appropriate equipment. All you can do until they arrive is continue to attempt ventilations.

If the child has not injured his neck or spine, position him on his back. Tip the child's head back with gentle pressure on his forehead and lift his chin. If the child has sustained a head, neck, or back injury, it is important to keep from moving his spine in any way. Move his lower jaw *only*, thrusting it forward, without moving his head or neck. This is called a jaw-thrust maneuver and is described in greater detail on pages 71–72.

Once the airway is in an open position, lean down so that your ear is close to the child's mouth with your head turned so you can watch his chest. Look for chest rise indicating the child is breathing. Listen for breath sounds with your ear. Feel for air on your cheek as the child exhales. If you look, listen, and feel and cannot detect breathing, you must breathe for the child.

If you attempt to breathe in this manner for a child and find that the air only leaks out around your mouth, the airway is blocked. Reposition the child's head once more, tipping the forehead back and lifting the chin, and try again. Because a child's head is much larger in proportion to his body than an adult's, it can be useful to place a small towel or wash cloth beneath his shoulders. If air still will not move in enough to lift the child's chest then something is blocking the child's airway.

If a foreign body is blocking the airway, you must take action to remove it. The Heimlich maneuver that can dislodge a foreign body in the airway is described below.

- You can open a child's airway simply by changing the child's position.

- Tilt the child's head back and lift his chin. If a child's head, neck, or back are injured, use a jaw-thrust maneuver described below.

IF A CHILD'S NECK IS INJURED

The simple maneuver described above to open a child's airway by tipping his forehead back and lifting his chin is sufficient to pull a flaccid tongue away from the back of a child's throat. But this maneuver requires manipulation of a child's neck. If the child has suffered a trauma or injury, manipulation of his neck in this manner may cause additional damage and even result in paralysis or death. Look at the circumstances at the scene. Did the child fall? Is he lying at the foot of a flight of steps? If he has been pulled from a swimming pool, did he dive in, striking his head on the concrete bottom? If you do not know, or if you suspect any possibility of trauma to a child's head, neck, or back, you must use an alternative method of opening his airway.

Turn the child onto his back by rolling him gently. Keep the head and neck as straight as possible and in line with the rest of his spine. If possible, have a second person hold his head and neck straight while together you roll the child slowly, like rolling a log. At this point, if a second person is there, he should continue to hold the child's head and neck straight by placing one hand over each of the child's ears and spreading his fingers to immobilize and splint head, neck, and back together.

To open the airway, place your fingers behind the child's lower jaw on both sides, just below his ears. Place your thumbs on the child's cheekbones, being careful not to injure his eyes with your fingers or fingernails. Now lift his *lower jaw only*, straight up, using slight pressure on his cheekbones to keep from lifting his entire head off the floor and inappropriately moving his neck. You must continue to hold his airway open in this manner, with only the lower jaw thrust forward, while you attempt to give breaths. Since we do not have

Jaw-thrust maneuver

three hands, you cannot squeeze off his nose when using this maneuver. To keep air from escaping, either blow into both his mouth and his nose or press your cheek against his nostrils to block them.

- Use a jaw-thrust maneuver to open an airway without moving a child's spine.
- Reposition the lower jaw only.

PRACTICE MAKES PERFECT

Opening an airway is one of the few maneuvers you can and should practice at home. *Chest thrusts, abdominal thrusts, mouth-to-mouth breathing and chest compressions should never be performed on any person who is not in need of resuscitation.* These maneuvers can harm a child or an adult. But it is safe and simple to practice opening an airway. It is also instructive to be on both the giving and receiving end. Lie on the floor and have someone else open your airway, using both the head-tilt-chin-lift maneuver and the jaw thrust designed to keep the neck from moving. This will help you to understand how little pressure and movement are actually necessary to open an airway and will allow you to feel more comfortable and confident if you ever have to use the skill.

- The head-tilt-chin-lift and jaw-thrust maneuvers can be practiced safely.
- Moving an airway into an open position requires very little pressure.
- Never practice chest thrusts, abdominal thrusts, rescue breathing, or chest compressions on anyone who does not require resuscitation.

CLEARING A BLOCKED AIRWAY

Anyone, at any age, can choke to death. Adults usually choke on food and usually when they are drinking alcohol, laughing, eating, and telling a good joke all at the same time. I pulled a piece of meat from a man's airway once that was so huge we could almost still recognize what part of the cow it was from. But children are at particularly high risk, and stupidity is not a prerequisite. As anyone who has ever played with children knows, discovery of the world around them requires that they touch, feel, and *taste* everything. Children want to put everything in their mouths, especially as they teethe and search for some object that will comfort their sore gums.

Young children choke on peanuts. Since they cannot chew them, they roll them around in their little mouths until a great big breath sucks them down into the airway. They may also choke on marbles, little plastic toy soldiers, grapes, hard candies, potato chips, coins, matches, cigarette butts, keys, plastic wrap, paper clips, raw vegetables, popcorn, and anything else imaginable that can fit inside a little mouth. Of many toddlers who choke to *death* each year, the foreign object found blocking their little airways is frequently a piece of *balloon*.

If your child is coughing forcefully or able to talk, stay with him but take no action. Children are frequently capable of clearing their

DID I MENTION PEANUTS?

I was one of only a few paramedics taking the Advanced Pediatric Life Support course (APLS) developed by the American College of Emergency Physicians and the American Academy of Pediatrics. Most of the students were doctors—interns and residents from area hospitals. It was one of the most valuable classes I have ever had the privilege of taking. Only portions of the course occur in a class-room setting. Most of our time was spent in small groups practicing hands-on skills and learning by talking ourselves through mock emergencies. As I sat with several young, new doctors in a small room waiting for our instructor, I listened as they debated how old a child should be before a parent should allow them to eat peanuts. They reached a consensus as the instructor walked in, deciding that nobody should be allowed to eat peanuts until they reach the age of thirty, and only then if they are not drinking alcohol.

own airways without injury or danger. Let them cough and sputter and move into whatever position is most conducive to expelling the object. It is when a child can no longer move air sufficiently to cough loudly or talk that he is in trouble. You, and anyone else who cares for your child, need to learn the Heimlich maneuver. For a child who is still awake, this means abdominal thrusts. For a child who is unresponsive, this means a combination of thrusts and attempts to open his airway and breathe for him. For an infant who is still awake, this means back blows and chest thrusts. For an infant who is unre-sponsive, this means back blows, chest thrusts, and attempts to open his airway and breathe for him. You need to apply this skill as soon as your child stops coughing on his own, begins to make high-pitched squeaking noises or gasping, begins to signal frantically that he can-not breathe, or if he begins to turn blue.

You must learn this skill. Help will not arrive in time. Unless you have a paramedic visiting with his equipment at the time your child chokes, EMS will not be enough. Paramedics who respond to assist children who are choking either find an alert child who is fine now that he cleared his own airway or someone at the scene knew how to perform the Heimlich maneuver, or they find an unresponsive child near death. Even in areas where EMS response times are minimal, the amount of time a child is without oxygen during a choking episode can be enough to kill him or cause extensive brain damage. Again, if you need a reminder: Don't feed young children peanuts.

- Anyone, of any age, can choke to death.
- Children are at very high risk of choking.

HEIMLICH MANEUVER FOR CHILDREN

If a foreign object is stuck in the airway and blocking air movement in and out of the lungs, force may be required to dislodge or remove it. The concept behind the Heimlich maneuver is to use the air trapped inside the lungs to blow the object up and out. This air is pushed upward by sharp thrusts against the underside of the *diaphragm*. The *diaphragm* is a large, muscular sheath that separates the contents of the chest from the contents of the abdomen and lies just below the lungs. To perform these thrusts move behind a standing child, wrap your arms around his waist, place your closed fist, thumb-side facing you, against the child's abdomen. Your fist should be above the child's belly button but well below the bottom of the breastbone. You must then push in quickly and sharply, directing your fist inward and upward by pushing it with your other hand. These thrusts should be provided until the object pops out or the child begins to breathe on his own.

If a child is unresponsive, or becomes unresponsive, position him on his back. If you can see an object in his airway try to remove it ONLY if it is easy to grasp. If you can see it but cannot reach it easily, your big fingers may simply push the object deeper into the child's throat. Straddle the child, placing one knee on the

Heimlich for children (awake)

floor on either side of the child's legs. Place the palm of your hand against the child's abdomen, staying well below the breastbone. Push upward (toward the child's head) and inward (toward the child's back) with sharp movements five times. Then move to the child's head to see if the object was expelled or if he is breathing on his own. Again, do not put your fingers in the child's mouth unless the foreign object is easily grasped. If the child is still not breathing, and you cannot see what is blocking the child's airway, tip his head back, lift his chin up, and attempt to give rescue breaths. If you are unable to move enough air to lift the child's chest and can feel air leaking out around your mouth, straddle the child again and perform five more thrusts. You must continue to attempt to clear a child's airway in this manner until help arrives or the child begins to breathe on his own.

Heimlich for children (down)

- If a conscious child is choking, stand behind him, reach around him with your hands, and perform abdominal thrusts.
- If a choking child is unresponsive, perform abdominal thrusts on the floor and stop after each set of five thrusts to try to give a breath.
- Remember to move the airway into an open position each and every time you try to give a breath.

HEIMLICH MANEUVER FOR INFANTS

Obviously, you cannot stand behind a small toddler or infant. In very small children and infants this maneuver can be performed on your lap, the kitchen table or counter, a coffee table, a changing table, or the hood of a car (make sure it is not hot!). For infants, abdominal thrusts with your giant hands may injure internal organs.

The necessary rapid increase in pressure inside a baby's chest can be made by turning a child face down on your lap and delivering sharp blows to his back. Use the heel of your hand and deliver the blows between the baby's shoulder blades. If the baby's head is tilted slightly down toward the floor, gravity may help to dislodge the object. Remember that infants have very weak necks. Their heads need to be supported with your hand. This is easiest if you support the child along the length of one of your arms, further supporting the arm with your leg, if necessary, cradling the child's face in that hand and performing the back blows with your other hand.

You can also turn the baby over, keeping his head at a slightly lower level than his feet, and perform chest thrusts. Again, you must support the baby's head. A little one's neck muscles are not strong enough to hold up his own head. Permanent damage can occur without your support. These thrusts are basically the same two-finger compressions you would use for CPR. In the event of a blocked airway, the goal is not to compress the chest to force circulation of blood, but to initiate a rapid, sharp increase in pressure in the lungs to blow the object out of the airway. If the child is awake, continue flipping the child back and forth, performing back blows then chest thrusts with

Heimlich for infants (awake) (back blows)

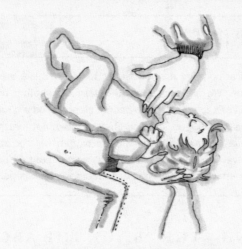

Heimlich for infants—chest thrusts

two fingers on the breastbone, just below the nipple line until the object is expelled or the baby begins to breathe. If the baby becomes unresponsive, stop after each set of five back blows and five chest thrusts and try to give a breath. If you are successful, give another.

Sometimes nothing will work to remove a foreign object and clear a child's airway until help arrives. Paramedics on the street or doctors in an emergency department will have an instrument, called a *laryngoscope,* which will allow them to visualize the upper airway, and long, curved forceps that are specially designed to pull objects out of the way. If the object is below the level of the vocal cords, an advanced intervention may become necessary. Continue performing the Heimlich maneuver until help arrives with advanced capabilities.

- If a choking infant is conscious, perform back blows and chest thrusts.
- If a choking infant is unresponsive, stop after each set of five back blows and five chest thrusts and try to give a breath.
- Remember to move the airway into an open position each and every time you try to give a breath.

DON'T SKIP TO "C"

Notice that at no point are you feeling for a pulse like they do in the movies. We are not trying to determine whether or not a child is in cardiac arrest. If you cannot clear a child's airway and move air, containing oxygen, into his lungs, it does not matter if his heart is beating. Circulating blood without oxygen will not save the child's life. Airways must be opened first, breaths must be provided second. Only then will you even bother to feel for a child's pulse.

BREATHING—THE "B" OF THE ABCS

Once a child's airway is opened, breaths can be given. If you are sure a child is not breathing, breathe for him. Once two good breaths are in the child, you should feel for a pulse. If there is no pulse, you must begin chest compressions as well. If you can feel a pulse but the child is still not breathing, you must breathe for the child.

Rescue breathing in a child—mouth-to-mouth seal

- Give one breath every three seconds for an infant,
- Give one breath every four seconds for a child aged one to eight.
- Give one breath every five seconds for a child over age eight.

This is called *rescue breathing*. You can count seconds by adding the words "one thousand" between the numbers (one-one-thousand, two-one-thousand, three-one-thousand). The actual timing is not so critical; breathing for a child who cannot breathe by himself **is** critical. Breathe for him. Breathe for him. Breathe for him. Sometimes a child who is not breathing will still have a pulse, and you will never need to continue to the "C" of the ABCs. But having a pulse is not enough. Children need air.

Air cannot be transferred to the lungs through any body orifice except the mouth and nose. Since these two airways combine into one airway at the back of the child's throat, if you do not block off his nose while breathing into his mouth the air will just blow out his nose. If you breathe into the child's nose and do not block off his mouth, the air will simply blow out his mouth. If a child is small you can prevent air from escaping by simply breathing into both his mouth and nose at the same time.

Rescue breathing in an infant—mouth-to-mouth and nose seal

You can tell when air is going into the child's lungs when you can see the chest rise. Enough air is in when the chest stops rising. When you breathe for a child, pretend that his lungs are like little balloons. If you blow a balloon up too much, it pops. The same is true of little lungs. The smaller the child, the smaller the lungs, the less air you will need to provide. With infants, the amount of air it takes to puff up your own cheeks should be sufficient. With larger children, larger breaths are necessary. But it is very easy, especially with adrenaline pumping through your own system, to blow too hard and too fast. This can rupture little lungs and make breathing for him even more difficult.

This usually occurs early in a resuscitation attempt. As with chest compressions, it is during the first minutes—when you are upset and scared and panic is pervasive—that mistakes are made. I have watched big, strong rescuers start chest compressions on frail, elderly adults, only to feel and hear breastbone and ribs fracture beneath their hands. Once the damage is done, it is impossible to take the compressions back. The same is true of breaths. If you blow all the air in your big, adult lungs into a child's tiny, tender lungs,

THE CHILD MAY VOMIT

Unfortunately, children vomit. A child may vomit even if he is not breathing. If you are moving air into his lungs, you may also be moving air into his stomach. Chest thrusts, abdominal thrusts, and unwanted air in a stomach can combine to cause vomiting. This vomitus must be cleared from a child's mouth and airway, or it will be sucked or blown into his lungs. Vomitus and lung tissue do not belong together. Not only will vomitus further block his airway, making it even harder for oxygen to be transferred into the bloodstream, the vomitus may damage lung tissue. Roll the child onto his side, use a finger to sweep his mouth and clear the vomit out, and begin the breaths again. Expect it. Anticipate it. Get it out.

the child's lungs may rupture. Air may leak into his chest around his lungs and push in, making subsequent attempts to inflate the lungs more difficult. It is easy to say, difficult but not impossible to practice. Remain calm. Begin slowly, gently, carefully. Once the chest stops rising, more air will not help.

- Give one breath every three seconds for an infant who is not breathing.
- Give one breath every four seconds for a child ages one through eight.
- Give one breath every five seconds for a child over age eight.
- Don't blow too hard—when the chest stops rising, more air will not help.

CIRCULATION—THE "C" OF THE ABCS

Now that you know how to open and, if necessary, clear a child's airway and breathe for him, you must check for a pulse. Remember that "A" stands for Airway, "B" stands for Breathing, "C" stands for Circulation. These are the ABCs of emergency medicine used by everyone from firemen to pediatric cardiologists. If a child does not have an open airway, oxygen cannot get in. If a child's airway is open, but the child is not breathing, oxygen cannot get in. If a child's airway is open and you are breathing for him, that oxygen is getting in but may not be getting to the organs that will begin to die without it. The oxygen is delivered to those organs by the blood, which is pushed around the circulatory system, made up of blood vessels, by the heart. The heart is just an organic, four-chambered pump. Its entire purpose is to push blood around. If it has stopped working efficiently, the blood is not circulating, oxygen is not being delivered to brain and other organ cells, and a child will die.

We can tell if a heart is pumping sufficiently if we can feel the pulsating movement of blood in a large vessel. In an adult or larger child (over the age of one) we can feel that pulsating movement easi-

Find carotid pulse

est in one of two vessels called *carotid arteries* in the neck. These arteries are located on either side of the *trachea,* that ribbed tube that runs up and down the front of the neck. Find that tube, which includes the Adam's apple, and let your index and middle fingers slide off to either side. Press gently and feel for at least ten seconds. Remember not to use your thumb, or you may simply be feeling your own pulse. It is best if you practice feeling for this pulse in a nonemergency setting, but do not hold pressure on this artery for more than the time it takes to feel the pulse. These arteries are delivering oxygen-containing blood to the brain. Pressure against one of these arteries can inhibit that flow and cause a person to lose consciousness. In a very young child or infant with their fat, multiple chins, it may be easier and safer to feel the brachial pulse on the inside (body side) of the upper arm between the elbow and the armpit.

If you have a child's airway open and you are providing needed breaths but you are unable to feel a pulse, you must begin chest compressions. If you are alone, you must continue opening the airway, giving breaths, and performing these compressions yourself. You must continue until help arrives and takes over. If you get to this point, the child is in cardiac arrest and you are performing CPR. This skill can and does save lives. It is worth all of your

Find brachial pulse

effort, every drop of sweat, and every last ounce of your strength. If you do nothing, the child will die. If you do your best, the child may live.

It is crucial to understand, however, that you may do everything correctly, you may perform this skill in an excellent, calm, efficient manner, and the child may still die. This is true of adults as well, and it is imperative that you begin knowing your efforts may be futile. You are making a last-ditch effort to keep a child from dying who is critically, possibly fatally ill. You try your best, and the child may still die. You do nothing, and the child will certainly die.

This is important to understand because anyone and everyone who has ever performed this skill on a child without success doubt themselves. "I should have done that first. I should have done that faster. I shouldn't have pushed so hard or so fast. I should have pushed harder or faster." This is true, not just of family members and bystanders, but also of EMTs, paramedics, nurses, and doctors. We all feel inadequate when our skills are not enough.

I have been involved in the attempted resuscitation of many people, both children and adults. The exact sequence of events as taught in CPR classes is almost never followed precisely. Any number of random events and extraneous factors will force rescuers to modify the steps to some extent. But that is why the simple acronym ABC helps so much. Open the airway. If they are not breathing, breathe for them. If they have no pulse, start compressions. Until help arrives there is nothing more you can do. When this simple skill does result in a life saved, it is the most exhilarating, joyous feeling you will ever know. It is always worth the effort.

Chest compressions require that pressure directed straight down against the breastbone collapse the chest one-third of the way to the floor. In a baby, this may be less than one inch and require only one or two fingers placed in the center of the front of the chest, just below the nipple line. In a child aged one through eight, this may be one to two inches and may require the palm of one hand. In a child over age eight, this means two hands pushing straight down toward the floor in a smooth, even manner about two inches. These compressions must be performed on a child lying flat

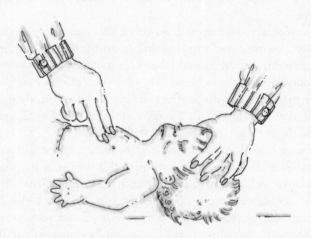

Two-finger compressions (baby CPR)

One-hand compression

**Locating proper hand positions and chest compressions,
both hands**

on his back on a hard surface. The necessary compression of the chest can rarely be achieved if the child is lying on a soft mattress, a couch, or the seat of a car. Compressions can decrease the volume inside the chest putting, pressure on the heart, theoretically squeezing blood out of the chambers and into the vessels. As you relax and raise your hands, the natural flow of blood should refill the heart's chambers. Your next compression should then force more blood out through the vessels. In reality, exactly how these compressions work is somewhat controversial. Nonetheless, it is the only known way short of open chest surgery and manual heart massage to circulate the blood.

Compressions should be performed to mimic a child's natural heart rhythm. The younger a child, the higher his normal heart rate, the faster you must perform these compressions. On adults and children over age eight, we try to perform eighty to one hundred compressions per minute. Maintain this rate by inserting the word "and" between each number (one-and-two-and-three-and-four-and-five). On a younger child, we try to perform compressions at least one hundred times per minute. For a child under age eight, leave out the word "and" between the numbers and simply count one-two-three-four-five. Taking a CPR class and practicing on a mannequin with a trained instructor guiding you will make you feel more confident if you ever need to use the skill. Following each set of five compressions, the child must be given a breath. This means reopening the child's airway each and every time. If the child vomits, roll him to the side and clear his mouth, roll him back and begin again. In past years, instructors and students became too focused on the minutiae or precise movements and sequences. Don't let precise movements and sequences interfere with the basics: Airway, Breathing, Circulation. It really is that simple.

Performing this skill, even on a small child, can be physically exhausting. A child without oxygen for more than four minutes may begin to experience permanent damage. If you are moving air in and circulating blood by performing CPR, the process of tissue death may take much, much longer. You are giving a child needed time with every breath and every compression. If the child is over age eight and an Automatic External Defibrillator (AED) is available, don't neglect the basics while you fiddle with a fancy machine. *CPR must continue while the machine is being hooked up.* Expect to become tired quickly. Begin gently and try to pace yourself. Make sure help is on the way.

When help arrives, they will continue what you have begun. Do not stop CPR as soon as you see them. They will need a moment to set up their equipment and will be grateful for your continued assistance.

- Compressions should collapse the child's chest one-third of the way to the floor.
- Use two fingers on an infant, in the center of the infant's chest and just below the nipple line.
- Use the heal of one hand on children ages one through eight, pressing straight down toward the floor.
- Use two hands on a child over age eight, as you would on an adult.

STOP THE BLEEDING

The other aspect to the "C" in the ABCs of emergency care also involves the circulatory system. If all of a child's blood leaks out, it can no longer perform its job of delivering oxygen to cells. A child's circulatory system is a fairly closed system of blood moving around through vessels from the heart to the lungs to pick up oxygen, back to the heart to be pumped throughout the body, then back to the heart. If the system begins to leak, whether inside a child's body or outside a child's body, the system will eventually shut down. Leakage inside the body can be due to internal bleeding or to faulty blood vessels. Physicians in the hospital must control blood and/or volume loss inside the body. Blood being lost outside the body can be controlled by you.

Applying direct pressure and holding tight for several minutes is usually sufficient to stifle the flow of blood. This is not appropriate if pressure blocks the child's airway or prevents him from breathing.

Optimally, sterile bandaging material should be applied directly over the wound. In an emergency, if no sterile bandaging material is available, any absorbent material or even your bare hand is sufficient. If a child is bleeding to death, the risk of infection associated with using materials that are not sterile is not a priority. Antibiotics to fight infection can be given later. Infection is no longer an issue if the child has bled to death. Remember, however, that diseases can sometimes be transmitted through contact with an infected person's blood. If you are not familiar with the child's medical history, you should minimize your direct contact with any blood.

Occasionally, direct pressure is not enough, particularly if a large vessel has been opened and the blood is squirting out or streaming out rapidly. If direct pressure does not stop the bleeding, it may be possible to find a pressure point above the wound to help impede blood flow. This is only possible if the wound is to an extremity (an arm or a leg). If the wound is located on the head, neck, chest, abdomen, or pelvis there are no appropriate pressure points. Continue with direct pressure only.

If the wound is located on an arm or leg, pressure can be placed on the artery above the wound. The word "above" in this context means higher up the arm or leg, closer to the trunk. For wounds to the hands or arms, find that same spot where you would feel for a pulse in a small child, between the elbow and the armpit on the inside (body side) of the upper arm, and squeeze. For a lower leg you can apply pressure behind the knee. If the wound is above the knee, you can apply pressure to the femoral artery, located near the groin, just to the injury-side of the pubic bone. Use the heel of your hand and press down, barely clearing the pubic bone to one side.

If direct pressure is not enough to stop the blood loss, or if the child has already lost a great deal of blood, there are other actions you can take while you wait for help to arrive. Keep the child very still and as calm as possible. Movement and excitement will elevate the child's heart rate and increase blood loss. The goal is to continue circulation of oxygen-containing blood to the brain. Gravity can work against you if the child is sitting or standing. The child should be lying flat. It may be helpful to raise the child's feet several inches off the floor. *This is NOT appropriate if one or both of the child's legs are injured, or if you suspect trauma to the child's neck or back.*

Monitor the child closely while you wait. Significant blood loss may eventually cause a drop in blood pressure and may lead to loss of consciousness. A child who loses consciousness may be unable to maintain his own airway. Be aware of mental status changes, and be prepared to open a child's airway, if necessary. And try to remember that there may be other injuries. In the rush to control that obvious and upsetting bleeding, people frequently overlook injuries that can be a greater threat. Your efforts to stop the bleeding should *never* involve manipulation of an injured spine or block a child's airway. If you are alone, breathing for a child in respiratory arrest is more important than pressure to stop the bleeding.

- Direct pressure will usually stop the flow of blood.
- Remember that exposure to blood can pose a risk of disease transmission.

WHEN IN DOUBT— REMEMBER THE ABCs

There are three actions that you can take to help your child while waiting for the ambulance to arrive that are always correct, never wrong. Open and, if necessary, clear his airway. Start the breathing. If you cannot feel a pulse, begin compressions. Stopping the bleeding usually requires simple, direct pressure on the wound. These are easy skills to learn and difficult to remember and perform when a child is in trouble. Practice helps.

- Make sure a child has an open airway, either by tipping the forehead back and lifting the chin, or using a jaw-thrust maneuver.

- If a conscious infant is choking, provide repeated sets of five back blows and five chest thrusts until the object pops out or until the infant becomes unresponsive.
- If an unresponsive infant is choking, stop after each set of back blows and chest thrusts and attempt to give a breath.
- If a conscious child is choking, stand behind them and use your closed fist to perform abdominal thrusts until the object pops out or until the child becomes unresponsive.
- If an unresponsive child is choking, position him on his back on the ground. Straddle him and provide five abdominal thrusts. Then move back to the child's head, open his airway, and pull out any foreign object you can see and retrieve easily. Attempt to give a breath. If his airway is still blocked, straddle the child again and deliver five additional abdominal thrusts. Continue until help arrives.
- If you can provide two gentle breaths, stop and feel for a pulse.
- If you cannot feel a pulse, begin CPR by providing five chest compressions followed by one breath. Remember to open the airway each and every time.
- Provide chest compressions for an infant using one or two fingers, pushing straight down on the breastbone, just below the nipple line. Compress the chest approximately one-third of the way to the floor.
- Provide chest compressions for a child over age one using the heel of one hand, pushing straight down on the breastbone, just below the nipple line. Compress the chest approximately one-third of the way to the floor.
- Provide chest compressions for a child over age eight the same way you would for an adult. Use two hands, one on top of the other, and push straight down on the lower third of the breastbone. Compress the chest approximately one-third of the way to the floor.
- If you can feel a pulse, but the child is still not breathing, provide rescue breaths. Give one breath every three seconds for an infant, one breath every four seconds for a child aged one

through eight, and one breath every five seconds for a child over age eight.

- Make sure help is on the way. Remember that you may become tired quickly. Pace yourself. Be gentle with breaths. Remain calm and remember the ABCs.
- Practice helps, both to perform this skill efficiently and to remember the correct steps. Reading this book is no substitute for taking a pediatric CPR course from the AHA or the American Red Cross. Take a class.

PART TWO

UNDERSTANDING TRAUMA

COPING WITH TRAUMA 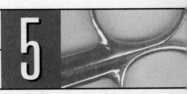 5

- ✚ Injuries are the Leading Causes of Death in Children
- ✚ Most Injuries are Preventable
- ✚ Trauma Medicine Saves Lives
- ✚ Coping with Trauma Care

✚ *When the family car was struck broadside, Mom's school-aged son's head slammed into the side window. It took a moment for her to react, to check that she and her husband were not injured, and to climb out of the car. She was a skilled surgical nurse. She had no training in car crashes and extrication, but this was her son. She immediately climbed into the backseat through the undamaged side of the car. Her son was unresponsive. He was slumped in the seat with his chin on his chest, and he was not breathing. She gently opened his airway. When he didn't begin to breathe on his own, she made a seal with her mouth over his, covered his nose with her cheek and began delivering gentle breaths while holding his head very still.*

By the time I arrived in my ambulance, her son had resumed breathing on his own, but he remained unresponsive. She moved out of our way

97

and used her cell phone to advise her coworkers at the hospital of her son's injuries and to alert the trauma team. My partner and I managed to slip a stiff collar around her son's neck and were carefully lifting him to a long board to protect his spine when he began to fight us. Flailing about indiscriminately, his kicking and punching were not from anger or fear or hostility. The combativeness was a sure sign of a serious head trauma. Keeping his airway open and an oxygen mask over his mouth and starting an IV while keeping him restrained on the board turned into a wrestling match. A police officer jumped into the driver's seat so my partner and I could work together during the short transport. Mom rode with us in the back of the ambulance and assisted in her son's care. Her son recovered fully from his intracranial bleed. Without Mom's actions, he may have died or suffered from permanent brain damage. She was, truly, her son's hero.

INJURIES ARE THE LEADING CAUSE OF DEATHS IN CHILDREN

In EMS, as in the balance of the medical community, emergencies are broadly defined as either trauma-related or medical in nature. Trauma emergencies involve an accident or assault with resulting injury. Medical emergencies involve illness. Preventable injuries are the leading cause of death for children. Injury-related death rates for all ages are highest in rural states like Alaska and Wyoming, lowest in states like Massachusetts and Rhode Island, where rapid access to high-level trauma care is possible. In addition, almost 40 percent of all emergency department visits are injury related. While most of these injuries are minor, from simple fractures to small lacerations resulting from falls, many are fatal, or permanently disabling, or disfiguring, and many involve children. Of over 92,000 unintentional injury deaths in 1998, over 41,000 were the result of motor vehicle accidents. But more than one-quarter of all accidental deaths occurred in the home.[1]

ARE YOUR PRIORITIES IN TUNE WITH REALITY?

As a paramedic, I was fascinated by a study published in the *Journal of Emergency Nursing*. The study discussed the results of interviews with 412 parents and caregivers of children being treated in the emergency department of a level-2 trauma center. Only half knew pediatric CPR. Less than half believed that most injuries could be prevented. Parents were far more concerned about assault and kidnapping than about leading causes of death in children, like motor vehicle accidents and drowning.[2]

MOST INJURIES ARE PREVENTABLE

Accidental injury rates remain so high, trauma care so prevalent, that the medical community refers to trauma as a "disease." Over the past three decades, research resources have been dedicated to finding a "cure" for this disease. That cure has come in the form of prevention strategies that work. They save lives and allow children to avoid disability, pain, and suffering.

Engineering and government controls have been used, where appropriate, to enforce these strategies. Every state and Washington, D.C. have motor vehicle child-restraint laws. Most have helmet laws. The Consumer Product Safety Commission (CPSC) has established safety standards for toys and cribs and infant walkers. But using the information gained from that research is really up to us. Injury prevention cannot be left entirely to legislators, physicians, nurses, and public-safety professionals. Primary responsibility for preventing accidents involving children rests with us as parents and caregivers.

We have made some progress, and injury rates have dropped modestly since 1970. This has been accomplished largely due to efforts on the part of the American Medical Association (AMA),

NO HELMET? NO BIKE

In June of 1994, a New York law mandated that children under age fourteen must wear helmets while bicycling. Helmet use reportedly rose from 2 percent to 26 percent. But a subsequent study in Buffalo demonstrated that only 31 of 208 children injured while riding their bicycles after the law was passed were wearing helmets. None of those who died were wearing helmets, and the cause of each of those deaths was head injury. Helmeted children were more likely to have sustained simple concussions and less likely to have suffered skull fractures and disabling brain injuries.[3]

We, as parents and caregivers, are not insisting that our children use these invaluable safety devices. We are not demanding that Hollywood stop showing movies with cool kids doing awesome stunts without protective gear. As a result, some of us are arranging funerals. Many others are buying wheelchairs and diapers for thirteen year olds. How can we rationalize lectures about strangers with candy without also insisting that no helmet means no bike?

American Academy of Pediatrics (AAP), American College of Emergency Physicians (ACEP), National Highway Traffic Safety Administration (NHTSA), National Safety Council (NSC), the Consumer Product Safety Commission (CPSC), and others. But we, as parents, are not doing enough.

TRAUMA MEDICINE SAVES LIVES

Trauma medicine has evolved to address this "disease." Trauma center care constitutes a frenzied, harsh alternative reality. Time is critical. Futuristic-sounding diagnostic tests and aggressive intervention, including major surgery, occur far in advance of piddling things like parental consent or referrals for second opinions. Success is measured in lives saved. Comfort and family-centered care take a backseat to survival. Lives take precedence over limbs, and nobody asks permission for these well-established medical priorities. If your child is flown or transported by ambulance to a trauma center following a serious accident, hold onto your sox and prepare for a long, cruel, roller-coaster ride.

Trauma medicine dictates the same attention to the ABCs of emergency medicine that begin in the street. Airway, Breathing, Circulation. A team approach is used, led by a trauma surgeon or specialist in trauma medicine. The team is composed from a variety of disciplines: from critical-care nurses and X-ray technicians to respiratory therapists, anesthesiologists, and numerous specialists. Even as a patient enters a trauma bay at the hospital, members are looking for a secure, open airway and evidence of adequate breathing. From a distance, they can look like a swarm of bees descending on the patient. How remarkable that so many providers can perform tasks requiring hands on the patient without knocking each other over.

Parents and family members are appropriately led away from the trauma bay. This serves a dual purpose. Loved ones are spared the emotional trauma of witnessing advanced interventions that can be terrifying to watch, and they are prevented from getting in the way. Trauma medicine is based on the concept of a "Golden Hour." Physicians have demonstrated that if breathing is adequate and both external and internal bleeding can be controlled within an hour of the injury, the potentially fatal effects of shock can be minimized. Speed is as crucial as skill.

But team members are cognizant of the presence of family and loved ones, and efforts are made to put child and family together as early as possible. There will also inevitably be one member of the team dedicated as a liaison. On many trauma teams, this is a member of the clergy. Your religious affiliation is irrelevant. They are there to offer spiritual support, certainly, but they are also members of the team. They have access to your child when you do not. They can speak to team members and the team leader even while initial resuscitation efforts are still in progress. This team member will be your greatest ally and your most valuable source of information.

At the hospital, while a variety of frenzied activity takes place, extending sometimes to twenty-four, forty-eight, and even seventy-two hours before a prognosis can be made with any certainty, parents and family members will sit in waiting rooms, stand in hallways, and stare out of windows. There is nothing so frustrating or upsetting as knowing that your child is in trouble and feeling unable to do anything for them. Most hospitals now know that even critically injured children and their families benefit from being together. Efforts will be made to allow you access to your child as soon as possible. During these hours frustration can overwhelm, tempers can flare. Parents and family members need to be extremely gentle with each other.

Use family and friends for anything you can think of. They want to help, too. Ask them for transportation assistance, fresh clothes, food, breaks, and reading material. Ask them to say prayers. Don't be afraid to ask them to stay with you if you need a hand to hold or a shoulder to cry on. When my own son needed more blood for transfusions than my husband and I could provide alone, I put out a call for help. I was awestruck by the response, especially from members of my sister's church nearby who didn't even know us. It was amazing and heartwarming to realize how many people wanted to help in any way they could.

It is a paradox that the professionals best able to help our children are sometimes the least capable of explaining what is going on. Doctors spend so much of their lives in a highly technical world, studying and treating the complex human organism, that they can sometimes forget how to speak without using technical words and medical terminology. The words they use can be many syllables long and meaningless to those without a medical education. They are so well trained that communication can be difficult. Doctors also tend to avoid absolutes. They may not say that your child may die. But if they say your child is "very sick," that is what they mean. If they tell you that things look better, or good, this may not mean that your child will be discharged tomorrow or with no permanent disability.

If you finish with an interview with the doctor and are left standing in the hallway scratching your head or with your mouth open and your eyes bugging out, find the nurse. Critical-care nurses are very special people. They may not offer a great deal of information before they are asked. Some people are not ready to hear what they need to hear and consider unsolicited information an intrusion. Once asked, these nurses can be generous and skilled teachers. They can explain not only how a ventilator works, but also why your child still needs one. They can explain the reasons for the constant blood tests in terms you will understand. They can tell you about every instrument and monitor attached to your child, and they will help you learn to assist in your child's care, where possible. They will show you where to find blankets, pillows, and coffee or apple juice at

RAPID, ADVANCED TRAUMA CARE MAKES A DIFFERENCE

Children's Hospital in Washington, D.C. is a pediatric trauma center. Over a single three-year period, the neurosurgical service at this hospital treated over one thousand head-injured children. Most of these head injuries were minor. But of those that were categorized as severe, 50 percent died who were transported from other hospitals for specialized care, and only 26.8 percent died who were brought to the trauma center directly.[4]

Other studies also show a lower death rate and higher survival rate of critically injured children brought to these trauma centers. The quality of prehospital care also makes a difference. In a study of over one thousand trauma-related fatalities in Kentucky, death rates were higher in rural areas, highest in Appalachia, and lower in areas of the state where twenty-four-hour emergency department care was available and prehospital providers were trained at an Advanced Life Support level.[5]

3:00 A.M. and they will believe you if you see something indicating a change in your child's condition.

Children benefit from having loved ones near. Even children in deep comas can hear you. They know when you are there. Your voice telling them you love them can comfort them. Your presence, your soothing voice, and your loving touch matter.

This level of trauma care saves lives. It is aggressive. It is also expensive, and thereby threatened by the evolution of "cost-cutting"

TRAUMA MEDICINE DESERVES SUPPORT

Doctors at New England Medical Center published a study in 1996 comparing costs, charges, and reimbursement rates for trauma patients to those for patients undergoing simple appendectomies. The study showed that insurance reimbursements for appendectomy patients averaged 72 percent of hospital charges, representing 112 percent of hospital costs, thereby generating revenue. These payments were usually received within 36 days of patient discharge. Reimbursement rates for severely injured trauma patients were only 63 percent of hospital charges six months after discharge, representing only 86 percent of costs, thereby costing the hospital money.[6]

Fortunately, the study also showed that these reimbursement rates were time dependent, usually while patients and families fought legal battles for coverage, and that eighteen months after discharge reimbursement rates climbed to 76 percent of charges, representing 103 percent of hospital costs. How unfortunate that the medical professionals saving our children's lives are forced to spend time on studies showing a cost benefit. How utterly inappropriate that they are waging this battle without the grassroots support of their little patients and their families.

managed care organizations. This is true of many academic or teaching hospitals. The revenue generated at these facilities supports, not just patient care, but also the training of new doctors, research to find new cures and treatments for diseases, and public education. A battle is being fought by physicians for the continued support of these centers without the assistance of the parents of the children being saved. And our help may be pivotal.

The next five chapters provide a comprehensive understanding of the most common *serious* injuries in children. I will not tell you how to wash skinned knees or tie pretty bows on bandages. Many simple first-aid manuals provide that guidance. Saving children's lives is the priority of these chapters—and this means asking you to consider some pretty scary stuff. The goal is not to frighten; rather the goal is to empower and to inform.

These serious traumas result from automobile accidents, burns, drowning, fractures, and head injuries. This is not the kind of information that can be retrieved easily and quickly in an emergency. When a child is not breathing, or is bleeding to death, we do not have time to grab a reference book. Learning about injuries and prevention strategies allows us, not only to help our children until professional help arrives, but also to keep our children from becoming injured in the first place. The next five chapters offer general information about specific injury mechanisms first, then provide instruction on helping a child until emergency providers arrive. Each chapter ends with the best injury-prevention information available from expert sources.

AUTHOR'S NOTE

My son, Larry, died a hero on June 25, 2001. He was swimming across a stretch of water when his friend, swimming behind him, developed a cramp. Larry immediately turned back in the water to help. We're not sure what happened after that. Maybe my son also developed a cramp. Perhaps Larry forgot everything he was taught in his American Red Cross Lifesaving class about the dangers of attempting an open water rescue alone. Perhaps he overestimated his own ability. Perhaps he ventured too close too soon for fear of losing contact with his friend in the murky water. Divers found both boys dead the next day.

Less than three months later, on September 11, 2001, a group of fanatics murdered thousands of innocent people in New York City and Pennsylvania and Washington, D.C. Heroes died that day as well. Knowing your loved one died performing a heroic act does not ease the pain. My son made a decision in an emergency and died trying to save a life. I am proud of him for trying to save his friend. But my son is still dead. I miss him desperately. I still cry in the predawn hours, and I still have difficulty making sense of his death.

I drafted the following information regarding Mass Casualty Incidents (MCIs) before my son's death. I haven't the heart to alter the text. Similarly, I do not have the courage to prepare an objective discussion of the events of September 11, 2001. I haven't the intellectual capacity to make sense of that chaos, nor do I trust those who claim they can. Mass murder by suicidal maniacs is not within my realm of understanding any more than the sudden deaths of two outstanding young men in a tragic swimming accident.

Still, I know why so many emergency service providers died in New York City. I know why firefighters attempting to gain access to those in need of rescue did not turn back in the stairwells. I can understand why a satellite command center was established in the lobby of a skyscraper that was about to collapse. I knew, as I watched the news, why so many law-enforcement officers, firefighters, and emergency medical providers were running *into* that disaster scene, even as the civilian population of lower Manhattan was streaming in the opposite direction. I have had the great privilege of working with men and women with that level of courage. My husband and I tried to raise our son with that same sense of caring, responsibility, and loyalty.

I will not critique the response on the part of the City of New York to an act of war. But I will ask that you consider what would have happened if this particular urban emergency response network had not been so well trained and prepared. How many thousands more would have died without the orderly, rapid evacuation of lower Manhattan? New York City had learned to respond to an emergency at the World Trade Center after a previous bombing. I attended a seminar following that earlier response, during which a New York City official attempted to share the lessons they learned with emergency responders from Pennsylvania. We have watched those heroes share their expertise, and the benefits of their experience, in urban search-and-rescues in Oklahoma City, and all over the world. They were our teachers in MCI response. They truly were, and continue to be, the very best, the finest, the bravest. I pray that all those who lost someone they loved during that attack know, as their hearts break over and over again in the early morning hours, that they are not alone.

I share this information regarding MCIs and the Incident Command System (ICS) used to respond to major tragedies humbly and with great respect for those who have dedicated their careers to this field. This information is provided in an attempt to empower and assist parents who may someday face a bus accident, a train wreck, or a school fire. While such incidents, like the drowning of two sweet, decent young men, are of much smaller magnitude than mass terrorist attacks, such smaller incidents can just as easily and cruelly devastate individual families. Nothing can ever prepare any of us for the kind of horror we endured on September 11, 2001. As America faces threats of more terrorist attacks in the future, we can be comforted by the extraordinary courage of those who serve in emergency services. We can trust in their training and preparation to guide us to safety, as those who died in New York City demonstrated so clearly. We can follow their orders in the midst of chaos, stay out of their way, stay off our cellular telephones, and pray for their safety, as well.

Over one hundred emergency providers responded to our call for help on June 25 and 26, 2001, in rural Pennsylvania. Professional divers, search-and-rescue teams, ambulances, and helicopters surrounded us. I did not go into the water. I tried my best to stay out of their way and allow them to do their jobs. Even as rescue efforts became a search for bodies, they refused to slow down. Thanks to their heroic efforts, I was able to hold my son in my arms one more time and kiss him good-bye—an opportunity many families of emergency responders who died in New York City on September 11, 2001, will never have. Perhaps I am just a bereaved mom, reaching and searching for comfort, but I honestly believe Larry and his friend, Matt, were embracing emergency responders on September, 11, 2001, and welcoming them into heaven.

MCIS AND ICS—LESSONS FROM COLUMBINE HIGH

The entire country was shocked and saddened by the shootings of students and faculty at Columbine High School in Littleton, Colorado, and by other similar shootings in American schools in recent years. Many of us watched the news in horror as the tragedy unfolded. Imagine what would have happened if law-enforcement officers and fire-department personnel had not rapidly secured the school. Parents, learning only that shots were fired and students were hurt, were trying to enter the school looking for their children. Some had to be restrained. What if emergency responders had not done this? Now, imagine more bombs detonating. How many hundreds more could have died?

Put yourself in the shoes of the emergency personnel in charge of that scene. You know children are hurt. You do not know how many. You do not know if they are already dead or bleeding and in need of medical attention. You do not know who the shooters are or how many are inside the school. You do not know what kinds of weapons they have or what kinds of bombs they are reportedly carrying. You do not know their intentions. Children and teachers are pouring from the school trying to escape. You cannot tell if they are victims or assailants. You call for assistance. An entire region of Colorado emergency providers responds to the scene, as well as thousands of parents, journalists, and curious bystanders. If that is not enough, news crews are filming every move you make, and second-guessing and debating every decision made.

Any incident where multiple patients are hurt or sick that has the potential to overwhelm local resources is called a Mass Casualty Incident (MCI). Emergency providers, including police, fire, rescue, and EMS manage such scenes using an Incident Command System (ICS). Overall scene management is initially designated to law enforcement. If the location of the incident is a crime scene, police will attempt to secure the scene for evidence collection. They are also dedicated to the safety of other emergency responders and the public. If a crime scene does not exist, law enforcement will turn over control of the situation to the fire department and fall into a support role, continuing to manage scene security and traffic. If the scene does not involve a need for fire or rescue personnel, the fire department will similarly support EMS in efforts to triage, treat, and transport patients as efficiently as possible.

In order to accomplish all of this, a command system is established as soon as providers recognize the nature and severity of the incident. Communications between and among law-enforcement, fire, and EMS providers is critical. Access to the scene for emergency vehicles must be established early. Dangers posed by any continuing threats must be eliminated. These may include fire, smoke, electrical hazards, unstable vehicles, collapsing buildings, flood waters, chemical exposure, more bombs, and armed criminals. Unless and until these threats can be mitigated, ambulances may stage blocks or miles away.

One single responder will be the incident commander. This is usually the highest-ranking fire-department officer at the scene. While this responsibility may be transferred as more highly trained personnel arrive, there will always be only *one* person in charge. Once police and fire officials order EMS into such a scene, areas will be blocked off and designated for specific activities. The incident commander will delegate responsibility for these sectors to other providers, and they will remain in communication with each other. Managing the logistics of such a scene can be like choreographing a ballet. Patients, scene hazards, scene access, vehicles, equipment, personnel, bystanders, media, and family members must all be considered.

Providers may use colored tarps or cones to identify each sector. One area will be used for extrication-and-rescue. This is inevitably the most hazardous area. Treatment of patients in the extrication and rescue sector is extremely limited. Patients will be moved as quickly as possible to a safer treatment or triage area. There they will be prioritized as critical and in need of immediate care or stable. Theoretically, a stable patient could remain in this area for an extended period as patients who are more critically injured are treated and transported from the scene first.

As in a hospital emergency department, providers are trained to treat and transport more seriously injured patients before providing care for those who are stable. A paramedic or EMT will be in charge of making these decisions and assigning each patient a priority rating. Triage decisions are rarely simple. Patients who are already in cardiac arrest may not be treated at all. Patients are considered high priority if they are having trouble breathing, if there is evidence of shock, or if they have an altered mental status. Those with minor injuries may be assisted much later.

MCIs can be described as barely controlled chaos. Those are the well-managed ones. The first responders at the scene are inevitably overwhelmed. They cannot treat everyone who needs help. They are trained to initially ignore individual patient needs and perform a size-up evaluation allowing them to communicate the need for additional resources first. Before they can open any single airway or stop the bleeding for any single patient they must let dispatchers know approximately how many patients there are, what fire and rescue equipment and personnel are needed, and ensure access to the scene for those trucks. They will also designate themselves initial incident command, turning this job over to higher-ranking officers as they arrive. Their responsibility is to ensure adequate scene management before treating anyone. Only when additional resources begin to arrive at the scene will providers have the luxury of the time and equipment necessary to administer care.

MCIs involving children result in very high adrenaline levels.

The stress can be enormous, and tempers can become short. Some providers will lose nonessential skills, like common courtesy. You may not be asked politely to move, you may be ordered. If you are looking for your children at such a scene, you are not likely to find much assistance or sympathy in the first few minutes. Eventually, as resources in the form of trained personnel and equipment arrive, order will be established. Even then, you may have difficulty locating your children. There will be one sector responsible for transporting all patients from the scene. The provider in charge of that sector may or may not know the names of individual patients as they are loaded into ambulances. The transporting units may be delivering patients to several different hospitals. Helicopters may be taking patients to distant hospitals.

While this may be very difficult, you must trust these providers to do their jobs. If they are restricting your access to certain areas, there is a reason. That reason may be your safety. They may be trying to allow medical providers to work without being constantly distracted by bystanders. Or they may simply be trying to identify patients by eliminating those not injured. Stay out of restricted areas. If enough resources are available, the incident commander will try to help family members find their loved ones. But their responsibility is to ensure that all patients at the scene are rescued and receive care. The enormity of this job may not allow them to assist individual parents.

According to A. J. Heightman, editor of the *Journal of Emergency Medical Services,* and an expert at MCIs and ICSs, 166 EMS providers and firefighters were assisted by 2 doctors and a chaplain at Columbine High. Two helicopters and forty-eight ambulances were used at the scene as well as ten fire trucks. There were nine hundred law-enforcement officers assisting at or near the scene by the time it was over. The two students who perpetrated this horrifying violence detonated over thirty explosives and fired over one thousand rounds of ammunition. Another sixty explosive devices were found in and around the school later. Over two thousand students, teachers, and administrators were evacuated. Twelve students and one teacher died. Over 160 patients were injured or ill. At least one of the paramedics at the scene worked to treat patients not knowing whether or not his own daughter, hiding inside one of the classrooms, was okay. The teacher who died that day was the stepfather of a local fire-department dispatcher. Several paramedics risked their lives repeatedly to rescue children who were still alive. Every single child at that scene who was still alive when rescued survived.

Those who respond to disasters and scenes of violence like that which occurred at Columbine High are members of the community. Firefighters, paramedics, and police are inevitably also local residents. It is not unusual for those managing the emergency to have loved ones inside, too. They also take orders, respond to the ICS, and perform tasks assigned to them. They know that the orderly management of such scenes is critical to saving lives. Stay out of restricted areas and follow instructions. This is the only way you will find your child, and it may be the only way you will find them alive.

The worst MCI in American history outside of war (prior to September 11, 2001) occurred when Timothy McVeigh's bomb exploded near the Murrah Federal Building in Oklahoma City. Video footage shows the first responding medical personnel being completely overrun by patients. Circumstances were as bad as they could be. The building was still collapsing. Many people were trapped inside and crying for help. Nobody knew if more bombs would go off. Children were being thrown into the arms of EMTs and medics as they arrived, many of them critically injured. Access to the scene was hampered by vehicles and damaged buildings blocking nearby streets. This was a crime scene. Preservation of the crime scene and evidence-collection efforts were initially abandoned in order to rescue victims. The fire department had nowhere near the resources necessary to perform a safe rescue effort inside the building in the first dramatic minutes after the blast, and still they tried. Vehicles near the building were in flames. Hundreds of people were stumbling around, bleeding, confused, and scared. Radio traffic was initially so intense that dispatchers were overwhelmed and effective communication was not possible.

Yet emergency personnel gained control of this scene very rapidly. Incident command was established. Sectors were identified and managed. Resources were delivered, and patients treated and transported to hospitals in incredibly short time frames. In the midst of all that tragedy were acts of heroism that will never be acknowledged. Now and then we see footage on TV of rescuers performing under harrowing conditions. These activities took place in Oklahoma City, usually in areas the cameras could not go. But every single emergency responder in that area who ever attended a training session or drill deserves our praise. The cooperation of many people and experienced leadership resulted in one of the most efficient and heroic rescues we have ever witnessed. Emergency responders all over the country were saying prayers that day, both for the victims, and for the men and women who answered that call for help. Details of that MCI will be used for many years to train new providers on how to do it right.

That bombing represented the worst of America. The evil necessary to plan and execute such terror is incomprehensible to true Americans. The response on the part of the emergency providers in and around Oklahoma City was our very best. The courage and skill of those rescuers and responders shames McVeigh and others like him. It is a reminder that real Americans are caring, supportive, generous members of a diverse and proud community. And it shows firefighters for what they are—community members prepared to risk their lives for us.

From school bus accidents to smoke in day-care centers, there are numerous examples involving many children that require an ICS. The goal of every single emergency responder at such a scene will be to save lives. Period. Not all of them will treat patients. Many will be delegated to retrieving equipment, communications, logistics, and scene management. They train and drill to prepare to handle these incidents. Follow their instructions and abide by their orders. Do not use cellular telephones that may interfere with urgent communications. Stay away from restricted areas. Find other parents, if possible, and let the incident commander know where you, as a group, are gathered. Make a list of all children you believe are at the scene, including name, age, gender, and clothing each child is wearing. Make special notes regarding any children with existing health problems or who may be taking any special medications. No matter how chaotic the scene may appear, the ICS works. Cooperation with emergency providers at the scene is the fastest and safest way to find your child.

AUTOMOBILE ACCIDENTS

6

✚ *When I arrived at the crash scene in my ambulance, Mom had already managed to wiggle her way out of the driver's window—or what was left of it. The car had rolled upside down and back again, collapsing the roof, leaving very little room between the roof and the tops of the seats. Her face was covered with blood, and she was hysterical. She wouldn't let anyone touch her. She just wanted us to help her babies in the car. Filled with trepidation, I managed to wiggle in through the same window Mom had used to climb out. I pulled myself across the driver's seat and managed to turn my hips so I could look into the backseat.*

Three sets of eyes stared back at me—two sets appeared terrified, but okay. The third set appeared curious, perhaps even amused. I checked the curious infant who was safely strapped into an infant car seat in the middle first. He appeared to be completely uninjured, his car seat remained tightly secured, and he giggled and babbled in response to my smile. I checked the school-aged sister to his left next. She still had her lap belt and shoulder harness tightly about her. Although terribly frightened, she, too, was okay. Finally, I turned to the toddler. He was also properly secured— in a booster seat with lap and shoulder belts intact—but he was too scared to answer my questions. I glanced down and saw a toy on the floor. "Is this a Pokeman?" I asked. About a wonderful Pokeman doll, he was willing to respond. Within a couple of minutes I was able to safely lift all three children to firemen standing by outside the car. The older children's level of fear was directly related to the blood on Mommy's face. Once we showed them that Mom would be okay, they were okay, too. Still, all three were transported with their mom to the hospital for evaluation.

T raffic accidents are the leading cause of trauma death for all of our children. They can also cause the most serious types of injuries, called *multiple systems trauma*. As the term implies, blunt and penetrating injuries to the head, chest, abdomen, pelvis, and/or extremities can combine to cause extensive brain damage, permanent disability, and injury to organs that may be irreparable. Inadequate breathing and blood loss result in shock, which can subsequently cause failure of the liver, kidneys, and heart. Swelling and bleeding can squeeze and suffocate brain tissue. Poisons are released into a child's system that can cause coma and death.

TRAFFIC FACTS

I n 1997, almost fourteen million traffic accidents were reported, resulting in over 14,000 deaths and over two million disabling injuries. The National Safety Council (NSC) estimates that a traffic death occurs every twelve minutes and a disabling injury every fourteen seconds. These accidents represent a cost of over two hundred billion dollars each year, more than twelve times the profit of Ford, General Motors, and Chrysler combined. From *Accident Facts*, a publication available from the NSC:[1]

- The highest rate of accidents occurs on Friday, but the highest rate of fatal accidents occurs on Saturday evening.
- Alcohol consumption was a factor in only 7 percent of accidents in 1996, but a factor in 41 percent of all traffic-related *fatalities*.
- Over half of all deaths involved passenger cars, but there were one hundred deaths involving bus accidents in 1997 and three hundred deaths involving motor scooters and motor bikes (smaller than motorcycles and usually driven by children).
- Of 12,300 people injured in 1997 in school bus accidents, 9,800 were students. Over 1,000 were injured in South Carolina!
- Included in the 1997 traffic deaths were 1,100 children under age four, over 1,400 kids ages five through twelve, and almost *6,000 teenagers*.
- Every single state and Washington, D.C., have had child-restraint laws since 1985.
- Child safety seats decrease fatal injuries by 69 percent in infants and by 47 percent for children ages one through four.
- Of 653 children under age five killed in traffic accidents in 1996, over half were *unrestrained*.
- Fatal accidents involved drivers under nineteen more frequently than any other age group.
- Fifty-seven hundred pedestrians were killed in 1997, and another eighty thousand injured. These accidents occurred most frequently when the pedestrian crossed or entered the street. Twice as many were killed between intersections as those crossing at intersections. While walking in the roadway, more deaths occurred if the pedestrian was walking with traffic than against traffic.

THE MECHANICS OF A CRASH

When a vehicle crashes, there are really three separate impacts. The first occurs when the vehicle strikes another vehicle, a tree, or bridge abutment. Glass flies, metal is twisted and torn, and anything inside the car not tied down is catapulted through the air. When children are unrestrained in such a vehicle, they become human missiles. They are thrown against the dashboard, windshield, the seat in front of them, or the doors and windows on either side with massive force. This is the second impact. Bones break and skin is torn open. The third impact occurs when the child stops moving, and the child's organs crash against the inside of the body. This third impact can tear major blood vessels and bruise and damage organs, including the brain, heart, lungs, liver, pancreas, spleen, kidneys, stomach, bowels, and bladder.

When pedestrians are struck by vehicles, similar damage occurs. Because children are shorter than adults, they are struck higher up on their bodies. Instead of a bumper striking and breaking legs, the major force of the impact is to their abdomens and chests, with the potential for more life-threatening injuries. Because children are lighter than adults, they are easily thrown—sometimes into the air, usually to the ground where they can be subsequently run over. If you look up and realize you are about to be struck by a car, you will naturally turn away from the vehicle. Children have a tendency to turn toward the vehicle and put their arms out to try to stop it. The car strikes them head-on; they are thrown either up onto the hood and windshield or to the ground for a second impact. They are sometimes then run over by the wheels.

- Unrestrained children become human missiles when a car crashes.
- Children struck by motor vehicles usually suffer more severe injuries than adults.

TREATING ACCIDENT VICTIMS

A t the scene of any accident, you must be concerned about your own safety first. Are power lines down and in contact with any vehicle? Are trucks involved that may be leaking hazardous fluids onto the roadway? Crash scenes are inevitably covered with broken glass and jagged pieces of torn metal. Hollywood has mistakenly taught us that crashed cars blow up and burn. They use explosives and fancy technology to create this effect. While there is always a danger of smoke and fire, crashed cars only rarely explode like they do in the movies.

If you are in one of the crashed cars, you are safest if you remain very still. The adrenaline rush and psychological shock in the aftermath of an accident can mask pain. You may not even realize you are injured, and movement can cause additional injury. I have seen people with broken legs trying to walk. People have jumped out of crashed cars only to be struck by on-coming vehicles unable to stop in time. In the absence of smoke or fire, stay exactly where you are. It is helpful, if possible, to turn off the ignition and set a parking or emergency brake. Otherwise, sit tight.

The dispatcher needs as much information regarding an accident as possible. To yell into the phone that there has been a terrible accident is not enough. The location must be given as precisely as possible. How many vehicles are involved? How many are injured? Are any victims unresponsive or severely injured? Are any victims trapped in the cars? Are there other dangers like continued traffic hazards, smoke or fire, wires down, leaking fluids like gasoline or diesel fuel? This allows the dispatcher to send appropriate fire and rescue resources immediately. Helicopters can be placed on standby. Extra rescue equipment can be added to trucks. More than one ambulance can be dispatched.

- Protect yourself first—a dead or injured rescuer cannot help a child.
- Climb out of a crashed car only if smoke or fire threaten.

- Turn off the ignition and set a parking brake, if possible.
- Provide emergency dispatchers with as much information as possible.

AT THE SCENE OF A CRASH

At the scene of a serious accident children must be kept as quiet, still, and calm as possible. There is usually no need to move or reposition a child before help arrives. Move a child only if his airway is compromised and he is unable to breathe, or if he is in danger of sustaining additional injuries from smoke or fire. In a serious crash, we must assume a child's spine may be injured. Any movement may cause additional injury. Movement may also increase bleeding. Stay with the child. If he is conscious, talk soothingly and calmly. If he is not conscious, monitor his airway closely and be prepared to use a jaw-thrust maneuver, if necessary, to keep it open. If he stops breathing, open his airway and breath for him, mouth-to-mouth, minimizing movement to his spine. If you are not familiar with the child's medical history, remember there is risk of possible disease transmission.

Unless external bleeding is extreme, either pumping or streaming out quickly, it can be ignored initially. The airway and adequate breathing are more important. If the bleeding is intense or upsetting

LEAVE IMPALED OBJECTS ALONE

If anything is impaled in the child, do not remove it, unless it is blocking his airway and keeping him from breathing. More damage can occur as impaled objects are removed than when they went in. Impaled objects must be removed by a physician or surgeon in the controlled setting of a hospital.

to the child, direct pressure is appropriate. When bones break they sometimes slice through the skin and may be exposed. These bone ends can be very sharp and can slice through your hand as well. Use caution. If you are sure the child's airway is open and the child is breathing well, direct pressure can be applied to smaller wounds.

Injured children must be kept warm and protected from the cold. Trauma patients are frequently delivered to the hospital with low body temperatures. Children and the elderly are at particularly high risk of becoming too cold. This is referred to as *hypothermia*. Allowing a trauma patient's body temperature to drop too low can make their condition even worse.

If the child is conscious, be honest with him. If he is clearly injured, do not tell him he is fine. Children need and respond to information just as adults do, but they may process this information differently. If a child tells you his arm hurts, agree that he has an injury to his arm. But be sure to add that the doctor can fix it. Children sometimes believe that if something is broken it will fall off or be thrown away like their toys. Ask him if it hurts him to breathe. If it does, have someone call the dispatcher back and relay this information to the medics. You can minimize his fear by remaining calm yourself. Keep him informed about what is happening, and remind him repeatedly that help is on the way. Reassure him that he is not alone. Make sure he understands that the accident is over. The worst is over.

- Keep injured children at a crash scene as still and quiet as possible.
- Children will remain calm if they believe somebody is in control—your voice should be soothing, calm, and confident.
- Injured children must be kept warm.
- Be honest with children and remind them often that help is on the way.

WHEN HELP ARRIVES

Once emergency crews begin to arrive, do exactly as they say. Prior to their arrival you must be extremely careful for your own safety. Once they arrive, this is their job, and they know what they are doing. Police will take whatever measures are necessary to control traffic hazards, including shutting the road down completely, if necessary. Fire personnel will address smoke, flames, and fluids in the roadway to eliminate fire hazards and manage any downed power lines. They will also stabilize the vehicles to keep them from rolling or moving and causing further injury to vehicle occupants. Nobody will tear victims out of the cars unless an immediate threat of fire exists. If a seriously injured victim can be moved from a vehicle easily, they will be transferred to a long board to protect their spines after a stiff collar is placed around their necks.

If a victim cannot be moved easily from a vehicle, or if portions of a vehicle are trapping them inside, power tools may be used to pry the car away from the patient. These tools, including the "Jaws of Life," can be very loud and scary. The Jaws of Life can move the dashboard or roof of a car away, but more metal will tear, more glass will break. The victims inside the car will be protected during this time, possibly even covered with a blanket or tarp. This can be horrifying for a child. Rescuers will try to provide information, and let victims know what they are doing and why so that the noise and movements make sense. But their jobs require extrication be performed rapidly. This is not always possible.

Medics will begin the ABCs of emergency care even while victims are still trapped inside crashed cars. Airways will be opened. If victims are unresponsive, their airways may be protected with endotracheal tubes even while they are still entrapped. Adequate breathing will be ensured. Oxygen will be administered. Necks and backs will be protected from unnecessary movement, and external bleeding will be controlled. All of this will occur as quickly as possible. As soon as a critically injured child can be moved safely from a vehicle, he will be sent to the hospital. Any additional treatment, like IV therapy to replace lost fluids, will occur in the ambulance or the helicopter. No provisions will necessarily be made for you to remain with your child. If you are also injured, you and your child may even be sent to different hospitals.

- Follow instructions given by fire, rescue, and law enforcement personnel.
- If vehicle occupants are trapped, they will not be pulled away from the vehicle—the vehicle will be pulled away from the patient.
- The ABCs of emergency medical care will begin inside a crashed vehicle and continue all the way to the hospital.

PREVENTING ACCIDENT INJURIES AND DEATHS

Want to avoid learning about multiple systems trauma and care at the regional trauma center after an automobile accident?

PUT CHILDREN IN THE BACKSEAT

You cannot see them as easily. They are more difficult to touch, to talk to, to discipline, to monitor. Live with this inconvenience, and they may live as well. Children of any age are safest in the backseat. If they are thrown forward, they impact the seat in front of them and not the rigid dashboard or windshield. While restraints will not always prevent death or injury, use of safety seats, booster seats, and seat belts gives your child the best protection and the highest probability of surviving a crash.

- Under one year and twenty pounds, babies should be in child safety seats in the backseat of the vehicle and *facing the rear*.
- These child-safety seats should never be placed in the front passenger seat if your vehicle has a passenger-side air bag.

- No children should ever be in the front with a passenger-side air bag. When an air bag deploys, it explodes outward at up to two hundred miles per hour. It will strike the safety seat and crush the baby's head. It will strike a small child and break his neck. Air bags save adult lives. Air bags decrease an adult's risk of death by 18 percent in frontal crashes, and 11 percent in all crashes. But they can injure and even kill children. Children under age thirteen, and even small adults, have an increased risk of fatal injury from these bags as high as 34 percent, especially in low-speed crashes.
- No baby should ever ride in anyone's arms in a vehicle. When the car crashes, the child will be torn from your arms—no matter how tight your grasp—and be thrown. While they are usually thrown to the floor, they can also travel through the windshield, the side window, or into the backseat.
- Over one year and over twenty pounds, a child should face forward.
- You must ensure that the safety seat fits properly into your car and is sufficiently strapped in place. Before placing a child in the seat, grab it and tug hard to each side, and forward, making sure the seat does not pull loose.
- When a child reaches forty pounds you don't need to stop making them sit in the safety seat. This is not a magic number. Children should remain in the most protective seat for as long as they are comfortable.
- When they outgrow the safety seat, they should be placed in booster seats until they are large enough for the lap and shoulder belts to fit securely, without covering necks or faces. Again, children are always safest in the backseat.

PREVENTING PEDESTRIAN ACCIDENTS

Children under age five cannot be expected to cross streets safely. They overestimate their own abilities, and underestimate the speed and direction of vehicles. Their poor judgment is a function of normal, healthy child development. No preschoolers should cross streets without adult supervision. A child can cross a street safely after age five, but only with proper training and practice. Stop at the curb. Look left. Look right. Look left again. Proceed quickly if the street remains clear. Cross only at intersections, when possible, and only if existing traffic lights are green in the direction the child is crossing. If school-aged children practice this skill with adult supervision, they can develop an appropriate respect for those two-thousand-plus-pound hunks of metal coming at them.

One surprising high-risk group includes toddlers in driveways. The crush injuries these small children suffer when the family car backs out and runs them over are devastating and tragic. Toddlers are small, difficult to see, and highly mobile creatures who can be in one spot one moment, and in a completely different area just seconds later. In a six-year review of pediatric pedestrian injuries involving just two trauma centers, 527 children were treated. Of these, 51 were hurt in their own driveways. All but 10 of these children were under age five. The death rate for all the other pediatric pedestrian accidents was 2 percent. For these little ones run over in their own driveways the death rate was 20 percent.[2]

- Never allow a child under age five to cross a street alone.
- Provide children with play areas away from streets and driveways.
- Children over age five must be taught how to cross streets safely.

HIGH-RISK MACHINES

Children love the excitement of motorized transport. Graduating from a bicycle to something with a motor is thrilling. From go-carts and scooters to dirt bikes, children quickly leave the driveway or yard and find themselves on streets with traffic or on rough trails in the woods. Children do not always wear helmets. And they rarely know the rules of traffic, or that they are not as easy for motorists to see as other vehicles on the road, or that wood trails can be blocked by low-hanging branches and wire fences. These children are at very high risk of injury and death.

All terrain vehicles (ATVs) can provide a wonderful adventure. Since the 1960s children and adults have used a variety of two, three, and four-wheeled motorized bikes for off-road fun. These vehicles have short wheelbases and low profiles, some resembling full-sized motorcycles, others more like souped-up rider lawn mowers. They are unstable and difficult for drivers on roadways to see. They are unregistered, and drivers in most states need no licenses for off-road enjoyment.

There were so many injuries and fatalities from the use and misuse of these vehicles that the Consumer Product Safety Commission (CPSC) and ATV manufacturers signed a consent decree in 1988 to engineer new safety standards. But a study from Pittsburgh that reviewed injuries and deaths attributed to these vehicles in the five years after that consent decree was signed clearly demonstrates continuing danger. Children are still losing control of the vehicles, falling off of them, and only 30 percent of riders bother to wear helmets.[3] The deaths and permanent paralysis of children allowed to "play" on these dangerous machines continues (I refer to ATVs as automatic trauma vehicles).

Motorcycles, like automatic trauma vehicles (I mean, ATVs), provide drivers and riders with fun, mobility, and freedom. Many adults disdain helmet laws, and Colorado, Illinois, and Iowa still resisted motorcycle helmet laws as of January 2001. Mandatory helmet laws exist in twenty states. In twenty-seven states the laws only apply to minors, with age limits ranging from eighteen to twenty-one. But in states with age limits associated with the helmet law, only about 50 percent of riders wear them; whereas in states with no age limits, use is close to 100 percent. According to the National Highway Traffic Safety Administration (NHTSA), motorcyclists were sixteen times more likely than car passengers to be killed in a crash in 1998. Half of those who were killed were not wearing helmets, and head injury is the leading cause of death in motorcycle crashes.

Adults, I suppose, have a right to be stupid (except that reckless-ness and unnecessary risk resulting in injuries increase the cost of health care for all of us). Children, while still under our supervision, have a right to be taught responsible and safe habits. Require helmets while riding motorcycles regardless of state laws. If your child insists on a motorcycle, make sure he receives adequate training and rides only with an experienced buddy for the first year. Learning to drive a motorcycle and learning to drive a car are two completely separate skills. While the rules of traffic are the same for all motor vehicles, motorcycles handle differently and require additional training.

I treated and transported an adult motorcyclist who had lost control of his bike while driving home quite intoxicated from a party early one morning. He and the bike had separated, and he had traveled more than fifty feet along the asphalt like a child on a slide. He was wearing a helmet, and I am confident that the helmet saved his life. But he wasn't wearing leather. The road successfully removed most of his skin. This type of injury is called road rash *and is similar to a severe burn.*

On the way to the hospital, as I started an IV, I asked him if he was going to stop wearing shorts, T-shirt, and sandals on his bike and start wearing leather and boots. He grunted. At the end of my shift I found him at the hospital. He had been taken to the burn unit first, where he had been "tubbed," allowing staff to scrub and scour off the remaining dead skin. Then he was wrapped like a mummy and sent to the shock-trauma unit. He didn't remember me. I told him about our conversation in the ambulance, when he had scoffed at my advice to wear leather and boots in the future. "Ma'am," he replied, "forget leather. I'll never get on a motor-cycle again."

- High-risk activities like riding dirt bikes, go-carts, and ATVs without appropriate training, supervision, and protective equipment, or riding motorcycles without helmets or adequate training are just that—HIGH RISK.

TEENAGED DRIVERS

F inally, it would be inappropriate to discuss the dangers posed to children by hazardous traffic without a discussion of teenaged drivers. Young drivers are, by definition, inexperienced. They do not yet know that wet leaves can be as slippery as winter ice. They are not yet skilled in braking, making sharp turns, or dealing with unexpected obstacles in the roadway. They are easily distracted and will

HOW TEENAGERS DIE

I n a study from New Hampshire reviewing one hundred fatal accidents between 1991 and 1996, more than three-quarters of the drivers were teens. There were five motorcycle deaths, four drivers who struck pedestrians, two drivers who struck children on bikes, and one car that was struck by an object falling off a truck. Of the eighty-eight single- or multi-car accidents, two-thirds of the drivers were males. The teenaged drivers were killed in 47 percent of these accidents. Sixty-two of the drivers had passengers, and passengers were killed in 55 percent of the accidents. Twenty percent of the accidents involved alcohol or drugs. Two-thirds of the accidents occurred between 10:00 P.M. and 6:00 A.M. Seventy-two percent of those killed were not wearing seat belts. And 59 percent of these accidents involved a traffic violation, usually speeding.[4]

The last year of this study (1995–1996) there were thirty fatal accidents causing thirty-three deaths. These accidents occurred on one-lane roads 90 percent of the time. Drivers were licensed less than one year 63 percent of the time, and less than six months 47 percent of the time. These accidents tended to occur before 11:00 P.M., and none involved speeding, alcohol, or drugs. These were not older teenagers drinking and driving late at night. This last group represents teens who die as a direct result of their lack of driving experience.

turn away from the road to talk, change the radio station, or reach for something in another seat. Since this is a fun, new experience, which lends them independence and mobility, their cars are frequently filled beyond capacity with friends. Teens tend to drive *too fast*. And they have the lowest rate of seat-belt use of any other age group.

Teenagers are also inexperienced consumers of alcohol. Even with strong grassroots organizations like Mothers Against Drunk Driving (MADD) and Students Against Destructive Decisions (SADD), adolescents are getting behind the wheel under the influence of alcohol and drugs. Combine novice driving skills with intoxication and we are left with some of the most gruesome, chilling accident scenes imaginable. Nothing is as upsetting to police, EMS, fire and rescue personnel as the sudden, violent deaths of a whole group of formerly strong, healthy kids. It happens too often, frequently around the time of high school proms, homecoming, and graduations.

The American Academy of Pediatrics (AAP) advocates graduated licensing procedures for young drivers, allowing for more time behind the wheel with experienced driver supervision before full driving privileges are granted. Instead of a learner's permit followed by a license in six months, young people should be granted provisional licenses after the learner's permit, allowing them to drive during daylight alone, but during high-risk periods (like after dark) only with an experienced, licensed driver for an additional period of time. The AAP also advocates curfews, a restriction on the number and ages of passengers, and zero tolerance for alcohol. All parents should consider driver education and/or defensive-driving classes for their children, whether individual state laws require them or not.

- Never allow teenaged drivers unrestricted access to a vehicle.
- Limit the number and ages of passengers they may have.
- Require seat-belt use all the time, all the way around the car.
- Impose a zero tolerance for alcohol rule even if you live in Wyoming or South Carolina where such laws still do not exist, or in Mississippi where the limit for minors is barely below that for adults.
- Never be afraid to take away the keys. Driving is a privilege.

BURNS 7

- **What Are Burns?**
- **Stop the Burning**
- **Look for Other Injuries**
- **EMS Treatment of Burns**
- **Prevention of Burn Injuries**
- **Fire Safety Basics**
- **Those Nifty Fireworks**

My younger sister, Terry, is a physical therapist. She worked for many years with head-injured patients in a large rehabilitation hospital. One morning she awoke to a day when Murphy's Law prevailed. Her husband was cranky; the children were unruly and dawdled through breakfast. She was late. After dropping off the kids, she had a flat tire. Nobody stopped to help her change it. By the time she arrived at work she was very late, and there were no nearby parking spaces. She had to park on the opposite side of the hospital from her office and walk. She entered the building through the burn unit. The moment she opened the door, she could hear the screams of a young child in the tub room. She knew from her own clinical rotation working with burn patients that the child was in a large bathtub and that dead, burned skin was being scoured away. She knew the child's screams were not from fear, but from pain. A woman stood leaning against the wall nearby with her face in her hands. Terry hurried to her office. Once inside she stood with her own back to the wall and took several deep breaths. Then she closed her eyes and said a prayer, thanking God for this glorious day, for her wonderful husband, for her beautiful, healthy children, and, most of all, that she was not that child's mom.

Burns are by far the most devastating injuries children endure. Burns are painful, they can be disfiguring, and they can kill our children. In 1995, fire and flames killed over nine hundred children.[1] Over half (57 percent) were under age four. That year there were also 260,000 emergency department visits due to burn injuries. In 1999, 2,895 people died in fires, 81 percent of them in house fires.[2] One-quarter of house fires occur between 4:00 P.M. and 8:00 P.M., after school but before many parents are home from work. But most *deaths* in home fires occur between midnight and 4:00 A.M. while families are sleeping.

WHAT ARE BURNS?

Burns are called *thermal injuries* and include more than just injuries in fires. Children are scalded by hot fluids, in bathtubs, in sinks, and from pots and pans on the stove pulled down by little hands. Children can similarly be injured by touching hot surfaces, from curling irons to stove tops and space heaters. They are also injured by electricity while playing with appliances, outlets, and extension cords. Together, thermal injuries are the second leading cause of trauma death in children.

Burn injuries can involve more than just the skin. The extent of a burn will result from two distinct factors: the temperature of the source of the burn, and the amount of time the child is in contact with that source. Children exposed to hot water at a much lower temperature than fire or flames for long periods of time can suffer burn injuries that are as deep as children exposed to high temperatures for short periods of time. The highest temperatures a child can be exposed to in a home environment are from electrical sources. These injuries occur in a flash, but can melt through skin, muscle, tendons, ligaments, and even damage bones. Never allow young children to play where they have access to a coffee percolator or extension cords. But children placed in tubs of hot water and left there for long periods can similarly suffer massive, life-threatening injury.

Burns are described by degrees or by general terms indicating the depth of the burn. First-and second-degree burns are called *partial-thickness burns*. Third-degree burns are called *full-thickness burns*. First-degree burns are comparable to sunburns. The area will be dry, red, and painful, but not blistered or wet. When the burn area contains blisters or pockets of pus, or when the area is wet or becomes waxy in color, it is considered second degree. The worst burns are white or black in color and dry—even leathery—and these areas may not be initially painful to a child because the nerves beneath the skin may also be injured. The extent of a burn may not be apparent initially. Burns can progress and develop from partial to full-thickness injuries over time.

A child's skin performs many important tasks for the body. It protects the tissue beneath the skin. It provides a barrier to infection. It helps the body to contain and manage fluids, and it provides the body with temperature control. When the skin is injured, fluids can be lost and the child's body temperature can drop rapidly. Replacement of lost fluids and body temperature maintenance will be mainstays of treatment later at the hospital. Antibiotics will be used to control infection. But at the scene, in those early minutes following an injury and after the burning is stopped, it is crucial that a child be kept warm.

- The extent of a burn depends on both temperature and time.
- Partial-thickness burns range from bad sunburns to burns containing blisters and pockets of pus that can become infected.

- Full-thickness burns are dry and leathery and may not be initially painful.

STOP THE BURNING

Burn emergencies require a departure from the normal ABCs of emergency care. Before treatment of any kind can begin, the burning must be stopped. Remember to protect yourself. If your child has been electrocuted, make sure that by touching them you will not become a part of the circuit yourself. If they are still in contact with an electrical source, use any nonconducting implement to separate them from this source. Thick wood or plastic will do, including broomsticks, large books, chairs, or other furniture that does not contain metal. If the child is in contact with any large power line, wait for trained rescuers. Remember that a dead or injured rescuer cannot help anyone. You cannot breathe for a child who has stopped breathing if you have been electrocuted also.

Stop the burning using any means available. Most school-aged children know to stop, drop, and roll if they are on fire. Suffocating

STOP, DROP, AND ROLL

If a child's clothing or hair catch on fire, his instinct will be to run to try and escape the flames. Running will only fan the flames and make the fire worse. Children must be taught to counter this instinct by learning and practicing how to "stop, drop, and roll." This lesson need not be scary for a little one. You are not frightening them, you are empowering them with a means of controlling a scary situation. A child can conquer flames by stopping where he is, dropping to the ground or the floor, and rolling with his hands covering his face. Running will feed the flames. Children can learn how to "stop, drop, and roll" as young as age three.

the flames by rolling a child on the ground or covering them with a blanket, sheet, coat, jacket, towel, or anything else available will extinguish most flames.

B urned areas should be cooled, but beware of the danger of lowering a child's body temperature too much. If possible, cool the burn only—not the whole child. If large areas of skin are involved and water is used, a child can become too cold (hypothermic) very fast. Wet dressings may cool the skin and soothe the pain, but further harm a child who has suffered burns to more than 10 percent of his body surface area. Do not try to pull burned clothing off the child; damaged skin may pull away also. Never apply butter, margarine, or oil to a burned area of any size. The oils only insulate the heat and allow damage to the skin to progress.

- Protect yourself first—it may save a child's life.
- Stop the burning.
- Cool the burn, but not the whole child.

LOOK FOR OTHER INJURIES

A ny child who has been severely burned is in danger of having sustained other injuries. The worst of these may involve inhalation burns. Call EMS immediately if the child is having trouble breathing, if he begins to turn blue, if he has soot or ash in his mouth or nose, burns to his face, or a hoarse voice. Make sure his airway remains in an open position and be prepared to breathe for him, if necessary. The danger from an inhalation injury involves damage to little lungs, but may also cause a little airway to swell shut rapidly.

While this is easy to say and very difficult to practice, ignore the burns at first. If the child is unresponsive, it may be due to lack of oxygen or inhalation of carbon monoxide or hot gases, or it may be due to a head injury. This may happen in a fiery car crash, or when a child jumps from a window attempting to escape a burning building. If a child has injured his head or spine, his neck and back must be protected from movement that could cause further injury. If he is unresponsive, he may not be capable of keeping his own airway open. Look for other damage, like broken ribs, that could cause difficulty breathing, or broken bones and external bleeding. Look for injuries that may represent the danger of internal injury and bleeding. All of these can kill a child before the burn injury.

When skin is burned it can melt into adjacent skin. If a child's hands are burned, and he is able to separate his fingers, place gauze or some other clean material between his fingers to keep them apart. The same is true of toes, ears that can become attached to the skin of the scalp, and genitals. Wrap the child in clean materials like sheets, and then in blankets to keep him warm (avoid wool). If you plunge a child into a shower or tub to stop the burning, or douse him with water, dry him immediately and keep him as warm as possible. Remember to look for signs of other injuries.

Minor burn injuries should be kept very clean, very dry, and, once completely cooled, covered with antibiotic cream and a dry dressing. A physician should evaluate any burn to a child if the area becomes wet, blisters appear, or the area becomes infected. Even minor burn injuries to children can become infected and can result in life-long scars. When in doubt, call your child's doctor for guidance.

- Remember to protect yourself first.
- Ignore the burn initially—look for other life-threatening injuries.
- Remember the ABCs—Airway, Breathing, Circulation.
- Cool the burn only, if possible—not the whole child.

EMS TREATMENT OF BURNS

When the medics arrive, they will repeat and continue what you have already done. They will ensure that the burning is stopped. They will look for an open and secure airway. In a child with an inhalation injury, the ALS provider may secure his airway with an endotracheal tube rapidly, before the airway can swell shut. Oxygen will be given to the child, and the child will be covered with dry, sterile sheets. The medic will also be looking for signs and symptoms of other injuries, taking precautions to minimize movement of a potentially damaged neck or spine. An IV may be established, but probably in the ambulance on the way to the hospital. If the child is conscious and in pain, analgesics (painkillers) may be given while the child is still in the ambulance.

Depending on the extent of the burn, as well as complications like inhalation burns and other injuries, the child may be transferred to a regional burn center. A doctor will make the decision and the arrangements. The transfer will be made by ambulance or by air medical transport—either a helicopter or fixed-wing aircraft with specially trained personnel—once the child's condition has been stabilized. This specialized, regional center may be close by or may be hundreds of miles away. You may not be allowed to accompany your child, and travel to and from this center may be burdensome. But if the decision has been made to make this transfer, the child needs the specialized treatment this center offers.

- Medics will also protect themselves, stop the burning first, and look for other injuries.
- Medics will also follow the ABCs—Airway, Breathing, Circulation.
- Burn centers save lives.

PREVENTION OF BURN INJURIES

Protecting your child from the harm of a home fire means protecting your entire family. Every home should have smoke detectors. Every home should have fire extinguishers. Every family should have fire drills, practicing the calm, orderly escape from more than one exit on a regular basis. Children must be taught never to reenter a burning home for any reason, and that they must not fear or hide from firefighters.

Children will play with matches and cigarette lighters. They will sometimes accidentally start fires. They will then run and not necessarily alert anyone to what they have done for fear of punishment. When a room becomes full of smoke, they will hide under beds and in closets. Firefighters eventually find them, sometimes too late, huddled together under blankets and mattresses, or in closets or bathrooms. Children should be carried during fire drills when they are still babies. Children can be taught to leave the house with you during a drill when they can walk, and they can learn to leave a house during a fire drill by themselves by the time they are three years old. The drills need not be scary. But the importance of leaving a burning house or apartment must be reinforced throughout childhood.

Protecting your child from other fire and burn dangers involve simple steps you can take that are age dependent. The most important step you can take to protect your infant or very young child is to make sure that the temperature of your tap water never exceeds 120°. If you live in a private home, this temperature can be controlled directly by altering the thermostat on your water heater. If you are unsure how to do this, call a service technician. If you live in an apartment or have no direct control over water temperature, have your landlord or building maintenance representative do this for you.

- Remember to check the batteries in your smoke detectors.
- A member of your local fire department can help you learn to use a fire extinguisher properly and safely.
- Fire drills should be an integral part of your family's life.
- Keep children away from matches and cigarette lighters.
- Monitor the temperature of your tap water.

FIRE-SAFETY BASICS

The guidelines below are directly from the American Academy of Pediatrics (AAP), the, Consumer Product Safety Commission (CPSC), and the National Fire Protection Association (NFPA). The NFPA is a nonprofit organization dedicated to fire-prevention education and adoption of standards to keep us safe. Thanks to this organization's diligent work, fire-related deaths have decreased by 50 percent during the past three decades. Protecting children from fire danger is their business.

- Smoke detectors should be located in hallways near all sleeping areas on all levels of a home. They should be located on the ceiling or six to twelve inches below the ceiling on the wall. Smoke detectors should also be located in the kitchen, basement, and workshops. Batteries need to be changed every year and checked every month. The smoke detectors should bear the label of an independent testing laboratory. These smoke detectors can decrease the risk of a family member dying by 50 percent. But the CPSC estimates that, at any given time, as many as 20 percent of all installed smoke detectors are not functional, usually due to dead or missing batteries.

- The best fire extinguishers for home use are multipurpose dry chemical extinguishers (also called A:B:C extinguishers). These are useful for fires involving combustible materials like paper and wood, flammable fluids like gasoline and kerosene, and electrical fires. The extinguisher must be checked monthly. These inexpensive devices are of no use, however, if nobody in the home is skilled in their use, and can be dangerous if used improperly. They must be pointed at the base of the flames using a sweeping movement. If you're unsure, have a member of your local fire department teach you and other family members how to use these devices correctly.

- Practicing fire drills in the home should be a regular family activity. From any given area of the house, especially bedrooms, children should be taught two ways of escaping. A designated meeting place outside the home should be established where all family members would find each other in the event of an actual fire. This is your opportunity to emphasize that children should leave the house or apartment immediately without changing clothes or collecting valuables and to never reenter a burning home or hide in closets or under beds. This is your chance to introduce your children to the concept that firefighters are "good" strangers who can be trusted in an emergency. This is the perfect time to reemphasize the need to stop, drop, and roll if clothes are on fire, to never open a door that feels hot, and that the best air to breathe in a smoke-filled room is near the floor. You should include baby-sitters and extended family members in these drills.

- Children can learn to ignite cigarette lighters and matches as young as two. These materials can be a huge source of curiosity for little ones who have no understanding yet of how rapidly flames and fire can spread. These materials should not be accessible to children.

- Children will also climb in kitchens, if necessary, to access cookies and treats. These goodies should not be stored above or near stove tops.

- Pajamas for children older than nine months should be flame resistant, snug fitting, or both. While they may look adorable, little ones wearing Mom or Dad's cotton shirt to bed are in great danger. This material burns rapidly, and the loose fit allows them to catch fire easily. When shopping, look for the tag or label telling you that sleepwear meets federal safety standards.

- Purchase antiscald devices for sinks and tubs, outlet covers and plates, and ground-fault circuit interrupters for areas where electric devices like shavers and blow dryers are used near water.

- Use the CPSP's "Your Home Fire Safety Checklist" to ensure your home is a safe place for your children to sleep. This and other fire-prevention material can be printed off the Internet or ordered using the addresses in the back of this book.

ABOUT THOSE NIFTY FIREWORKS

No book written about children by a paramedic would be complete without space dedicated to fireworks. According to the Centers for Disease Control and Prevention (CDC), 8,500 injuries occurred from the malfunction or careless use of fireworks in 1998. Instead of allowing children to play with explosives, why don't we just take one child out of every classroom in America and remove a hand, an eye, an ability to hear, or permanently scar their little faces. No parent should place a sparkler or package of firecrackers in the hand of a little one without attending a screening of photographs showing how horrifying these injuries can be. Imagine what a child looks like after placing a lit M-80 in his mouth. Why is it necessary for EMS providers to carry fingers wrapped in plastic to the hospital along with their terrified little patients every single July Fourth weekend? Orthopedic and plastic surgeons have plenty of business without this crazed demand for their services as we celebrate Independence Day.

Fireworks are made from explosive materials. They explode. They blow up. They detonate. They discharge. They burst violently. Sometimes they explode before a child expects this to happen. Sometimes they explode outward in a direction a child does not anticipate. When the explosive material burns, even with those cute little sparklers, temperatures can exceed 1,000°. The pressure from even a small explosion can rupture nearby eardrums. The force of the explosion can be sufficient to separate body parts.

Sale of firecrackers containing more than two grains of powder, reloadable shells, cherry bombs, aerial bombs, and M-80 salutes is prohibited under the Federal Hazardous' Substances Act. Really? Somehow word of that prohibition is not reaching the parents of thousands of children harmed by these materials each year. Still wondering whether you should buy these great toys for your child? Request permission to ride along as an observer in the back of any ambulance next July Fourth—but only if you have a very strong stomach.

- Never give children fireworks.

DROWNING 8

- Sad Drowning Facts
- Treatment for Drowning
- EMS Treatment for Drowning Victims
- Preventing Drowning Emergencies.

By the time I arrived in my ambulance on a cold winter day as backup for the City of Allentown EMS, the municipal firefighters and medics already had the scene under control. The car was discovered upside down in the water of a drainage canal by passers-by. Divers were working to extricate three teenagers from the crashed car. None of the children were breathing. Nobody knew how long the boys had been in the water. As each teen was pulled to shore, CPR was initiated and resuscitation efforts were continued throughout transport to the hospital. While I helped in the initial attempt to resuscitate one of the boys, my assistance was not needed during transport. I had the great privilege of remaining behind and monitoring and treating the firefighter/divers taking turns in the cold water.

Although none of the boys ultimately survived, the rescuers at the scene could not be sure of the outcome at the time. Divers returned to the water

140

repeatedly, risking their own lives, in the hopes of saving even one child's life. Most of the divers I cared for that day were also parents. None of them wanted to take a break, or warm up, or let me take their blood pressure. They just wanted to get back in the water. While I grieve for the loss of life at that scene, I know that everything humanly possible was done to save those boys, and I am proud that I had the opportunity to care for true heroes. Those stubborn, courageous divers remain in my thoughts and prayers every day.

W hen a child drowns, they are submersed in water or some other fluid long enough to cause exactly the kind of oxygen starvation to the brain that CPR is intended to prevent. Only 90 percent of drowning victims actually inhale the fluid; the remaining 10 percent suffer a spasm of their airway, preventing both water and air from entering the lungs. When fluid does enter the lungs, it doesn't always suffocate a child directly, but may simply wash out chemicals called *surfactants* that are necessary to keep the lungs inflated. When a child is deprived of oxygen, they are said to suffer *hypoxia*. A total lack of oxygen is called *anoxia*. Hypoxia, or an "anoxic hit," can cause the brain to swell, organs to shut down, bleeding into a child's gastrointestinal system, respiratory distress syndrome, and heart failure, even if a child survives the initial trauma.

Oxygen deprivation for as little as one minute can cause loss of consciousness. Children submersed for several minutes will usually be okay if they are resuscitated rapidly at the scene. Children submersed for longer periods may die, or they may survive with massive, permanent brain damage. Even children who appear to be okay following a near drowning incident may suffer from brain swelling or kidney failure six to twelve hours later. For many children a prognosis can be made when they first arrive at the hospital. If CPR is still in progress, the child will likely die. The sooner a child begins breathing again—either on his own or with your assistance—the greater his chance of survival. A child pulled from the water who is not breathing must be resuscitated immediately. Continued oxygen deprivation will guarantee death.

Despite occasional reports to the contrary children pulled from cold water often die. You may have read reports in the news about children pulled from icy water after submersions in excess of an hour who live. The reason is that a child who is too cold will suffer from hypothermia, but the kind of hypothermia that can protect the brain from lack of oxygen must be induced very rapidly and can only occur in water that is less than 5°C or 41°F. Unfortunately, most swimming pools and lakes and rivers where children swim are not cold enough to be protective in this manner.

SAD DROWNING FACTS

According to the American Academy of Pediatrics (AAP) and the National Safety Council (NSC), over six hundred children from infancy to kindergarten drown each year. Half are under age three. Over one-third are one year olds, making drowning the second leading cause of injury death for this age group. Another five hundred who die each year are teenagers. For every drowning death, the NSC estimates there are four nonfatal submersion injuries. Not surprisingly, the death rate rises during summer months, peaking in July. More deaths occur in California, Texas, and Florida, where temperatures make swimming more popular than in other states. Of the six hundred youngest victims, half die in backyard swimming pools. Of these, 70 percent die in pools at their own home; another 20 percent die in pools at relative's homes. Three-quarters of these children drown while being supervised by at least one parent.[1]

School-aged children who drown are less likely to be in the backyard pool and more likely to be in natural bodies of water like the ocean, rivers, and lakes. Boys have six times the drowning rate of girls, black children have twice the drowning rate of white children and children with epilepsy drown at four to ten times the rate of children without epilepsy. While the highest drowning rate is for one year olds, the second highest is for those aged fifteen to twenty-four. Half of the drowning incidents involving this older age group involve alcohol.

If you were asked to locate objects in your home representing a danger to your children, you might pick up a power tool, a box of matches, or an extension cord. You would probably not point to that five-gallon plastic bucket used for washing the car or mopping the floor. The Consumer Product Safety Commission (CPSC) issued a warning about these buckets. Because their sides are straight, and because with even a small amount of water in the bottom they are heavy enough to be difficult to tip over, they are easy for toddlers to pull themselves up on and fall into headfirst. Because they do not tip over, the babies drown. The CPSC claims that fifty children ages eight to fourteen months die this way each year.

- Little ones out of sight for mere minutes can drown in back-yard swimming pools.
- Half of teenaged drowning deaths involve alcohol.
- Children can drown in buckets and bathtubs—not just in pools.

TREATMENT FOR DROWNING

As you pull any child from the water, you must decide rapidly if he may have suffered a head or neck injury. Diving accidents, when a child strikes his head on a solid surface in the water, account for one-eighth of all spinal cord injuries. Half of these victims become quadriplegics, with no ability to move their arms or legs. If a child appears to have suffered a head or neck injury, use a jaw-thrust maneuver to open his airway. If there is no sign of neck injury, tip his head back, lift his chin, and look, listen, and feel for breathing. If he is not breathing, begin mouth-to-mouth or mouth-to-mouth-and-nose ventilations. If you are able to provide two good breaths, stop and check for a pulse. If you are unable to feel a pulse, begin CPR. If you are able to feel a pulse but the child is still not breathing, you must continue breathing for him. Immediate resuscitation at the scene is crucial. Do not wait for police, EMS, or Superman.

The child is oxygen starved. Someone must breathe for him if he is not breathing on his own.

While a child may or may not have water in his lungs, he will almost certainly have swallowed water. These children may vomit copious amounts of this water back up, making mouth-to-mouth breathing more difficult. When he begins to vomit, roll him onto his side, wipe his mouth clear, roll him back, and begin again. If he begins breathing on his own, keep him on his side to help him keep his airway clear. If the child is breathing, or begins to breathe on his own, remove wet clothing and wrap him gently in warm blankets. Once oxygen begins to circulate through a child's system, hypothermia is no longer helpful and may be harmful. Warm him.

- Minimize movement to a child's spine after any diving accident.
- Remember the ABCs—Airway, Breathing, Circulation.
- After successfully resuscitating a child, keep him warm and make sure a physician evaluates him.

EMS TREATMENT FOR DROWNING VICTIMS

When the medics arrive, they will continue CPR all the way to the hospital, if necessary. They will secure the child's airway with an endotracheal tube, ventilate him with pure oxygen, monitor the child's heart rhythm, gain IV access, and administer powerful drugs, as needed, to stimulate the child's heart. At the scene of a child in cardiac arrest, a flurry of very rapid activity takes place. Providers will not remain at the scene very long. Most of the resuscitation effort will take place while the ambulance is moving toward the hospital. Questions may be thrown at bystanders while many other activities are taking place. Medics will need an estimate of how long the child was missing and the temperature of the water. They may not even ask the child's name, but will need age, medical history, a list of any medications the child takes, and information about allergies to medications. Everything else will wait until arrival at the hospital.

Again, an emergency physician at the hospital must evaluate even children who are rapidly resuscitated at the scene. Children who are awake and breathing well will be monitored closely for signs of swelling in their brains or other damage from lack of oxygen.

- Protect yourself. A drowned rescuer cannot help anyone.
- The faster a child is assisted in breathing, the greater the child's chance of surviving.
- Open a child's airway and, if he is not breathing, breathe for him, breathe for him, breathe for him. In no other injury setting is training in pediatric CPR so critical. Take the class.

PREVENTION

The best prevention of drowning for young children is close supervision when they are in or near the water and elimination of access to that water without the supervision.

- Pools should be fenced in.
- Fences should be at least forty-eight inches high and vertical slats should be no more than four inches apart.
- Gates should be self-closing, locked, or with latches a child cannot reach.
- Gates should be designed to open away from the pool, so children cannot accidentally push their way into a pool area.
- There are a variety of pool covers and alarms available, but if money is tight, at least invest in a poolside telephone. This will not only allow you to summon help quickly, but keeps you from leaving the poolside to answer the phone while the children are playing.

Siblings should not be expected to supervise younger children. This goes for the bathtub as well as the swimming pool. Bathtubs and buckets should be emptied after use and never left with standing water inside. Children with epilepsy must be monitored very closely and should learn to shower instead of bathe in a tub of water at an appropriate age. Swimming lessons for children under age three may not help and may even encourage a little one to think he can jump in when adults are not around. But swimming lessons after age five can someday save your child's life. Use of personal flotation devices (PFDs) like life jackets should not mislead you into thinking children are safe without supervision. While they are extremely important protective devices, especially during boating and water sports, children still need to be supervised closely. PFDs should be approved by the U.S. Coast Guard, be sized to fit your child properly (so the child cannot slip out), and be designed to keep a child floating faceup.

Finally, children can also drown in hot tubs, whirlpool baths, and spas. The high water temperature in these spas can overwhelm a child who has not yet reached puberty. Even adults can become drowsy and drown if the water temperature exceeds 104°F. The CPSC reports seven hundred deaths in these spas since 1980. One-third of these victims were under age five. While new drain covers have been designed to prevent hair entanglement, at least forty-nine people have been held under the water by the power of the suction at the drain, and at least thirteen have died. The powerful suction of the drains in both spas and pools has entrapped body parts as well, sometimes leading to disembowelment or death.

Keep water temperature in spas below 104°F. As in any body of water, children must never be left unsupervised. This means eliminating access if you are not there with them. Make sure the tub has at least two drains to dilute the power of the suction and that covers meet current safety standards and are intact and functioning properly. Know where the pump cutoff switch is located so that you can turn it off quickly.

- Eliminate access to water when you are not there to supervise children.

- Empty buckets and bathtubs after use.
- Children need supervision even while wearing flotation devices.
- Children need supervision even if they have had swimming lessons.
- Keep water temperature in spas and whirlpools below 104°F.
- Maintain drain covers and pumps in pools and spas. Make sure you know how to shut off pumps.

FALLS AND FRACTURES 9

- ✚ **Why the Spine Is So Important**
- ✚ **Treating Suspected Spinal Injuries**
- ✚ **Treating Other Broken Bones**
- ✚ **Open Wounds**
- ✚ **EMS Treatment Will Depend on Your Child's Condition**
- ✚ **Preventing Falls and Fractures**

✚ *The little girl tripped—not surprisingly—on the brand-new deep pile carpet in her brand-new home. The way she landed surprised all of us. With her arms out to her sides, she sprawled across the hallway and her head slammed straight between the carved wooden rails of the brand-new banister. When she tried to get up, she realized her head was stuck, and she couldn't back out. Mom tried to help her, and the more they pushed and twisted without success, the more they both began to panic. Mom's frantic call for help was difficult for the dispatcher to understand. Because she claimed her daughter was trapped, he sent both an ambulance and the fire department. So many volunteer firefighters responded to assist, we all couldn't fit in the brand-new hallway of the beautiful new house.*

I initially ignored the fact that the child was stuck and made sure her airway was open and she was breathing adequately. I then looked for signs of a head injury, or a neck or back injury. Nothing was broken, and the tender spot on the side of her head appeared to be a minor bump. As I evaluated her, both she and her mom began to calm down. After determining the little girl was not seriously injured, I turned to Mom. Her daughter would be just fine, but her daughter's head was not going to come out of this predicament the same way it went in. Mom, realizing that one of the posts would have to go, looked briefly at the beautiful new carved wooden banister, took a deep breath, and turned to one of the firemen. He looked back at Mom, turned to me, gazed down at the little head trapped between the posts, and said, "I'll go get a handsaw." As she gently stroked her daughter's hair, I could almost hear Mom wondering to herself if this would be covered under her brand-new homeowner's insurance policy.

C hildren and adults fall down. Children and the elderly are at higher risk than others of serious injury from falls though. The younger and smaller a child, the lower the height necessary to result in serious injury or death. Children falling or jumping from roofs can be compared to infants falling from a bed to a ceramic tile floor. Both the distance of the fall and the material on which a child lands will be predictors of injury. It is also important to know how the child fell. What part of the body did he land on?

From infant walkers crashing down the stairs, to toddlers falling backward on steps and landings, there is no end to the manner in which children can sustain injuries. They fall from monkey bars and swing sets. They fall off the sides of slides instead of rocketing down the middle to a soft landing. They crash into stationary objects while sledding and skiing. They run through sliding-glass doors and crawl out of windows. They slip in bathtubs, and fall off cabinets and dressers. They can land upside down when a really awesome jump flings them completely off the bed. Children can become entrapped in escalators and caught beneath automatic garage doors. Both power tools and simple tools like scissors can injure children, and they may topple from ladders and handrails and banisters.

There are 206 bones in the human skeleton. Children have found ways of breaking almost all of them. Some of the ways children find to hurt themselves are so bizarre that medics, doctors, and nurses will look at you, lift an eyebrow, and cock their heads. They can fall from trees and fall from horses. They can run out of the bushes and trip in front of rider lawn mowers or fly off water tubes being pulled by motor boats with enough force to be paralyzed for life.

We will never stop children from being hurt entirely. There will always be bumps and bruises and cuts. Sometimes they will need stitches, and sometimes fractures or sprains or strains will result in slings, casts, and crutches. No amount of supervision will completely prevent your child from these typical childhood injuries. However, the prevention strategies listed at the end of this chapter can minimize the risk of injury for your child, and there are actions you can take to protect your child from further harm when accidents do occur.

WHY ARE SPINES SO IMPORTANT?

A child's back and neck are made up of exquisitely shaped bones called *vertebrae*. They are basically doughnut-shaped, rounded, and with holes in the middle. Between each vertebra are discs that act as shock absorbers and keep each bone in its place. Through the center of these vertebrae, which are stacked like a pile of doughnuts on a stick, is the spinal cord. This is a major-league power line from the brain to the rest of the body. Between each vertebra and disc, smaller lines run outward toward the body's extremities. These are peripheral nerves. Nerves control both movement and sensation. If anything cuts one of these lines, or impinges on them, the nerves cannot function correctly. They may short out completely, or they may send inappropriate messages back to the brain.

If there is a break in the spine, and the spinal cord is injured, all messages between the brain and the rest of the body below the injury will be affected. The higher or closer to the brain the injury occurs, the more the body may be disabled. Breaks that include injury to the spinal cord in the neck may result in complete paralysis and sometimes death. Breaks that are lower may affect the legs only. High injuries that damage many nerves may even disable the muscles a child needs to breathe, resulting in dependence on a mechanical ventilator.

A film star who played Superman, Christopher Reeve, suffered such an injury when he fell from a horse. Mr. Reeve is one of my heroes. He has not only survived, but flourished. He has been challenged and remains in a wheelchair. But he has not been defeated. He remains a talented, creative, active man, with both theatrical and altruistic pursuits. It is wonderful that he can continue to be such an uplifting, courageous, and decent role model for our children even when he no longer has a cape flapping behind him.

Spinal injuries resulting in paralysis are not the end of the world for children either. Many paralyzed children lead long, productive, happy lives. But Mr. Reeve may not have survived at all without rapid, appropriate treatment at the scene. The same is true of our children.

- Fractures to the bones of the spine can damage nerves in the spinal cord.
- Movement of a fractured spine can result in death or permanent disability.

TREATING A SUSPECTED SPINAL INJURY

S igns and symptoms of an injured spine can be subtle and difficult to detect. Based strictly on the way a child is injured, we must sometimes *assume* a child's back or neck is hurt and protect him by minimizing movement until diagnostic tests at the hospital prove us wrong. A medic will always assume that your child's spine may be injured if he has sustained a serious head injury. Any force strong enough to knock a child unconscious may also have been strong enough to injure his neck.

Some clues that your child may have an injured spine include an inability to move, or weakness, tingling, or numbness in arms or legs. Pain may or may not be present. If your child feels pain in his neck or back, assume it is injured. Even children who are preverbal will let you know when movement hurts. In the absence of clear signs and symptoms, however, remember to review the mechanism of injury before moving an injured child. If you believe your child has an injured spine keep him very still. If he begins to vomit, roll him onto his side, keeping his head and neck in line with the rest of his body—like rolling a log—and immobilize him to the greatest extent possible. Be prepared to use a jaw-thrust maneuver to open his airway and to breathe for him, if necessary. You can review the jaw-thrust maneuver in chapter 4.

Rescuers will continue this immobilization and protection of the entire spine until arrival at a hospital where X rays can definitively find or rule out injury. Medics usually use the same assessment techniques and criteria for choosing this level of immobilization that doctors use to decide to x-ray a child. Doctors and medics are not X ray machines. If the signs and symptoms and/or the mechanism of injury suggest the possibility of spinal trauma, the child will remain immobilized until X rays are evaluated. Most ambulances have special pediatric immobilization devices that are shorter and narrower than the long boards used for adults. These pediatric boards are also padded. If the ambulance does not have special pediatric equipment, the medic may use sheets or blankets to secure your child safely on an adult board.

If your child is not conscious, a medic may intubate him to ensure a secure, open airway, to provide adequate oxygen, and to prevent him from breathing any vomit or other fluid into his lungs. This airway can be removed later if the support of a ventilator is not needed.

- Always review the mechanism of injury before moving a child.
- Use a jaw-thrust maneuver to open the airway of an injured child who is not breathing.
- Minimize movement of an injured child who is breathing on his own.

TREATING OTHER BROKEN BONES

Fractures of other bones take many forms. Most of us know some-one who has broken an arm or a leg. But bones in the back, neck, and hips can also be fractured, as can ribs, collarbones, and facial bones. Frequently when an arm or leg bone is broken, the child will have heard or felt a snap. He may not be able to move the injured area, or he may feel pain when he tries. A fracture may be "open" or "closed." If the fracture is open, the skin has been torn and pieces of bone may be visible. Remember that these bone fragments may be very sharp and can slice through your skin as well. If the fracture is closed, it may be obviously deformed and bent in the wrong direction, or it may be straight and difficult to assess. Sometimes, until X rays are taken and evaluated it is impossible to tell the difference between a bone that is broken and a sprain or strain.

Check airway and breathing first. If there is a possibility of spinal trauma, do not move a breathing child. An injured child should be moved only if he is not breathing and the child's position makes it impossible to open his airway using a jaw-thrust maneuver. If the child must be moved, keep the head and body in line and immobile to the greatest extent possible. Move him only as much as necessary to use a jaw-thrust maneuver and breathe for him. If a child is breathing, use direct pressure to stop any bleeding. Prevent movement of an injured arm or leg by creating a splint. This can be as simple as rolling up a newspaper and attaching it to the arm with tape or gauze. A proper splint can be made of any rigid material, from cardboard to broom handles. It should extend from the joint above the injury to the joint below. It can be padded for comfort using towels, pillows, or sheets. The injured area should be splinted in the position found. Do not try to straighten a fracture or push a bone back into place.

A larger broken bone, like an upper leg bone, may require that you hold it with your hands until medics arrive. Large bones can cause bleeding inside when they break. Bone fractures can also cause damage to nerves, tendons, and ligaments. Movement can increase this damage. It can also cause severe pain. When medics arrive, they may leave the injured arm or leg exactly as you have secured it, or they may need to remove your splint and apply their own. A medic will need to know if there is a pulse, providing evidence of blood flow, below the injured site. If there is inadequate blood flow below the injury, they may have to reposition the arm or leg. Do not do this yourself.

Fractures to the upper leg, called the *femur,* can be very painful if they remain unstable during transport, and they can result in extensive bleeding inside. While the amount of internal bleeding from a closed femur fracture may not endanger a child's life, if that blood loss is combined with blood loss elsewhere, from a scalp laceration or other internal bleeding, it can become dangerous. If appropriate, medics may use a special splint that looks like a metal brace to apply traction on a broken femur. When this splint is applied, the medic must pull gently on the child's leg. This can be very painful for the child, but the intense pain only lasts a moment. Once secured properly, it will give the child a great deal of pain relief and prevent the unstable leg from moving during transport.

- Minimize movement to a broken bone by applying a splint.
- Splints can be made from any rigid material and padded for comfort.
- Never manipulate a fracture or try to push a broken bone back into place.

OPEN WOUNDS

F ractures may require evaluation by a radiologist, a specialist who interprets X rays. This usually means a trip to the emergency room. Only rarely will a pediatrician or family physician's office have appropriate X-ray equipment. The same is true of cuts and lacerations that may require stitches. Cuts are deep enough to need special care in an emergency department if the bleeding will not stop, or if they are very deep, if they contain debris you cannot clean out, or if fatty tissue is exposed. If you cannot clean a cut out well using cold water and soap, or if the bleeding does not stop after you apply pressure for five minutes, you need to seek assistance.

To apply direct pressure, place a piece of sterile gauze or clean bandaging material over the wound and press firmly. If blood soaks through the bandaging material, do not remove it; just add more on top. Do not delay the application of pressure to a heavily bleeding wound while you rummage through cabinets looking for clean bandaging material. Use whatever material is at hand—like your husband's shirt! The risk associated with infection can be addressed later. Infection doesn't matter if a child has bled to death. Your doctor may be able to treat minor cuts and lacerations at the office. If the bleeding is not severe, call the doctor for assistance in determining where you should take the child for treatment. If the blood is pouring or squirting from a wound, if you believe a bone may be broken, or if your child has signs or symptoms of head or spinal trauma, call EMS.

- Apply direct pressure to a bleeding wound until the bleeding stops or help arrives.
- Heavy bleeding requires prompt action. Don't waste time looking for sterile bandaging material.
- If the child is a stranger, remember the risk of communicable illness and minimize your direct contact with any blood.

EMS TREATMENT WILL DEPEND ON YOUR CHILD'S CONDITION

In the ambulance, the medic will converse with a physician, if necessary, to decide whether or not to activate the trauma team. Most broken bones and cuts and bruises do not require the assistance of a trauma team. Even a potentially injured spine may not represent the level of life-threatening injury necessary to mobilize a whole team. The medic may or may not choose to start an IV. If blood loss from external wounds or possible internal bleeding is severe, or if your child is showing signs of shock, an IV may be started to administer fluids and replace volume. While medics carry painkillers, like morphine, these are only used if absolutely necessary. They reduce pain, but they can also mask neurological problems, lower your child's breathing rate, and prevent your child from keeping an open, secure airway. Painkillers will only be administered before arrival at the hospital if the medic is convinced that these potential side effects do not represent any additional danger to your child.

Once at the hospital, your child will be moved to a bed in the emergency department and treated by an emergency physician. It is important to point out that whether your child is transported by ambulance or by private vehicle, he may not be treated immediately. Hospital emergency departments use a system called *triage*. This allows them to treat the most seriously injured or ill patients first. Patients are not seen in the order they arrive. They are seen based on a priority system that depends on the nature and severity of the child's injury in relation to the condition of others in the emergency department. If your child's injuries are major or life threatening, he will be cared for immediately. Broken bones without complications and minor lacerations may result in a wait.

Emergencies are great equalizers. Your income, title, level of education, skin color, ability to pay, religion, sexual preferences, nationality or citizenship, gender, age, your name in lights, or your picture on a poster at the post office will not make a difference. Security is tight in hospital emergency departments, particularly in inner-city neighborhoods. Staff members do not like loud and obnoxious people who distract them from providing care. They do not hesitate to throw such people out. This is not one of those situations where the squeaky wheel gets the grease.

Be prepared to answer the same questions over and over again. The first emergency provider at the scene of the accident, whether in your home or on the street, may be a police officer. He will ask, "What happened?" You will then hear this same question from the EMTs and the medics. As described earlier, the EMS providers will need a great deal of information, from name and address to medical history, medications, and allergies. Once you arrive at the hospital, this questioning will begin all over again. The nurse will need to know, the admissions clerk will have questions, and by the time the doctor walks in and asks, "What happened?" you will want to pull out your hair and scream.

While the need for these repeated questions is sometimes a function of poor communication or bureaucratic inefficiency, they also serve a purpose. The police need to understand the nature of the problem. This will allow them to communicate with EMS by radio and let them know if additional resources are needed. The EMTs and medics also need to know, but in greater detail. The hospital administration needs to know business-related details like insurance subscription data and religious affiliation. The nurses need to know what the medics know, and both the doctor and the nurses will be asking you to repeat everything to ensure no important information was missed or overlooked.

If your child fell from his bike and has a scalp laceration that needs stitches, did he also land on the handlebars? Should the doctor have a high degree of suspicion regarding internal as well as external injuries? It is amazing how often areas of the body that do not hurt when the medic asks at the scene, begin to hurt by the time a child arrives at the hospital. The entire assessment, from airway and breathing to a head-to-toe evaluation will be repeated. This is the only way additional injuries will not be missed. While the emergency physicians will treat some injuries themselves, they may call in specialists for others. They may insist that an orthopedist, a neurologist, or a surgeon evaluate your child. And the questions will begin yet again.

- Medics will take action necessary to protect your child from further harm.
- Broken bones and open wounds do not always require care from a trauma team.
- Emergency department visits sometimes require patience from patients.

PREVENTING FALLS AND FRACTURES

Providing appropriate supervision can prevent many of the injuries children sustain from falls of any kind. Inappropriate use of equipment, tools, and machines by little ones is usually a matter of Mom, Dad, or baby-sitter saying, "No." But even children with diligent, comprehensive supervision will find ways of getting hurt. Here is a list of prevention strategies from the American Academy of Pediatrics (AAP) and the Consumer Product Safety Commission (CPSC) that provide additional protection:

- Stairways must remain uncluttered and well lit.
- Install window guards to prevent children from climbing out and falling.
- Balconies must be high enough to prevent children from climbing over them.
- Slats in railings and banisters should be spaced close enough to prevent children from slipping through or becoming entrapped.
- Doorknob covers, locks, and/or safety latches should be used to secure unsafe areas.
- Gates should be used to eliminate access to stairways, but children can choke or be strangled by the types with accordion tops; use the types with rigid top bars.

- Bathtubs and tiled bathroom floors should be covered with skid-resistant materials.
- Sharp corners on coffee tables and furniture at the level of a child's fall should be padded.
- Window blind and curtain cords without safety tassels should be cut or tied to keep them out of a child's reach.
- Design of play-equipment areas should include a soft "fall zone." Padded carpeting inside and energy-absorbent material outside can prevent serious injury.
- Specifications for outdoor play equipment like swing sets and monkey bars should include a "fall zone" that extends both beneath the equipment and at least as far from the equipment as the height of the equipment. A six-foot high slide, therefore, requires a six-foot radius of soft material around the slide.
- The soft (energy-absorbent) material recommended by the AAP includes pine bark, wood chips, and loose fill, as well as more expensive synthetic materials. The material must be thick enough to cushion a child's fall. Outdoor play equipment should never be placed over asphalt, cement, or packed dirt.
- Play equipment should not be high enough to allow a pre-school child to fall more than five feet, or older children more than six feet, and only onto a soft surface.
- Play equipment should be spaced far enough apart to allow children to exit slides or swings without colliding with other children.
- Play areas outside should be fenced. Fences should be at least four feet high and well maintained. Fences should be at least six feet from play equipment like slides and swings.
- Climbing equipment, like monkey bars, must be anchored in concrete, with the concrete covered with energy-absorbing material. This equipment should be free of sharp edges or holes large enough to entrap body parts.
- Swing sets must similarly be anchored in concrete covered with energy-absorbing material. The swing seats should be made of soft material like canvas or plastic, not wood or metal.

- Swings should be at least twenty-four inches apart, and at least thirty inches from the frame.
- Plastic slides are less likely to become blistering hot in the sun than metal slides and are less likely to develop sharp, jagged edges.
- Slides need guard rails both at the top platform and along the slide itself. The AAP suggests that a hill be constructed of soft material beneath the slide, so that if a child falls off, they roll down the hill and do not fall straight to the ground.
- Other types of play equipment like seesaws, merry-go-rounds, and rockers need to be checked frequently to avoid sharp edges and ensure adequate handholds, footrests, and seats. Tires used on playgrounds must be checked for metal projections of the steel belts through the rubber.
- Do not purchase a backyard trampoline. If you already have, take it down. These contraptions are great fun, but represent a serious danger to your children. Trampolines can be used in organized gymnastics or sports classes, but only with appropriate, trained supervisors, thick mats, and protective measures in place. In 1996 alone, there were 83,400 trampoline-related injuries. Two-thirds of these injuries were to children ages five through fourteen, but children under age five had the second highest rate of injury. Most occurred in the backyards of private homes. Many involved fractures that required surgery. Others resulted in serious head and spinal injuries. Get rid of them.
- Infant or baby walkers do nothing to help your child learn to walk. There is even limited data that suggests a delay in walking may result from use of these convenient baby minders. While they may provide a little one with exercise and mobility, they are dangerous. Infant walkers that pound down the stairs with your child onboard cause devastating head injuries and fractures. While new standards require the base of these walkers to be wider than a standard door opening to prevent falls, they do nothing to prevent children from reaching hot surfaces and dangling appliance cords or prevent them from

falling into tubs, toilets, and pools. The Consumer Product Safety Comission (CPSC) claims that 14,300 injuries from these walkers occurred to children younger than fifteen months in 1997, and that there have been at least thirty-four deaths because of them since 1973. The AAP has recommended a ban on these devices.

HEAD TRAUMA 10

- ✚ Facts About Head Injuries
- ✚ Assessment and Treatment of Head Trauma
- ✚ Treatment of Head Trauma at the Hospital
- ✚ Preventing Head Injuries

I was called to help a child struck by a car while riding her bicycle within minutes of my coworker, Bruce, having left on an identical call. Bruce and his partner took off for one end of town; my partner and I left for the other side. Although Bruce and I were far from each other, we were about equidistant from the regional trauma center. Bruce and his patient arrived at the hospital long before we did. Bruce worked up a sweat, had his red lights and sirens going the whole time, and arrived at the hospital a full twenty minutes earlier. After assessing our patient at the scene, my partner and I slowed down. We used no lights or sirens, we stopped at red lights with the rest of the traffic, and I had an amusing conversation with my delightful little patient on the way. My patient had a small laceration to her ear that required stitches and a sore neck. Bruce's patient had a fractured skull and permanent brain damage, among other injuries. My little patient was discharged from the hospi-

tal that afternoon with wound care instructions and Tylenol. Bruce's patient survived, but spent weeks in the hospital and months in rehabilitation. The difference? My little patient was wearing her bicycle helmet.

C hildren have no business using toys that allow them to travel at high speeds without also using helmets. Our skulls and facial bones create a cavity inside our heads called a *cranial vault*. Inside this protected vault is a very important organ, the *brain*. Brain tissue is soft and easily damaged. It is not in direct contact with the skull; it is surrounded by membranes and a small amount of fluid that acts as a cushion to further protect the soft brain, rather like the yolk of an egg floating in the white material inside the shell.

When a large enough force is applied to the skull, it can break just like an eggshell, spilling brain material out. Most doctors and trauma team members never see children with this level of head injury. We do not even attempt to resuscitate children with these types of injuries who are no longer breathing. We simply call the coroner or the medical examiner and pray we will not still be at the scene when Mom and Dad arrive and the screaming and crying begin. We are not insensitive. We are, perhaps, too sensitive. Knowing that our skills and experience will not save a life hurts. When a child is involved, you will see even the biggest, toughest EMS, fire, and police providers biting their lips and turning away. And we can become angry when we know that a simple helmet may have prevented the tragedy.

Even if brain matter doesn't spill out, damage to that soft, complex organ can be fatal or result in devastating permanent disability. Blood can leak into the space between the brain and skull causing pressure, or into the brain tissue itself. Swelling can squeeze brain cells and cut off the oxygen supply through tiny vessels. Depending on the location of the damage, the child may lose sight, hearing, speech, memory, movement, intellect, personality, or all of the above. Sometimes surgery can help save a life. But the extent of the damage and the level of permanent disability may not be known for as much as a year after the injury occurs.

FACTS ABOUT HEAD INJURIES

- From a study in Florida reviewing 211 children injured while riding their bikes, the mean age was ten years. Seventy-nine percent were boys. Eighty-four percent of the injuries occurred when the bikes collided with automobiles. Almost half of these children suffered head injuries. Only three were wearing helmets. Six children died.[1]
- From a study at just two Georgia trauma centers over five years, 69 children were killed in accidents: four were bicyclists. Two of them died as a result of severe head injuries. None of them were wearing helmets.[2]
- In 1997, there were seven hundred fatal bicycle collisions with motor vehicles and 48,000 injuries. The highest rate of death occurred in children ages five through fourteen.[3]
- In a study from Chicago reviewing over four thousand bicycle injuries to children using the National Pediatric Trauma Registry (NPTR), only 3 percent were wearing helmets. Five percent of the children were preschoolers. The preschoolers were less likely to have been injured in the street and more likely to have been hurt in the driveway or yard. Only two of these little ones were wearing helmets.[4]
- A study out of Boston using the NPTR identified over six hundred children aged five through nineteen injured while rolling on skates or boards between 1988 and 1997. Three-quarters were boys, and almost half were injured on roadways. More than one-third sustained head injuries. This included over half of those on skateboards, about one-third of those on in-line skates, but less than one-fifth of those on traditional roller-skates. The skateboarders were eight times more likely to have severe injuries than the roller-skaters, and the in-line skaters were twice as likely.[5]
- In a study from Philadelphia, 107 children were identified who were injured while bicycle riding. Seventeen of these children were injured by the bicycles' handlebars. These were usu-

ally minor crashes or simple falls when the bike stopped moving and the child landed on or was impacted by the handlebars. The resulting abdominal injuries were frequently severe, including lacerations and damage to liver, spleen, kidneys, and pancreas.[6]

ASSESSMENT AND TREATMENT OF HEAD TRAUMA

When a child is injured while riding a bicycle, skateboard, in-line skates, or regular roller-skates, it is crucial to review the mechanism of injury. How did he fall? How fast was he moving? On what part of the body did he land? Head injuries are common, and if the

---

PROTECTIVE POCKET MASKS

Protective pocket masks are available at most medical supply stores and many pharmacies. Some are too large to fit into a pocket, others are so small they fit on a key ring. They are inexpensive and allow you to help both children and adults in a medical crisis without worrying about disease transmission. Along with a plastic barrier to prevent direct contact between the user and the patient, the good masks have a small one-way valve to prevent fluids from backing up. You simply unfold them, place them over the mouth and nose of the child, pinch off the child's nose right through the plastic, and form a seal with your mouth directly against the mask. I have one in the glove compartment of my car, another in my purse, and a third on my key ring. While they may be too large for use on infants, these masks are cheap, life-saving tools. If you have never used one or practiced with one in a CPR class, be sure to read the directions *before* an emergency occurs.

head has been hurt, the neck and spine below may also be damaged. If your child sustains a head injury, assume that he may have injured his neck as well. Keep him as still as possible. Scalp lacerations can cause massive bleeding. The amount of blood can be frightening to both you and the child. While holding head and neck in line as much as possible, simple direct pressure should stop any bleeding. If it does not, continue holding direct pressure until help arrives.

The blood may also make it difficult to see injuries to the skull below. If the skull is obviously fractured, do not push on the broken bone. If there is anything stuck in the wound, leave it alone. Removing it could increase the bleeding or cause additional injury. If the child is unresponsive, you must protect his airway using a jaw-thrust maneuver and breathe for him if he stops breathing on his own. If you are not familiar with the child's medical history, you must remember the risk of possible disease transmission and consider protecting yourself, both by using a pocket mask and by minimizing direct contact with any blood.

Hundreds of thousands of children will fall from their bikes or while skating, or have minor collisions with vehicles or stationary objects. Most of the injuries they sustain will be minor scrapes and bruises. But if they land in a manner that results in a blunt trauma to their abdomens, or if they sustain a head injury, they need to be evaluated by a physician. If a child loses consciousness, call 911 and monitor his airway closely. Even if he regains consciousness, he needs to be transported on a board and with a stiff collar in place that will protect his spine. In addition, he may lose consciousness again or begin to have seizures, and these conditions are best handled in the back of an ambulance by trained providers.

Loss of consciousness, even if it is brief, is just one sign of a possible head injury. Others include:

- Pupils that are not the same size
- Weakness or paralysis
- Abnormal breathing

- Bleeding from the nose or ears
- Sleepiness
- Vomiting
- Headache
- Speech or vision impairment
- Dizziness
- Irritability or combativeness
- Loss of bowel or bladder control in children who are fully toilet trained
- Loss of memory
- Seizure activity

These signs and symptoms may not become apparent until later. Any child who has taken a nasty spill, even if he was wearing a helmet, must be monitored closely. If any of these signs or symptoms appear, a physician should evaluate the child.

- Do not be distracted by minor bleeding that can look scary. Remember to protect a child's spine.
- Head injuries can be difficult to detect immediately after a fall. Continue looking for changes in your child up to twenty-four-hours after a nasty spill.
- Never hesitate to call your child's doctor if you are unsure.

TREATMENT OF HEAD TRAUMA AT THE HOSPITAL

Even at the hospital, head injuries can be difficult to evaluate. After providers have ensured that the child's airway is secure and he is breathing adequately, tests will be run to find evidence of damage. The child will be x-rayed to find or rule out injury to the neck and spine. The child will also have a full neurological examination. The child may then be sent for a CT scan. When to send children with

HEAD-INJURED CHILDREN MUST BE MONITORED

In a study from Salt Lake City, the charts of 508 head-injured children were reviewed. There were 313 children who had normal or unremarkable neurological examinations who became sleepy, began vomiting, had headaches, suffered loss of consciousness, became irritable, developed amnesia, or suffered seizures. An abnormal CT scan was detected in 88 of these children. Four required surgery.[7] This is why close monitoring of children by skilled providers is so important. The neurological examination will reveal most injuries, but subtle head trauma may not cause immediate neurological deficits or become apparent until later.

minor head trauma for a CT scan is controversial in some hospitals. These tests are expensive. The test will be ordered if the neurological examination shows evidence of an abnormality. If the exam is normal, doctors may choose to monitor the child closely, but delay further testing.

- CT scans are not always necessary following a minor head injury.
- Doctors may choose to monitor your child closely for changes.

PREVENTING HEAD INJURIES

When you think of young children under age five, think of cartoon characters with their big heads and little bodies. These children have a different center of gravity than older children and adults. They lack coordination and motor skills. They do not belong on skateboards. If your child tells you he will just die if he is not allowed to have a skateboard, make it a special treat when he reaches double digits, and make sure he is also equipped with helmet, knee and elbow pads, and wrist guards. Campaign in your neighborhood, if necessary, for a separate, safe area to use bikes, boards, and skates that is away from streets, traffic, and obstacles.

The type of skates your child should use is similarly age dependent. Roller-skates are safest, but if your child insists on in-line skates, make sure the rules are clear. Mixing skaters and traffic is deadly. Take them to an empty parking lot or area closed to traffic. Helmets and other protective gear should be mandatory. Helmets should fit snugly. Your child's head should not be bouncing around inside a helmet that is too big. Helmets must be secured with a chin strap. The strap must fit tightly against your child's chin and still allow him to open his mouth; it shouldn't be hanging loose. Helmets should be certified by one of the following four organizations:

- American National Standards Institute (ANSI)
- American Society for Testing and Materials (ASTM)
- Snell Memorial Foundation
- Consumer Product Safety Commission (CPSC). Look for this label on any helmet manufactured after March 1999

It is usually not the parent who decides a child will not wear a helmet. It is usually the child complaining that the helmet is uncomfortable or makes him "look like a nerd." The helmet rule has to be mandatory and nonnegotiable. No helmet? No bike. No helmet? No skateboard. No helmet? No skates. No protective equipment? Play something else.

Helmet manufacturers go to great lengths to make these devices attractive and "cool." They come in every color imaginable and sometimes with glitter and gold sparkles or fancy logos and pictures. If children are introduced to helmets as necessary from the first day they ride a bike or don skates, they will not consider them intrusive or uncomfortable. It also helps if Mom and Dad are using the equipment as well, providing responsible role models.

Children need to be taught the rules of traffic and how to use hand signals. They should not be allowed on bikes or skates near roadways at dusk or after dark. They should wear brightly colored clothing and have reflectors on the fronts and backs of their bikes. Children should only ride bikes that are appropriate for their size. A child should be capable of keeping both feet on the pedals throughout a full rotation while sitting on the seat. If they must stand or leave the seat to maintain contact with the pedals, the bike is too big. Children should only ride a new bike after they have demonstrated proficiency at this skill.

- When children ride bikes, skateboards, or skates, they sometimes fall down or lose control of their direction and speed. When this happens in traffic, tragedy strikes. If they are not wearing helmets, the head injuries can be devastating and even fatal.
- Signs and symptoms of a head injury may not be apparent immediately following the fall. A physician should immediately evaluate any child who loses consciousness after a spill. Less obvious signs of a possible head injury include pupils that are not the same size or pupils that do not contract equally when exposed to a bright light. Still other signs include unusual weakness, changes in mental status, vomiting, seizures, disturbances in vision or speech, inappropriate sleepiness, irritability, and amnesia.
- If a child's head has been injured, his neck or spine may also have been injured. Call EMS for any child who has suffered a serious head injury so that he can be transported with protective spinal-immobilization equipment in place.
- Toys like bikes, skates, and boards should be appropriate for the child's age, size, and skill level. This is a parent's judgment call. If you are uneasy watching him, take the toy away until he is older and bigger.
- Find a safe area away from traffic for the children to have fun.
- Younger children require adult supervision.
- A simple helmet can prevent devastating brain injuries and save your child's life.

PART

THREE

UNDERSTANDING ILLNESS

ALLERGIC REACTIONS AND ANAPHYLAXIS

11

- ✚ **What Is an Allergic Reaction?**
- ✚ **What Is Anaphylaxis?**
- ✚ **What Anaphylaxis Looks Like**
- ✚ **Treatment of Anaphylaxis**

✚ *At first, the car crash appeared to be a simple tragic accident. A vehicle had left the roadway and struck a tree. The old man still sitting in the front seat was clearly no longer alive. I gathered the information I needed for my report, requested that the coroner respond to the scene, and began writing my trip report. Then I glanced up and noticed a state trooper wandering around in the roadway looking puzzled.*

I left my paperwork behind and followed him, looking back at the scene through his eyes. This narrow country road would not allow a car to travel at high speed without losing control. Accidents were frequent along this lane. Yet I could see no skid marks on the asphalt—no indication that the driver had ever used his brakes. Tire prints in the soft shoulder suggested the car simply left the road and bumped into the tree, as though randomly. I walked back to the car and inspected the damage to the front end again. I have seen cars bent so completely around a tree that the engine

173

compartment no longer existed. The damage to this car was minimal. The windshield was cracked but not shattered. Similarly, the elderly man in the driver's seat showed few signs of injury even though, by the time the crashed car was discovered, he had been dead for some time. I realized his seat belt was not fastened. His left arm was entwined in the fabric, as though he had unfastened the belt after the crash but hadn't managed to remove it entirely.

While crash victims sometimes die from heart attacks or strokes and not from injuries during the crash, this man's autopsy uncovered no evidence of heart attack or stroke. The medical examiner discovered a fresh bee sting on the man's leg. The man's medical history contained documentation of a severe reaction to bee stings in the past. And the postmortem revealed signs of an anaphylactic reaction. Whether he was stung and tried to drive himself to the hospital, or was stung while driving and chose not to pull over and request help, the crash hadn't killed this poor man; a bee had.

WHAT IS AN ALLERGIC REACTION?

Substances that cause some people to have allergic reactions are like poisons for them. If a child is allergic to a substance and it is allowed to enter his body, his body automatically responds to defend itself. Substances that can trigger such reactions are called *antigens*. A healthy human body views an antigen as an enemy attempting to invade—like a poison. The antigens are frequently, in fact, bacteria or viruses. The body's immune system takes immediate action to defend the castle. This highly sophisticated system first produces antibodies and sends them out to capture and attach themselves to the antigens, forming bulky complexes. These large molecules are then rounded up by immune system soldiers called *neutrophils* and *macrophages* and are escorted out of the body. In addition, the immune system has a diligent bookkeeper in charge of cataloguing and remembering every single invading antigen so that if a similar enemy invades in the future, the antibodies can be produced quickly. A healthy immune system can ward off antigens without a child ever becoming aware war was being waged.

Unfortunately, some protective antibodies are more aggressive and creative than others are. They may insist on enlisting the assistance of cells capable of producing a chemical called *histamine*. A powerful agent, histamine works behind the front lines to further protect the body from invasion. The gate across the moat is raised. Barriers are erected to block avenues leading into the body. Usually, this amounts to little more than watery, weeping eyes, sneezing, and coughing to flush the antigen out. Sometimes, the upper airway will begin to swell closed, and the smaller airways will constrict to prevent entry of more offending antigens through the respiratory system. A child may begin drooling, and swallowing may become difficult. Blood vessels near the surface may dilate, resulting in red, blotchy skin that may feel warm and may itch. Some of the smallest vessels may even begin to leak, causing pockets of fluid beneath the skin that we call *hives*. The nervous system may be called into action, causing a sympathetic response, including a rapid heart beat and profuse sweating. If the gastrointestinal system's assistance is called upon, a child may develop nausea, vomiting, and diarrhea as the body tries to rid itself of the offending invader.

When those very creative antibodies demand a release of histamine, the body's response is what we call an *allergic reaction*. Many people have immune systems that react in this way to prevalent antigens like pollen, dust mites, and mold spores. Others react to the dander or saliva from cats, dogs, and other household pets. A child's gastrointestinal system may respond to certain foods like milk, fruit, fish, or nuts. With young children we may have trouble figuring out what causes an allergic reaction. When symptoms make a child very uncomfortable, or if the immune response aggravates other conditions like asthma, it may be necessary for a doctor to test the child by exposing him to very tiny amounts of a variety of antigens to determine what antigen is causing the allergic reaction.

- Our bodies view antigens as poisons attempting to invade our bodies.
- When we have an allergic reaction, histamine is released to help the body rid itself of the invading antigen.

WHAT IS ANAPHYLAXIS?

Occasionally, the immune system flips out and completely overreacts to an invading antigen. Large amounts of histamine and other chemicals may be released, causing the body to defend itself in a manner that can actually cause its own death. This is called an *anaphylactic reaction* and this is not the same as a typical allergic reaction. In an effort to prevent continued exposure to an antigen, a child's body can begin to shut down very, very fast. Airways can swell shut completely, not allowing a child to breathe at all. The dilation of blood vessels can cause a precipitous drop in blood pressure that can prevent the heart from doing its job of delivering oxygen to cells. A child may pass out and go into irreversible shock. An anaphylactic reaction to an antigen is rare, but it can be deadly and it can occur very rapidly.

This overwhelming reaction on the part of the immune system sometimes occurs after exposure to certain antibiotics, like those from the penicillin and cephalosporin families. Anaphylactic reactions may also be triggered by aspirin and nonsteroidal anti-inflammatory drugs (NSAIDs) like ibuprofen. Some children may develop reactions to shellfish or the venom of bees, wasps, or ants. Initial symptoms will be a flush color or rash, sweating, coughing, difficulty swallowing, and/or tightness in the child's chest. As airways begin to shut down, the child may begin to wheeze or you may hear stridor. His voice may change and become very hoarse. He may become very weak or dizzy. Eventually, as his blood pressure drops, he will pass out.

It is not surprising that a drug called an antihistamine, like diphenhydramine (Benadryl) will work to block the effects of the histamine. Available at any drugstore, diphenhydramine will help to alleviate the symptoms of most common allergic reactions. If a child is having an anaphylactic reaction, however, the oral diphenhydramine may not be enough or may not be absorbed into the child's system fast enough. A child experiencing an anaphylactic reaction requires a different and more powerful drug, called epinephrine.

Instead of blocking the effects of histamine, epinephrine causes the exact opposite effects. Blood vessels constrict to maintain a normal blood pressure. Swelling is diminished. Airways dilate. Epinephrine is a prescription drug, however, and must be injected beneath the skin to be effective.

- An anaphylactic reaction occurs when the immune system flips out and attempts to protect the body in a manner that can cause its own death.
- Anaphylaxis is rare, but can be life threatening.
- One treatment to counter the histamine release in a typical allergic reaction is an antihistamine like diphenhydramine (Benadryl). The best treatment for anaphylaxis is epinephrine.

WHAT ANAPHYLAXIS LOOKS LIKE

According to The Food Allergy & Anaphylaxis Network (FAAN), anaphylaxis causes as many as two hundred deaths every year. As soon as your child begins to manifest signs of an allergic reaction that you have never seen before, like sneezing and itchy, watery eyes, call your doctor for an appropriate dose of over-the-counter diphenhydramine. If a child develops signs or symptoms of anaphylaxis, if he suddenly has a rash and/or hives and begins to wheeze or complain about difficulty swallowing or breathing, call EMS. Signs and symptoms of anaphylaxis include:

- Flush, pink or red color
- A rash and/or hives
- Swelling
- Profuse sweating
- Rapid breathing
- Difficulty breathing
- Difficulty swallowing
- Wheezing or stridor

- Dizziness or fainting
- Nausea/vomiting
- Diarrhea

An anaphylactic reaction is an emergency. If you suspect your child is having a rapid allergic reaction, do not hesitate to call for help. Remember that anaphylaxis is different from a typical allergic reaction. Deterioration in a child's condition may be rapid and severe.

- If your child is suffering from anaphylaxis, you do not have time to call the doctor for advice—call EMS.
- The effects of anaphylaxis can cost a child his life in minutes.

TREATMENT OF ANAPHYLAXIS

The best and most effective treatment of anaphylaxis is prevention. And the only true means of preventing an anaphylactic reaction is *avoidance.* Once you determine that your child is allergic to a substance, extraordinary measures may be necessary to prevent exposing your child to that antigen. If your child is allergic to dogs, bringing a puppy into the house will not "beef-up" your child's immune system and eliminate the allergy. While some children "grow out" of allergies and develop the defenses necessary to avoid reactions in the future, some children become even more vulnerable over time. If your child's initial reaction to an antigen was mild, it does not mean that the next exposure will also be mild. Subsequent exposure may result in a far more dangerous—and even life-threatening—reaction.

Your child may react to food products. Nuts (especially peanuts), fish (especially shellfish), milk, eggs, soy, and wheat are frequent antigens. Alerting school officials and the school nurse to your child's allergies is important, but not enough. Pack a lunch for your child that you know is free of antigens and do not rely on the school cafeteria staff. Encourage your child to wash his hands before and after meals. Make sure he knows not to share food, utensils, and food containers with other children. Pack a place mat or large napkin for the table as well. Some children are so sensitive to specific antigens—like peanuts—that even peanut butter not cleaned properly from a cafeteria tabletop can bring about a reaction.

Your family should learn to read all food labels. If a product does not have a label, do not even open the product. Learn all the different ways your child's antigen may be labeled. "Hydrolized vegetable protein," for example, may contain peanut oil. Canned soups that contain shellfish may not be called "Clam Chowder." As your child grows, he should learn to read the labels also. He should be encouraged to talk openly about his allergy and inquire about cooking methods and ingredients when eating meals away from home. Younger children should be taught how to alert an appropriate adult as soon as they begin to feel the symptoms of a reaction.

If your child is allergic to bees, wasps, yellow jackets, or some other critter, become familiar with his environment at home, school, day-care facilities, and friends' homes. Areas where your child plays should be free of nests. Garbage cans should be securely closed at all times. Some children are allergic to latex, a material used to make the gloves worn by doctors and nurses and dentists. You may have to remind the medical provider about your child's allergy each and every time you have an appointment. Whether your child's allergy is to a medicine, like a specific antibiotic, or foods, or latex, or critters, he should wear medical-alert jewelry. In a nursery setting, infants should wear badges. If his allergy is severe or he has suffered an anaphylactic reaction in the past, the doctor should prescribe a dose of epinephrine. Also known as Adrenalin, epinephrine is a very powerful drug and is only prescribed for children who are believed to be at risk for a life-threatening reaction. The decision to prescribe epinephrine must be made by a physician.

An older child capable of learning to administer the medicine himself should be allowed to carry the medicine with him at all times. The medicine is frequently dispensed in single-dose automatic injectors that resemble pens. A popular trade name is EpiPen®. The epinephrine can save a child's life. But it can also be dangerous if administered incorrectly (injected into the thumb) or inappropriately (if the child is NOT having an anaphylactic reaction). The injections are painless. Patients sometimes question whether or not the medicine was injected and try to test the pen with a finger. The epinephrine, if injected into a thumb, can cause such severe vessel constriction that permanent injury may result. Training for proper use of this medicine is crucial. So is the amount of the dose. An adult's dose of epinephrine should never be given to a child.

You may be required to sign a waiver to allow your child to keep the epinephrine with him at school. Some schools may insist the medication be maintained at the nurse's office or some other central location. Do not *ever* sign a waiver releasing the school from liability for not assisting your child. Administering the epinephrine properly requires training, and a child suffering from a reaction may need assistance. The school should be held responsible for your child's safety and well-being during school hours. Your child's teachers and other staff members must be given training to help your child. Insist on that training for staff members and assistance for your child if it becomes necessary. Remember that, like most medications, epinephrine doses can expire and prescriptions may need to be refilled. Your child's epinephrine dose should never be locked away in a drawer that is difficult to access in an emergency.

Even if your child was prescribed a dose of epinephrine and given the training to inject the medicine, he needs to be evaluated by a physician as soon as possible after administering a dose. A single dose may not be enough. Remember that epinephrine is a very powerful drug that can cause side effects. Look at your child. If he is still experiencing signs and symptoms of anaphylaxis, call EMS. If not, call your child's doctor for guidance. A child with a history of anaphylaxis should be monitored closely for six to twelve hours following exposure to a known antigen.

While waiting for an ambulance, make sure exposure to the antigen has been eliminated. Move your child to a different room or outside if necessary. Have the child lie down. Remember that the reaction could cause a rapid decrease in the child's blood pressure. A rapid decrease in blood pressure may result in dizziness, lightheadedness, and fainting. A child who becomes unresponsive may need your help keeping his airway open. This usually means simply tilting his head back and lifting his chin. If the child vomits, roll him onto his side and keep his mouth clear. If the child stops breathing, begin mouth-to-mouth, or mouth-to-mouth-and-nose rescue breathing as described in chapter 4. If you cannot detect a pulse, begin pediatric CPR. If you know how to use a child's automatic epinephrine injector, and he has not used it yet, you may inject the medicine into his leg or arm even if he is already unresponsive or CPR is already in progress.

EMS will ensure an open airway and adequate breathing with supplemental oxygen while rapidly transporting your child to a hospital. If nobody else at the scene is trained, an EMT may be able to help your child use his own automatic epinephrine injector. An Advanced Life Support provider may be capable of starting an IV to replace lost fluids and maintain a normal blood pressure. Depending on your child's condition, the medic may administer diphenhydramine directly through the IV. Usually, though, a medic will also inject an appropriate dose of epinephrine. In some parts of the country, both drugs may be administered.

A medic may also intubate a child before his airway can swell shut or take other necessary actions to ventilate a child adequately until arrival at the hospital. Ensuring adequate breathing and maintaining a normal blood pressure are the mainstays of treatment of anaphylaxis. While these reactions in some people can take as long as an hour to develop, others may die without treatment in minutes. Anaphylaxis is an acute medical emergency.

- Rarely, a child's immune system will overreact to an invading antigen and result in a life-threatening anaphylactic reaction. If an allergic reaction is minor, call your doctor for an appropriate dose of diphenhydramine (Benadryl). Call EMS first if your child shows signs of a rapid, acute reaction.
- Children known to have severe allergies should wear medical-alert jewelry or a badge in a nursery setting.
- If your child's doctor prescribes an automatic epinephrine

injector, ensure that your child and all those who care for him know how to use the device.

- Sign a waiver, if necessary, to allow your child to carry a dose of epinephrine with him at all times at school. Never sign a waiver releasing the school from responsibility for your child's well-being. Enlist your child's doctor's help if you have trouble.
- Have a child who has been exposed to a known antigen lie down and keep him as calm as possible.
- While waiting for help, remember the ABCs of emergency care. Airway, Breathing, Circulation.

Allergic reactions can exacerbate asthma. Asthma is an illness of the lower airway that can also threaten a child's life. The next chapter deals with a wide variety of breathing difficulties, including asthma. This is not a comprehensive list of all reasons for children to have trouble breathing. The next chapter focuses on those illnesses that sometimes bring about a life-threatening emergency.

BREATHING DIFFICULTY

12

- ✚ The Respiratory System
- ✚ Causes of Respiratory Distress
- ✚ EMS Treatment of Respiratory Distress

Mom met us at the door and carried her son to the ambulance without assistance. She was extremely anxious about her son's condition. He had become ill the previous morning, and she had watched in dismay as his temperature skyrocketed even with appropriate doses of Tylenol. Even more upsetting was the child's respiratory condition; he was working hard to breathe and barking like a seal when he tried to cough. Her greatest concern was that her three-year-old son had already experienced one febrile seizure during an illness months earlier, and she was scared that he might seize again while she tried to drive him to the hospital herself. While her son's condition did not deteriorate during the transport and he did not have a seizure, I consider her use of an ambulance as entirely appropriate.

Together, we unwrapped his many layers of damp clothing and checked a rectal temperature. His fever was 104°. We applied a sensor to his toe, called a pulse oximeter. His blood oxygen levels were normal except during his spastic coughing spells, when the levels would plummet. We applied an oxygen mask, and I completed my assessment of her son. No additional treatment was necessary prior to arrival at the hospital, but by this time the little fellow was beside himself with discomfort and distress. Keeping the child secured properly on the stretcher and talking to the doctor at the hospital at the same time became impossible. I finally managed to report, "Three-year-old male, alert and oriented, flush, rectal temperature of 104, pulse oximeter between 90 and 98 percent, and he sounds like this:" I then held the open mike near my little patient as he barked his croupy cough. The doctor chuckled as he thanked me for my succinct report. This little boy's diagnosis of croup would not be the doctor's greatest challenge this night. Unfortunately, the family's insurance company later refused to pay for the emergency transport.

A basic understanding of the respiratory system is enormously helpful when trying to evaluate a child's condition. Not all breathing difficulties are a result of illness within this system. An increased respiratory rate, also called *tachypnea* (ta-kip-nia), can result from metabolic imbalances like that which can occur during the onset of diabetes, from pain felt in other areas of the child's body, and from fever due to infection elsewhere. But understanding how the respiratory system works and learning a few simple terms can help you to understand the reasons behind a child's difficulty breathing and allow you to better communicate with your child's doctor.

THE RESPIRATORY SYSTEM

Human beings metabolize nutrients from food sources and turn them into energy. The process of metabolism is similar in some ways to building a good campfire. Our campfire will burn if we have wood, air containing oxygen, and a source of ignition. The wood is carbon based, just like most of our food. The carbon and oxygen burn, producing heat, and create by-products of combustion like carbon dioxide and water. These by-products drift away passively with the smoke from our fire. Metabolism is similar to combustion. We also use carbon-based molecules from our food, and combine them with oxygen to produce by-products of metabolism like carbon dioxide and water. Instead of heat, we manufacture energy in this way. This energy can be used by individual cells in a variety of ways and can even be stored for use later.

We are capable of continuing to convert carbon-based molecules into energy in the absence of oxygen for short periods of time. This is called *anaerobic metabolism.* It is extremely inefficient, and produces by-products that can be poisonous to our bodies. Like smothering a fire, in the absence of oxygen the process of metabolism will eventually stop, and cells will die. When enough individual cells die, the organ of which they are a part may also begin to die. The first organs to fall victim to this form of cellular suffocation are the brain and heart. Our bodies are also very sensitive to excessive accumulations of the waste products. If we are unable to rid the system of the waste carbon dioxide, it can build up and actually change the pH of our blood, wreaking havoc in many body systems. We need to pull the oxygen in and get the waste products out efficiently or illness will result. So we must breathe in, and we must breathe out for the system to function properly.

We suck air into our lungs by using the intercostal muscles in our chest walls. These muscles pull our ribs up and out. We also contract our diaphragm, that large muscular sheath that separates the contents of our chests from the contents of our abdomens. As the diaphragm pulls down toward our feet and our intercostal muscles pull our ribs up and out, the volume inside our chest cavity increases. In order to balance the pressure inside our chest with the atmospheric pressure outside our chest, air rushes into our lungs. This air contains approximately 21 percent oxygen. The rest of the air is made up of gases for which we have no use, like nitrogen and argon. We may use 5 or 6 percent of the oxygen in the air we breathe in, blowing what we do not use back out when we exhale. We also exhale the waste products of metabolism, like carbon dioxide and water, and the nitrogen and other air gases that we do not need.

WHY CPR WORKS

I f we used all the oxygen we inhaled for metabolism, there would be no residual oxygen in the air we breathe out. If this were true, CPR would not work because we would not be providing oxygen in the air we were breathing into someone else's mouth during resuscitation. Because we only use part of the oxygen we breathe in and the rest is exhaled, we can blow into someone else's mouth and still provide them with needed oxygen.

We breathe in by sucking air through our noses and mouths. When we have sinus congestion, it is not unusual to breathe all the air we need in through our mouths alone. As we sleep, sometimes with closed mouths, we may suck all the air we need in through our nostrils. These two body orifices provide the pathway for air to enter our lungs. They meet in the back of our throats to form a single pathway. If we need to blow air into a nonbreathing person's lungs, we must force the chest to rise and push the diaphragm down. We will not be providing the pressure necessary to lift a chest and fill lungs if the air is simply leaking out somewhere else. If we blow into the mouth, we must pinch off the nostrils or air will simply blow back out the nose. If we blow into the nose, we must block off the mouth. Either blow into both at the same time, as with a small child, or block off one of these orifices.

After the airways through our nose and mouth combine in the back of our throats, called the *pharynx,* the air is drawn across the voice box, called the *larynx.* This movement of air over vocal cords as we exhale allows us to speak. If we are not breathing in and out, or if our vocal cords are damaged or have been removed, we are not capable of speaking normally. People who have suffered from cancer of the larynx and have had their vocal cords removed sometimes use a device to mimic the resonance produced by the missing voice box that allows them to produce words. People who depend on machines to breathe for them, called *ventilators,* can sometimes create enough pressure as they exhale to produce sounds over their own vocal cords. The famous actor, Christopher Reeves, requires such a machine to breathe for him because the nerves that control his ability to lift his ribs and pull down his diaphragm have been damaged. But he is still able to manipulate the pressure sufficiently to create a voice. In his audio book, *Still Me,* the patterns caused by the use of his ventilator are barely perceptible.

After the air passes across the vocal cords, it travels through a long, round, cartilaginous tube called the *trachea.* Find your breastbone that travels up the center of the front of your chest. At the very top of this bone you will feel a notch. Your top ribs attach to your breastbone here and form a small valley. If you let your fingers move straight up toward your head they will feel that round, flexible trachea. It will feel uncomfortable to press on this tube. This is, in fact, what is compressed when someone is strangled. With too much pressure this tube can be compressed and flattened, not allowing for air movement and breathing.

Immediately behind your trachea is your esophagus. This is the wonderful, soft, flexible tube that allows us to swallow chocolate. This is the tube that leads food and drink to our stomachs for further processing so that we can metabolize it. But how does the chocolate know to go down the esophagus to our stomach and not down the trachea to our lungs? How does air know to travel down the trachea to the lungs, and not into our stomachs through the esophagus? We have a gatekeeper called an *epiglottis.* This small flap of tissue will allow air into our trachea as we breathe, but will quickly move to close off the trachea to protect the airway when we swallow. This diligent little gatekeeper knows to cover our airways to allow a sip of water to be swallowed and to enter our stomachs, and to open when we take a breath. It rarely knows what to do with a little plastic soldier, a piece of balloon, or how to react when a peanut blocks the way.

Just below that notch at the top of our breastbone, the trachea splits back into two separate airways. We have two lungs, one on the right side of our chest and one on the left. The trachea literally splits off into two separate airways to deliver air to both lungs. These separate airways leading to two different lungs are called *bronchi.* They lead to more splits and smaller and smaller branches to the airway as they supply all of our lung tissue with air. The airway at this point can look like an upside-down tree, with smaller and smaller limbs, branches, and twigs separating out from the common trunk. These smaller branches are called *bronchioles.* Eventually, the air finds its way into *alveoli,* air sacs that resemble tiny bunches of grapes. These air sacs fill and expand like tiny balloons. It is through the walls of these tiny balloons that oxygen enters the bloodstream through tiny blood vessels called *capillaries* that surround them, and waste carbon dioxide and water are transferred back into the lungs to be exhaled.

The term *respiration* describes the entire process of providing needed oxygen molecules to cells that will die without them and the elimination of waste products. Respiration includes the gross movement of a variety of muscle groups to suck air, containing oxygen, into the lungs as well as the exchange of oxygen molecules for waste products, which occurs at a cellular level. Inadequate respiration can result for many reasons. The muscles that allow a child to raise his chest and pull down the diaphragm may be weakened or injured. A foreign object may be blocking the airway. Swelling may narrow or completely occlude air passages. Fluids and thick goo may coat the smaller airways, blocking airflow. The oxygen may not be capable of passing from the alveoli to the bloodstream. The circulatory system may not be capable of transporting the oxygen molecules to the cells. The cells may be so damaged that they are incapable of utilizing the oxygen. The cells may be incapable of efficiently transferring waste products back into the bloodstream to be transported back to the lungs. Or the lungs may be incapable of expelling these waste products during exhalation.

If something goes wrong at any point in this process, metabolism cannot be accomplished efficiently and a child may become ill. Figuring out which part of the process is not working results in what doctors call a *diagnosis.* If the diagnosis is a bacterial infection, an antibiotic may help. If the diagnosis is the onset of a disease process, like diabetes, treatment plans can be developed. Sometimes the diagnosis involves an illness for which there are not yet good cures, like cystic fibrosis. Rarely, a diagnosis involves a sick heart, and may even result in major surgery. Usually, the diagnosis is of a viral infection that the child can overcome with close monitoring or symptomatic treatment alone and without complication.

- An understanding of the respiratory system and familiarity with some of the more common reasons for children to have trouble breathing can help you to better communicate with your child's doctor and to recognize when emergency help is needed.

CAUSES OF RESPIRATORY DISTRESS

The only clue that a child is acutely ill may be the changes in color, respiratory effort, and level of consciousness described in the preceding chapters. Determination of a diagnosis and development of a long-term treatment plan is the role of the physician. Bringing the child and physician together is the role of the parent. Keeping an acutely ill child alive until arrival at a hospital is the role of EMS. Illness that develops slowly or becomes chronic can be managed in the doctor's office and should not involve ambulances and emergency departments. Many such illnesses are not described here. Illnesses of sudden and acute onset may require emergency medical assistance. Some causes for a child's condition to become life threatening are described below.

The upper airway consists of the mouth, nose, and throat above the level of the voice box. The trachea, bronchi, bronchioles, and alveoli are all parts of the lower airway. A frequent cause of difficulty breathing that can involve either the upper or lower airway is foreign body airway obstruction. Choking incidents that require the Heimlich maneuver are acute. When the upper airway is completely occluded, the child cannot breathe and the need for help is obvious. But you may not have noticed your child inhaling something. Even they may not realize they have something blocking a lower airway or only partially blocking the upper airway. They may simply experience a sudden, acute episode of difficulty breathing. Children are sometimes not diagnosed as having a foreign object in the lower airway until they receive X rays. Doctors find coins, needles, pins, and food. Onset will still be sudden. You may hear stridor or wheezing. If a child begins to turn blue or starts gasping for air, call EMS. Foreign material lodged in the lungs can also result in infection, called *aspiration pneumonia*.

PERTUSSIS (WHOOPING COUGH) Another illness that can involve both the upper and lower airways shouldn't even exist anymore. There is a vaccine for **pertussis**. Unfortunately, some parents are concerned about reactions to the vaccine and refuse to have their children immunized. Many other children are not receiving regular, preventive care and immunizations. This illness is reappearing with alarming frequency in some communities. Instead of being wiped off the face of the earth, this illness is back, placing all of us at greater risk. I have been forced to undergo prophylactic antibiotic therapy following exposure to one of my little patients with pertussis.

Pertussis is a bacterial infection that can cause persistent coughing spells. When these prolonged coughing episodes end, the child, starved for air, takes in a huge, "whooping" breath. The coughing episodes can be severe and cause the child's color to change. High fever may be present, and the child may suffer seizures.

CROUP The common name for a viral infection below the level of the epiglottis, this is also called *viral laryngotracheobronchitis*. Croup causes stridor and a mild fever, but the hallmark of croup is a foghorn cough that sounds like a seal barking. It frequently strikes children between the ages of one and three, and occurs most often during winter months. The evening of the second day of illness is usually the worst time for children, with improvement and recovery taking several more days. A child will usually be comforted by fifteen to twenty minutes in a steam-filled bathroom, a cool mist humidifier, or exposure to the cool night air. Many children survive croup with no need for emergency care. Children should be kept well rested and well hydrated (push the fluids).

Occasionally, croup can overwhelm a child. The stridor should be heard only when the child exerts himself. If the stridor can also be heard while the child is at rest or if the child's level of respiratory distress becomes moderate (working hard to breath, paleness, and pallor) call the doctor back. If the child becomes exhausted, begins to gasp for air, begins to push you away, or seems breathless, call EMS. Severe presentations of croup can require intensive care and medications to control the inflammation and dilate the airways.

EPIGLOTTITIS   Infection and inflammation of the epiglottis. If not treated, the swelling associated with this inflammation can cause complete airway obstruction. Onset can be rapid (over several hours) and may include fever, difficulty swallowing, and respiratory distress. Children suffering from epiglottitis are usually between two and seven years of age and frequently insist on that tripod position to help them breathe. They will begin to drool because swallowing hurts so much. And they will look very sick. The major cause of epiglottitis used to be an influenza virus. Since the advent of the flu vaccine, the most common causes are streptococcal and staphylococcal infections that will usually respond to antibiotics. But the acute onset of epiglottitis can be life threatening. Call EMS.

PHARYNGITIS   The throat is also called the *pharynx*. The infection and inflammation of the pharynx is called *pharyngitis* (i.e., a sore throat). Sometimes infection to the back of the throat or the tonsils can become severe. An abscess is an inflamed area of soft tissue that fills with pus. If an abscess forms around the tonsils (**peritonsillar abscess**), or in the back of the throat (**retropharyngeal abscess**) it can become so swollen with pus that the child cannot swallow, and it can even begin to block the airway. Pharyngitis (a sore throat) is rarely dangerous, frequently bacterial in nature and may respond to antibiotics. A physician should see a child if a sore throat becomes severe and lasts throughout the day or persists for more than two days. If an abscess develops rapidly, before a child can be seen by a physician, it can become life threatening. Children with retropharyngeal or peritonsillar abscesses will be sick, they will have extremely sore throats and they may be drooling. They may also be running fevers.

ASTHMA   The most common illness of the lower airway is asthma. Depending on the type of asthma your child has, it may be triggered by environmental allergens, exercise, stress, irritants like cigarette smoke, or even something as subtle as changes in temperature and humidity. Asthma is occasionally misdiagnosed. Children with environmental allergies sometimes wheeze. This does not necessarily mean they have asthma. Children, particularly those without consistent medical care, are sometimes diagnosed with infection and offered antibiotics. Antibiotics do not cure asthma.

During an acute asthma attack, the lower airways become inflamed and begin to swell. As they swell, the space through which air must move becomes more and more narrow. When you whistle, you force air through a tiny opening between your lips. This is the same whistling sound air makes while trying to move through many constricted lower airways as the child exhales. We call it *wheezing*. The airways may be narrowed even further by an accumulation of thick mucous that can occlude the smallest airways entirely. And the bronchi and bronchioles can begin to spasm. All of this can combine to make it nearly impossible for an asthmatic child to breathe. The harder he works to breathe, the more frightened he will become, and the more bronchospasm may occur.

Acute asthma attacks are treated with medicines to open the airways, called *bronchodilators*. These medicines are usually administered in metered dose inhalers or nebulizers designed to aerosolize the liquid and allow it to be breathed directly into the lungs. They work rapidly to increase the inside diameter of airways and improve breathing. They also, however, affect the heart. These medications can cause an increased heart rate, trembling, and sometimes lead to nausea and vomiting.

When to use bronchodilators, how frequently a child needs the medicine, and how much medicine to give involves development of a treatment plan by a qualified physician for each individual child. In addition, medicines are sometimes needed to prevent the inflammation and swelling in the first place. These are corticosteroids. They sometimes also come in the form of medicine to be inhaled. But this is preventive medicine. Corticosteroids are of no use during acute attacks. It is important to determine what triggers an asthma attack. These triggers can be anything from a household pet to the brand of shampoo you use. Dust mites, mold spores, perfumes, or pollen can all be triggers for individual children. Different kids can have different triggers. Successful treatment of asthma is possible, but requires diligence on the part of both the physician and the parent.

When a child's asthma attack becomes acute, when he can no longer move adequate volumes of air without great effort, his color will begin to change. Working hard to breathe is exhausting. He may become agitated and upset, or his level of fatigue may cause him to begin to lose consciousness. EMS can take a number of actions to control an asthma attack, depending on the level of training of providers and local EMS protocols. At the very least, they can provide supplemental oxygen and mechanically assist your child in breathing if necessary. When Advanced Life Support providers are available, they can provide additional nebulized bronchodilators and will be capable of intubating your child, if necessary. Bronchodilators can then be administered through a bag valve device attached to the endotracheal tube, and sufficient pressure can be used to push oxygen through narrowed airways until further treatment at the hospital.

PNEUMONIA This can be due to either a viral or bacterial infection. A physician should see children younger than three months of age who are ill and have a constant cough immediately. These babies may or may not be running a fever. Older children with pneumonia usually do run fevers, they will have an increased respiratory rate, they will be sick, and they will be coughing. Again, anytime illness combines with difficulty breathing or an increased respiratory rate, it is time to involve your doctor. As fluid accumulates in the lower airways, you may be able to hear rales or a bubbling sound when you place your ear against the child's back, but even with a stethoscope the fluid can be difficult to hear. The child may also be wheezing and you may be able to hear him trying to cough up the thick, wet mucous that is invading his little lungs.

When a child becomes overwhelmed, his color will change. He may begin to struggle and work hard for each breath. Coughing spells may induce bronchospasm, making breathing even harder. He may become exhausted. If these changes are gradual, you may have time to travel to the doctor's office. If changes are sudden and dramatic, do not hesitate to call EMS.

APNEA VERSUS BREATH HOLDING

There is a huge difference between episodes of apnea that can occur during infancy and illness and breath holding on the part of a toddler. Apnea during infancy may occur for several seconds and be normal and not indicative of illness. Apnea lasting more than twenty seconds (which, for a mom or dad, is a very, very long time) may be due to illness, and you should call your doctor. But in older children, like toddlers, breath holding may be part of a typical temper tantrum. Approximately 5 percent of children between the ages of six months and five years will have breath-holding spells. The spells usually last less than one minute and are frequently preceded by an upsetting event—like being scolded, disciplined, or told, "No!" These spells are usually harmless. You should still consult your physician who can rule out any physical abnormality and may be able to recommend behavior-modification strategies to stop these episodes.

Sometimes a child cries so hard that he literally cannot catch his breath. Sometimes these episodes are entirely manipulative on the part of the child, and he needs to be taught better ways of venting his anger. Nevertheless, children can actually cause themselves to pass out or can appear to have seizures. Even if a child holds his breath so long that he passes out (and that is one angry little dude), his natural reflexes will take over, he will begin to breathe normally again, and he will wake up.

BRONCHIOLITIS   A similar viral infection of the lower airway, usually seen in children under two years of age. The viruses that cause bronchiolitis frequently strike during early winter months. A child's respiratory rate may increase, and you may be able to hear wheezing, rales, or wet coughing when you listen with your ear to the back of your child's chest. The child may be working so hard to breathe that you can see retractions, sinking of skin between ribs and above the collarbones and breastbone as the child tries to inhale. Children with bronchiolitis are susceptible to periods of apnea, when they stop breathing entirely. Periods of apnea may be the only signs of illness. While this illness is viral and may not respond to antibiotics, secondary infections can occur. These children may need intensive support in a hospital. Involve your doctor early, keep the physician informed about any changes in your child's condition. Do not hesitate to call EMS if changes are sudden and dramatic, or if your child begins to stop breathing for more than twenty seconds at a time.

SPONTANEOUS PNEUMOTHORAX   Occasionally, a small rupture can occur to lung tissue. Air can leak out of the lung and build up inside the chest, pushing in on the lung and making it difficult for the lung to inflate properly. A **spontaneous pneumothorax** will cause a child to feel a sudden onset of pain on one side of his chest and may cause difficulty breathing. Sometimes these ruptures are small and limited, and can heal by themselves with no special treatment. Sometimes a spontaneous pneumothorax can be massive and keep a child from using one entire lung. The rupture itself may not show up on an X ray, but a collapsed lung will. Treatment usually involves insertion of a tube into the child's chest, between the ribs on the affected side, to draw the air out and allow the lung to reinflate.

This treatment can rarely be performed in a doctor's office. The level of urgency needed to treat a spontaneous pneumothorax depends on the child's condition. If the pain and difficulty breathing are mild, your doctor can direct you to an appropriate facility for treatment. If the pain or amount of respiratory distress is acute, call EMS.

- The level of a child's respiratory distress can be described as minor, moderate, or severe. A physician should evaluate a child in minor respiratory distress during illness.
- When a child begins to struggle to breathe, his condition must be monitored by a physician more closely and may require intervention.
- Severe respiratory distress signals the possible onset of respiratory failure, and you should not hesitate to call for emergency help.

EMS TREATMENT OF RESPIRATORY DISTRESS

There are many different reasons for a child to develop respiratory distress. The paramedic or EMT will not offer you a diagnosis or attempt to treat a specific illness. A diagnosis will become important later. In an emergency, giving the illness a name does not matter. Regardless of the reason, a child who cannot breathe adequately needs supplemental oxygen and, sometimes, mechanical assistance. If bronchospasm is present, an Advanced Life Support (ALS) provider can administer appropriate medications even as they travel toward the hospital. Airways can be secured and steps taken to hydrate a child and bring down a fever. It is not unusual for significant improvement in a child's condition to occur during the ride in the ambulance.

In an ambulance, supplemental oxygen can help perk a child up and keep him more alert. Medicine can be given to dilate airways and make breathing easier. Fluids can be given to a child already dangerously dehydrated. The greatest value to ambulance transport, however, is that professional treatment can be provided immediately if the child turns that corner and begins to suffer respiratory failure. When a child cannot get enough oxygen, brain cells begin to die. Even if a child who has been oxygen starved can be resuscitated, brain damage may result. As soon as you become anxious about your child's level of respiratory distress, call your doctor. Call EMS if changes are sudden and acute.

- A child may have difficulty breathing for many reasons. When a child is in acute distress, the reason for this difficulty—the diagnosis—doesn't matter. Giving the illness a name will not make it go away.
- Call for help.
- Remember the ABCs of emergency medical care.

Many of the illnesses described above involve the potential for fever. A child with a fever can scare any parent. A child can become very uncomfortable and weak. While fevers rarely require emergency intervention—over-the-counter medications and plenty of fluids are usually enough—a rapid increase in body temperature can cause a child to have a seizure. Seizures can be frightening for parents who have never witnessed one before and should trigger automatic calls for help for children who have no seizure history. The next chapter will help you to better understand fevers and seizures.

FEVERS AND SEIZURES

13

- ✚ **What Is Fever?**
- ✚ **Treating Fever**
- ✚ **Fevers and Seizures**
- ✚ **Seizure Management**

✚ *All we were told as we dodged traffic toward the home was that a two year old was in cardiac arrest. Repeatedly, cars refused to pull over and move out of our way. As I left the passenger seat of the ambulance, the dispatcher informed me that we were already six minutes into this call. Three long flights of concrete steps led to the garden apartment where neighbors were already gathering. I carried a jump kit containing IV equipment and drugs, a cardiac monitor, and an oxygen tank. Somewhere on the second flight of steps I paused to catch my breath and yelled up the stairs to ask if the child was breathing. "NO!" I hurried up the remaining stairs, entered the apartment, and had to push my way through several people.*

He was lying on the living room floor and completely unresponsive. His airway was open and blood covered one side of his face. He was breathing. He was also covered with layers of heavy clothing and soaking wet. As

*my partner fitted a small oxygen mask over his face I attached a pulse
oximeter probe to his finger and listened to his lungs. As I listened I
allowed my body to relax and my own respiratory rate to return to a normal level. Another febrile seizure.*

WHAT IS FEVER?

Our bodies have an internal thermostat set within a narrow range to
keep us healthy. When our body temperature begins to drop
below that normal range, our metabolic rate increases. We shiver and
heat is generated to help bring the body temperature back up into
that normal range. When the thermostat senses that we are too
warm, we sweat. The perspiration evaporates into the air currents
blowing over the layer of moist skin, taking heat away with it. The
tiny blood vessels closest to the surface of our skin dilate, bringing
the warm blood closer to the surface where it can be cooled and giving us a flushed color.

The body's thermostat is controlled by the hypothalamus,
located deep in our brain. When a microorganism like a virus or bacteria invades a child's body, the hypothalamus may reset the child's
thermostat to a higher temperature, attempting to make the environment hostile to the invaders. The new, higher temperature range will
be reached by the same increase in metabolism that causes shivering.
Hence, the term *fever and chills.* The human body does this on purpose to cause the invading microorganisms to die, or at least to convince them to go somewhere else to live.

Different microorganisms, also called *pathogens,* need different
elevations in body temperature to be convinced to leave a child's body.
Some viruses need a very high temperature. Others may require relatively mild temperature elevations to find a child's body an unwelcome
home. Temperature elevation is a child's natural method of combating
infection. Most of the time a parent can welcome a fever as a sign that
their child's immune system is functioning properly. Unfortunately, a
child can feel very uncomfortable as this battle is waged.

General guidance is offered below for interpretation and management of a child's fever. But fever is one of those general subjects that parents should discuss with their child's physician, preferably prior to the onset of any illness. Different doctors may choose to handle varying levels of fever differently in individual children, depending on the known or suspected diagnosis. Emergency care is rarely needed. When EMS or emergency department care is necessary depends less on the number on the thermometer and more on the child's appearance and behavior. Remember to watch for changes in level of consciousness, skin color and tone, and difficulty breathing to call for help. If a fever becomes dangerously high, other signs will be abnormal and you will already know to call for help.

Rectal temperatures are more reliable and accurate than oral (under the tongue) temperatures, tympanic (ear) temperatures, or axillary (armpit) temperatures. Only rectal temperatures should be measured in infants and very young children. Your child has a fever if rectal temperature is above 100.4, oral temperature is above 99.5, or axillary temperature is above 99.0 (temperatures measured in degrees Fahrenheit). In children older than three months, a fever can be a healthy sign that your child's immune system is functioning properly. It is time to call the doctor and discuss your child's condition if your child is younger than three months and rectal temperature exceeds 100.4. Or if a child aged three to six months has a fever above 102. Or if a child older than six months runs a fever above 105.

Remember that appropriate treatment of the underlying infection may or may not warrant a prescription for an antibiotic. Viral infections do not respond to antibiotics. It is not always necessary to obtain a culture, grow an organism in a laboratory, and identify it exactly (which can take days) to decide if it is a virus or a bacteria. Physicians can frequently diagnose the nature of the causative infection based on the clinical presentation of the child and the parent or caregiver's description of the course the illness has taken. Be sure to tell the doctor about all of your child's symptoms to assist him in making this diagnosis, including any rashes your child may have or areas of skin that appear bruised, headache, a stiff or sore neck, and any unusual weakness. A physician will rarely prescribe an antibiotic without examining the child personally unless someone else in the home has already been diagnosed with an infection or he is aware of a specific infectious agent rocketing around our schools and day-care centers.

We must train ourselves to be content with over-the-counter treatment of symptoms like fever, when appropriate. In a 1999 study published in the journal *Pediatrics*, 96 percent of 610 pediatricians surveyed claimed they were asked for antibiotic prescriptions by anxious parents when the medicine was not indicated, 48 percent sometimes felt pressured to do so, and one-third admitted that they sometimes complied with these requests.[1] The abuse and misuse of antibiotics can cause some microorganisms to become resistant to standard therapies. The emergence of drug resistant infectious illnesses places all of us, including our children, at higher risk.

It is time to call EMS or take your child to the nearest emergency department when the child becomes excessively weak. If he suffers sudden changes in mental status and is no longer alert and oriented, you need emergency help. If his color becomes suddenly too pale or he begins to turn blue and develops difficulty breathing, call EMS. Emergency help is needed in these situations regardless of the number on the thermometer. Fever itself can cause the child harm if it exceeds 107, but this is a very rare occurrence, and the child will almost certainly be suffering from the symptoms noted above as well. Fevers should be measured and tracked to assist the physician in a diagnosis, but the exact number is rarely relevant in an emergency.

- Any child under three months of age with a fever must be evaluated rapidly by a physician.
- Most fevers in children over age three months are a good sign that our children are developing healthy immune systems.
- Most fevers do not require emergency care.

TREATING FEVER

Treating a fever at home is different than caring for a child while you wait for the ambulance. The mainstay of treatment for fever is an over-the-counter antipyretic, like acetaminophen (Tylenol), or ibuprofen (Advil). Never give a febrile child aspirin. Aspirin administration has been linked to Reyes syndrome, a serious illness that can attack the brain or liver following bouts of flu or chicken pox. Be very careful and precise with doses. If you are unsure about an appropriate dose or frequency of administration, call for your doctor's assistance. In a 1997 study, one hundred caregivers of children in a pediatric emergency department were asked to measure a correct dose of acetaminophen, based on a child's weight and the package instructions. Over half were unsuccessful, usually measuring too little medicine.[2] One of the clues a doctor uses to diagnose a child's illness is whether or not they have responded to acetaminophen or ibuprofen. If the child has not responded simply because the caregiver did not give enough medicine, this may result in unnecessary additional testing or treatment. Similarly, overdoses can be toxic.

A child with a fever should not be bundled up in layers of heavy clothing. Light pajamas and a light cover are enough. The child should be kept well hydrated. This means as much fluid as they care to drink without forcing it down, which could result in vomiting. There are special children's drinks on the market that have higher concentrations of electrolytes than pure water (like Pedialyte for babies or even Gatorade for older children). But any clear fluids are appropriate, as are ice chips, popsicles, and Jell-O. Avoid milk products and acidic juices that could upset their tummies. If the fever in a child over six months of age rises above 105, and the child is very uncomfortable, a lukewarm bath or a sponge bath with lukewarm water may help. But do not use cold water. This can bring a child's temperature down too fast and can cause them to shiver, defeating the purpose by generating more heat. NEVER use rubbing alcohol in a sponge bath to bring down a child's fever. The inhaled fumes are toxic and may cause your child more harm than any fever.

Once a fever has caused other acute symptoms, like changes in level of consciousness, difficulty breathing, and sudden changes in skin color and tone, you need help. Do not give the child anything more by mouth. If he becomes unresponsive or suffers a seizure, he may be unable to control his airway and he may choke on any vomitus. Monitor his airway closely. Unwrap any layers of heavy bedding or clothing. Remember: Lukewarm sponge baths are okay; cold water is not. Never use rubbing alcohol.

When EMS arrives, they will assure that your child's airway is secure, provide supplemental oxygen, and continue trying to gently cool the child. If the child is dehydrated, Advanced Life Support (ALS) providers will be capable of administering fluids through an IV. EMS providers will need to know if your child has received any medications like acetaminophen or ibuprofen, how much and when. When your child is very ill, keep a log of any medications you give him, how much of what medicine was given, and the time. It can be very hard to remember later when you are worried and upset.

Not all fevers result in seizures. Only about 4 percent of children experience febrile seizures. Children can run very high fevers with no danger of a seizure. And children typically run fevers that are higher than an adult's. When you have personal memories of feeling horribly ill with a fever of only 100°, it can be scary to look at the thermometer after taking your child's temperature and see numbers as high as 103, 104, and 105. The real threat represented by the number on the thermometer is the underlying cause for the rise and how fast it became elevated, not necessarily how high the number is.

The major threat associated with a high fever is dehydration. When their body temperatures begin to rise, children perspire. Their skin will become clammy and wet. This is the human body's natural way of attempting to cool itself down. As the perspiration evaporates it draws heat out of the body. When children become both hot and dry, they may no longer be capable of using this natural mechanism, and they may already be dangerously low on fluids.

When you place a wet towel in a clothes dryer with the heat setting on low, it will eventually become dry as the water in the towel evaporates. If you put the heat setting on high it will dry much

HOW HIGH IS HIGH?

A standard old wives' tale claims that a child with a very high fever can suffer brain damage. This is not strictly true. A child may experience brain damage if body temperature rises too high. But normal *fevers* do not usually produce this level of body temperature elevation. Children left alone in parked cars on hot days with closed windows die this way. Children left to play in the hot sun for extended periods or trapped inside sweltering apartments can suffer from a severe rise in body temperature that can cause coma and even death. This is called *hyperthermia,* or *heat stroke,* and represents a life-threatening emergency. Typical body temperature elevations associated with fighting infections rarely endanger a child, unless he is also lying in the hot summer sun, lying in a bed next to a hot radiator, or trapped inside an excessively hot environment.

faster. A very high temperature can result in the loss of large amounts of fluid from a child's body, and this can occur quickly. This fluid must be replaced. This can be especially difficult if the child is also vomiting and unable to drink enough. It is sometimes first necessary to use medications to control the nausea and vomiting in order to allow the child to drink enough fluids to keep up with the losses. As fluids leave the body, so do important chemicals called *electrolytes.* When the concentrations of these electrolytes in the bloodstream become unbalanced due to dehydration, a child may begin having difficulty breathing, may suffer mental status changes, and may even experience dangerous heart rhythms. Untreated, dehydration can kill a child. The fever itself cannot.

- Acetaminophen and ibuprofen can help bring a fever down and make a child more comfortable. Never administer aspirin.
- Make sure the child receives plenty of fluids.
- Lukewarm sponge baths can also provide comfort. Never use alcohol.

FEVERS AND SEIZURES

I was precepting a nurse with no previous prehospital experience. He was a talented and highly skilled intensive care nurse but accustomed to working in a well-lit, immaculately clean hospital environment. He was not used to uncontrolled scenes, communicating over the radio, or treating patients in the middle of the highway. These should have been his greatest concerns. Instead, as we talked in the garage next to our ambulance, he admitted that he was worried about facing a child in cardiac arrest and taking appropriate actions without someone telling him what to do next. While he had cared for many critically ill children, and had been involved in several efforts to resuscitate children in cardiac arrest, there had always been a doctor there calling the shots and making decisions.

We reviewed the protocols for treating pediatric cardiac arrest, and I reassured him that he would remember the proper steps. I also told him that children in cardiac arrest were rare in the prehospital environment, and that most pediatric cardiac arrest calls were actually children having seizures. If they have never witnessed a seizure before, parents are so sure their child is dying that they scream to the dispatcher on the telephone that the child is dead. Just as I was explaining this, the tones dropped for a code 7C. Seven, in this region, stood for cardiac arrest. The "C" stood for child. I looked at my precepting nurse with years of intensive pediatric care under his belt and watched all the color drain from his face. He spent a lot of time taking deep breaths on the way to the call. Our patient had, indeed, suffered a febrile seizure. She did just fine. Although it was not the cardiac arrest call he had feared, my precepting nurse did a truly wonderful job. He was going to be a terrific prehospital provider.

When a child seizes or has a convulsion (the terms generally mean the same thing), it is as though an electrical storm passes through his brain. Nerves fire in rapid, random fashion and overwhelm normal brain processes. The child no longer has any conscious control over bodily functions. His eyes may roll back in his head. His body may become as solid and rigid as a board, or he may jerk around in violent spasms. He may lose control of his bladder and/or bowels. Normal breathing patterns may be interrupted. Children sometimes begin to turn blue. The child may bite down on his tongue or cheek, and blood may spurt from his mouth. He may make gurgling sounds similar to the "death rattle" heard in dying adults.

Children frequently vomit during seizures or immediately after a seizure; and this, combined with incontinence, can seem like their little bodies are emptying out. Without normal breathing patterns, they can be deprived of oxygen long enough to make their color change—sometimes to a waxy, colorless pallor, sometimes to a dark, dusky shade of red. In can look as though a child is being electrocuted, zapped by a mysterious force that is tearing him apart, or like his life is being sapped from his body. As a parent stands by helplessly while a child seizes, a minute is still only sixty seconds. But seconds can last hours and days and years.

Seizures in children can occur for many reasons. Children with epilepsy or seizure disorders associated with brain abnormalities can seize often, sometimes even several times during a single day. These seizures are sometimes so commonplace and caregivers so well trained in protecting a child during the seizure that no doctor is called, no ambulance is summoned. But when a child seizes for the first time, either due to the onset of a treatable illness like epilepsy or due to a sudden rise in fever, caregivers are frightened out of their minds; ambulances are always—and should always—be requested. Even if a child has been ill and running a fever, until he or she is evaluated by a physician, it is impossible to be sure that the seizure is fever related (febrile). It is also impossible to know how long the seizure will last.

While most febrile seizures are self-limiting and relatively short in duration (less than five minutes), some seizures are prolonged and require intervention. Worse, some children develop a condition called *status epilepticus,* when a seizure does not stop. Even in children with seizure disorders, a seizure can be caused by other conditions like oxygen deprivation, low blood sugar, and metabolic imbalances that require emergency medical care. Not all seizures are due to fevers.

Even if you recognize early that a child is ill and take all the appropriate steps to care for him, he may have a seizure. Even if a fever does not exceed 105°, if it rose very fast it could cause a child to seize. Sometimes this happens so fast that a parent or caregiver did not even realize the child was ill. Again, a seizure may have nothing to do with a child's body temperature. Children can experience seizure activity after a head injury. The head injury may have seemed minor and/or may have occurred hours earlier. Children may seize if they are deprived of oxygen for too long, if they have ingested certain poisons, if they have received an overdose of a drug—either intentionally or accidentally. A child may seize if his blood sugar level drops too low; these children do not necessarily have to be known diabetics.

A qualified physician should always evaluate children who seize with no history of prior seizure activity. An ambulance is critical. Parents can be so upset that they may crash their cars on the way to the hospital with the child. And the child may seize again during the ride. In the ambulance, providers can continue to protect your child from further harm, monitor his airway, and provide supplemental oxygen. ALS providers can look for signs of head trauma, check your child's blood sugar level, administer fluids, monitor changes in cardiac rhythm, and, if necessary, administer medication to arrest a second seizure (usually diazepam).

- About 4 percent of children will experience at least one febrile seizure.
- One-third of the children who have one febrile seizure will have another.
- Nine percent of children who have one febrile seizure will have three or more.
- Less than 5 percent of children who have febrile seizures will develop epilepsy.
- A family history of febrile seizures places your child at higher risk.
- Febrile seizures occur most frequently between five months and five years of age.

- Children are at highest risk (seizures occur most frequently) during the terrible twos.
- Most febrile seizures are benign, self-limiting, and harmless.
- Fevers necessary to trigger a febrile seizure can result from common illnesses like ear infections, tonsillitis, and upper respiratory infections.
- Even when fever is present, a seizure may have been caused by other factors, such as poisoning or overdose, exposure to toxins, head injury, electrolyte imbalances, low blood sugar, and dehydration.
- Fever and resulting febrile seizure can occur within forty-eight hours of vaccination for pertussis or within seven to ten days of measles immunization.
- Fever and febrile seizure may occur with potentially life-threatening infections like meningitis, meningococcemia, and encephalitis.

SEIZURE MANAGEMENT

As with most pediatric emergencies, the most difficult challenge you will face when a child seizes is to remain in control. Parents and caregivers rarely understand what is happening to the child at first. There are many different types of seizures, so even if you have seen someone seize before, this may not be how your child presents. Once a parent realizes that a child is no longer in control of his body, it is very easy for panic to set in. Anytime you become so frightened that you lose the ability to think, remember that acronym, ABC. A stands for Airway, B stands for Breathing, C stands for Circulation. Protect yourself, protect the child from further harm, make sure help is on the way. Anything more requires special equipment and specialized training.

- Move your child to a carpeted floor or soft surface so that he does not injure himself by banging into furniture or falling off the bed.

- Make sure there is nothing blocking his airway. Remember that a child can seize as a result of oxygen deprivation. Be prepared to use the Heimlich maneuver if a foreign object is in the way.
- Children who seize may vomit. Position them on their side, if possible, to allow vomitus and saliva to drain out. Be prepared to clear any vomitus out of their mouths.
- Do not try to place anything into their mouths, like a bite block. If they bite down, as many children do when they seize, this may cause additional injury.
- Do not place your fingers into their mouths. Seizing children do not just bite down; their jaws may clamp down *hard*. Even young children can break your finger! If they vomit, roll them all the way over onto their tummies and let gravity be your friend. A bulb syringe can be helpful. If you don't have a bulb syringe, a turkey baster can be used to help clear their mouths. Do not insert anything past the child's teeth or beyond the gum line.
- Children do not swallow their tongues. If they begin to make strange breathing noises tip their heads back and lift their chins, or use a jaw-thrust maneuver to open their airways
- Children may suffer breath-holding episodes while seizing. These rarely last more than ten seconds, and the child will usually begin to breathe again on his own. If he does not, you may have to begin rescue breathing. This means one breath every three seconds for an infant, one breath every four seconds for a child over age one, and one breath every five seconds for a child over age eight. Remember to tilt the child's head and lift the chin—or use a jaw thrust—to move the tongue away from the back of the child's throat.
- A child will not necessarily become conscious again immediately after a seizure. He may experience a "postictal" period of deep unconsciousness. The jerking and shaking will stop, but he may not wake up right away. You may have to help him to maintain an open airway during this period, which can last for several more minutes. Consciousness may return slowly.

- If the child stops breathing completely, you must begin rescue breathing. You must also check for a pulse. If he does not begin breathing on his own, stop and recheck a pulse after every few breaths. If your child goes into cardiac arrest and you are unable to feel a pulse, you must begin chest compressions. Remember that pediatric CPR can save a child's life.
- Make sure help is on the way.

Seizures do not always result from fevers. Head trauma, low blood sugar, and oxygen deprivation are other causes noted above. Another cause of seizures is poisoning. Many poisons can cause a child to seize. Sometimes we must become detectives to discover the reasons for a seizure, such as an accidental exposure to a poison. The most important aspect to poisoning that parents should understand is that all accidental poisonings are preventable. The next chapter will explain how to prevent these tragedies.

WHEN POISONS GET IN

14

- ✚ Accidental Poisoning
- ✚ Poisoning Prevention
- ✚ Treatment of Poisoning Victims
- ✚ Inhalant Abuse
- ✚ Intentional Overdose

✚ *I responded to a call for a pediatric poisoning. My partner and I climbed into our ambulance and hit the siren as we left the station. It had been a long, difficult shift, and we were both exhausted. A pediatric poisoning can be anything from a toddler who tries to find out what bleach tastes like to a teenage suicide. Either way, I was distracted by my aching back and concerned about the fact that I was behind on my paperwork. Halfway to the scene the dispatcher informed us that he had additional information about the call.*

"Go ahead."

"A four-year-old male has eaten an entire bottle full of his grandfather's nitroglycerin tablets. Caller is hysterical. Nothing further on the child's condition at this time."

"Copy."

Nitroglycerine tablets are tiny, white pills. They are rarely dispensed in childproof containers as they can be difficult for elderly cardiac patients to open when needed. They have a very bitter taste. The medicine is absorbed through mucous membranes. When placed beneath a patient's tongue, the medicine melts and is absorbed and metabolized rapidly. While nitroglycerine can bring fast relief to a cardiac patient having chest pain, the drug's effects may only last a few minutes. The drug relaxes smooth muscle, including blood vessel walls, and can dilate blocked or clogged coronary arteries, allowing more blood to flow through. As the blood vessels relax and dilate, the patient's blood pressure can drop quickly. In a patient with a high blood pressure, this may be beneficial. In a patient with a normal blood pressure, this can be dangerous. A single, tiny nitroglycerine tablet is a very powerful drug. This child ate an entire bottle?

As my partner switched to a more obnoxious siren to convince other drivers to pull over and get out of our way, I remember lowering my head into my hands. We would not arrive in time. When we get there, I thought to myself, this child will already be dead. The drop in blood pressure will be overwhelming. The child's only chance will be if we can bolus him with enough fluid to convince his heart to continue pumping. *Instead of feeling the adrenaline rush of an exciting challenge ahead, I felt only trepidation and exhaustion.*

When we were cancelled just a block from the scene, I proceeded in anyway. The request for the coroner that I expected never came. The bottle the child was found playing with had been empty. Grandpa had discovered his new bottle from the drugstore in his jacket pocket—still full. The child was alive and well and squirming in Mom's arms. Grandpa was sitting on the steps of the porch with tears still drying on his cheeks. Such a lucky man, *I thought.* Too many grandparents learn this horrifying lesson with tragic results.

Poisonings take many forms. They may be accidental, as when a toddler eats something in the medicine cabinet or out of Grandma's purse. They may be intentional, as when a teenager eats a bottle full of Tylenol in a suicide attempt. They may be incidental and the result of exposure to a substance the patient is allergic to, like a bee sting. Poisons can enter the human body in many ways;

they can be ingested—or eaten, they can be inhaled into our lungs when we breathe, they can be absorbed through our skin or mucous membranes, and they can be injected through a needle or stinger.

ACCIDENTAL POISONING

Child death rates have decreased dramatically since the Poison Prevention Packaging Act of 1970, which required that we all use those bothersome child-protective caps for prescription and many over-the-counter medications. I am one of those adults, however, who can have so much trouble opening one of these caps that I will ask my son to open it for me. Children as young as three and four can learn to maneuver many of these caps. Many oldsters and those who suffer from arthritis and disabilities have difficulty opening these containers. They can simply ask the pharmacist to place their medication in a nonchildproof bottle. Unfortunately, Grandma's pocketbook can be a huge source of curiosity for a little one.

Even with significant decreases in poisoning incidents, over one million children under age six were poisoned in 1996,[1] which represents over half of accidental poisonings in patients of all ages. Not all poisoning incidents are deadly or even life threatening. Many children—after consultation with a poison control center and the child's doctor—can be cared for at home without going to the emergency department. Following any poisoning event you must *look at your child*. If he has an altered mental status, if he is having trouble breathing, or if you see dramatic changes in his skin color and tone, call EMS. Even if he is not ill, you must call the nearest poison control center and/or your child's doctor immediately.

Sometimes the substance your child has taken or been exposed to is not toxic. In these cases you may be capable of treating poisonings in your own home with the assistance of a poison control center or your doctor and without emergency help. So what does the child look like? How is he acting and responding to you? Is he still alert? Or is he becoming drowsy? Is he having trouble breathing? Is he turning blue? Call EMS.

POISONING PREVENTION

Not surprisingly, the most commonly ingested poisons are substances found easily and routinely around a child's home. These include cosmetics, plants, cleaning products, cough syrups, and analgesics like acetaminophen, ibuprofen, and aspirin. Lower yourself to the floor and crawl around your home at a toddler's level. You will be shocked by the dust bunnies under the bed (I'm always horrified). But you will also be surprised at how accessible many deadly poisons are for a child. From detergents and drain cleaners to nail polish remover and insect sprays, these materials are rarely in the high, locked cabinets where they belong. The long version of this list is below. But if you try to smell and taste these products yourself, you will understand why many such exposures are minimal and may not require treatment. Have you ever tried to drink furniture polish? Yuck!

Your child should not have access to the following:

- Laundry detergent, dishwasher detergent, bathroom cleaners
- Mouthwash, perfume, cologne
- Drain cleaners, bleach, disinfectants
- Gasoline, kerosene, lamp oil
- Insect sprays, pest repellents, mosquito repellents
- Paints and paint thinners
- Tobacco products
- Rubbing alcohol
- Furniture polish, metal polish
- Nail polish remover, nail polish
- Spot removers

The most dangerous poisoning events occur when a child consumes one of the substances listed below. It is crucial, whether you call poison control first, your doctor, or EMS to know *what* your child consumed, an estimate of *how much* he may have ingested or inhaled, and an estimate of *when* he was poisoned. The poison control center will also need to know your child's age and how much he weighs.

IRON How unfortunate that the vitamins we give our children can also be dangerous. We buy them intentionally in wonderful flavors and shapes to make them fun to take every day. But in large quantities these vitamins can be very dangerous. They usually contain iron. In large doses, iron can cause severe liver damage and even shock. They are also frequently left in a convenient location like the breakfast table. These vitamins should be in child-proof containers, locked in high cabinets, or both.

OVER-THE-COUNTER MEDICATIONS These include acetaminophen, ibuprofen, aspirin, cough syrup, decongestants, expectorants, and allergy medications, and they can kill our children. If you are not sure how much the child consumed, and he does not appear to be ill, call your doctor or the nearest poison control center. Many of these medications may not result in immediate symptoms like altered mental states or difficulty breathing. If your child is very ill, or you believe he consumed large quantities of these substances call EMS.

HYDROCARBONS These are a group of chemicals that include gasoline, kerosene, diesel fuel, solvents, paint thinners, and many of the constituents of polishes, cleaners, adhesives, glues, and paints. If the child inhales these chemicals into his lungs, a form of pneumonia can result that can be life threatening. If he has ingested these chemicals and vomits, he is at greater risk of aspirating this material into his lungs. Untreated, ingestion of hydrocarbons can result in damage to kidney, liver, and heart tissue.

ALCOHOLS These include liquor. Alcohol intoxication can kill a child. Even older children and teenagers can die from the effects of liquor. Your twelve-year-old daughter can die from drinking too much vodka at a party. You ten-year-old son can die from drinking too much grain alcohol at his friend's house. Young people are inexperienced drinkers and rarely know when to stop. Alcohol can kill them or make them critically ill. Alcohol can also cause them to lose the inhibitions that allow them to follow rules and make good choices. Motor vehicle crashes, fights, and rapes can ensue. Alcohol is also a constituent of some mouthwashes, colognes, and perfumes. An alcohol called *methanol* is probably in your windshield washer fluid. An alcohol called *ethylene glycol* is a component of your antifreeze. The garage can be a very dangerous place for a toddler. These substances can cause a life-threatening drop in blood sugar level.

CYANIDE   If you think you have no cyanide in your home, think again. Cyanide may be a constituent of your silver polish or nail polish. It is also frequently contained in insecticides and pesticides. I worked for an environmental protection agency for several years. In order to determine if my self-contained breathing apparatus mask fit me properly, I was led into a tent filled with almond extract fumes. If I could smell almonds, my mask didn't fit properly. The odor of almonds may signal exposure to cyanide. Or cyanide exposure may not be discovered until a physician reads the product label. The containers should be delivered to the hospital with the child. There are antidotes for cyanide exposure. Unfortunately, children may not survive long enough to receive these treatments if they ingest or inhale too much.

NARCOTICS   Heroin is only one derivative of the poppy plant. Another is man's greatest gift, a pain reliever called *morphine* (although morphine is now manufactured synthetically, it was originally derived from opium, the same substance used to produce heroin). Some cancer patients and others who suffer from retractable pain take large doses of narcotic painkillers on a daily basis. These include morphine and morphine derivatives, codeine, Demerol, Darvon, Darvocet, and Dilaudid. While these medications are necessary and important therapies for those with serious illnesses, they are very strong drugs and can cause coma and death in a small child when ingested by accident. A drug common to every paramedic's jump kit is called *Naloxone,* which can reverse the effects of some of these drugs and save a child's life if administered in time.

ANTIHYPERTENSIVES   Drugs like clonidine (Catapres) are used to maintain a normal blood pressure in adults who suffer from high blood pressure. Any drug capable of bringing a high blood pressure down may cause a normal blood pressure to fall too low. If a child ingests an adult dose of one of these medications, a severe drop in the child's blood pressure may result. Not all of these medications dilate the blood vessels like nitroglycerine can. Some act directly on the heart. All high blood pressure and cardiac medications must be kept strictly out of a child's reach.

CORROSIVES   These include both strong acids and strong alkalis. Drain cleaners, lye, oven cleaners, those nifty blue or green solids we place in the toilet tank to turn the water blue or green, and many other household chemicals fall into this category. As with hydrocarbons, do not induce vomiting. These chemicals can burn soft tissue. They may cause more damage coming up than when they went down. Have the child drink milk or water to dilute the poison and call poison control immediately. Your need for emergency help will depend on how much of what substance was ingested.

ANTIDEPRESSANTS   At one time, many people took a class of antidepressants called *tricyclics.* Tricyclic antidepressant over-doses were treatment nightmares for paramedics and doctors. Adults and children alike frequently died. Today, while many new antide-pressants on the market are not quite so deadly, they can still cause critical illness and death when ingested in large quantities. It is extremely important to determine how much of the medication a child took. If you have no idea how many pills were originally in the container, assume they were all consumed.

ORGANOPHOSPHATES   These are frequently constituents of insecticides, pesticides, and rodenticides. Exposure can cause a massive response on the part of child's nervous system that can result in coma and death. Call the nearest poison control center immedi-ately if your child has been exposed to a substance intentionally designed to kill critters. The word "organophosphate" may not appear on the label. If possible, deliver the container to the hospital with the child. If the child is not alert, call EMS first and prepare to manage your child's airway and breathe for him if necessary.

SMOKE   Smoke inhalation can also be life threatening. Inhalation injuries associated with fires can be more deadly than the burns a child may receive. Smoke can contain carbon monoxide, particulate matter, and toxic gases. Your highest priority should be to move the child to eliminate exposure to the smoke or gases and call EMS. Never take chances with an airway that may swell shut. In addition, if the level of carbon monoxide in a child's bloodstream becomes too high, the red blood cells are deprived of enough oxygen. Sometimes children must be transported or flown to specialized hospitals that have hyperbaric chambers capable of clearing the carbon monoxide from the child's bloodstream.

CRITTERS   A variety of deadly critters live in the United States. These include brown recluse spiders, black widow spiders, and scorpions. Snakes that can be deadly to a child include pit vipers and coral snakes. While some children can exhibit anaphylactic reac-

LICE REMEDIES

I responded to help an elderly female in a nursing home. For unknown reasons, this woman suddenly began to experience seizures. The seizures seemed to come and go. Staff believed the woman was suffering from a stroke. By the time I arrived at the hospital with my patient, a supervisor at the nursing home had discovered the nature of the problem and called ahead to the emergency department. The patient had head lice. She had been given repeated treatments with a shampoo preparation containing *lindane*. Lindane is an insecticide and can get rid of lice. But lindane exposure can also result in neurological problems and seizures. Read the label carefully, use only as recommended, or ask your pharmacist for lice treatment that does not contain this potent insecticide.

tions from simple insect stings like bees, wasps, and yellow jackets, these bites are typically just painful and involve localized swelling. If the swelling begins to block the airway, call for help. If a child is stung many times, however, the amount of venom injected can be fatal even if the child is not allergic. Some marine animals can also inject toxins into a child's body, including jellyfish, stingrays, and some sea urchins. Treatment is standard for all such attacks. Remove the child from the environment where he was stung and prevent any additional harm. Keep the child quiet and calm. Apply ice to the affected area. Tourniquets are *not* appropriate. Constricting bands, like rubber bands or stretch bandages can reduce blood flow and reduce the release of a toxin into the bloodstream. But judging how tight to make a constricting band is difficult, and eliminating blood flow to a limb entirely may result in an unnecessary amputation. Make sure help is on the way.

PLANTS AND MUSHROOMS   These can also be deadly. If toddlers are in the house, potted plants must be kept off the floor and out of reach. You should know the name of every plant and flower they could find attractive and possibly tasty. If you do not know the names of any plants, take a sample to your local nursery or florist for identification. Outside, young children must be supervised at all times. As they grow, children need to be told that they may not eat berries, mushrooms, or other plants. They should not be allowed in areas that were recently sprayed or treated with fertilizers or insecticides.

Surrounding my home in Pennsylvania are naturalized jonquils, daffodils, and crocuses. Dutchman's-breeches, jack-in-the-pulpit, and skunk cabbage abound. I have sweet peas and wisteria adding beauty to the natural hemlocks and rhododendron. Inside my home are a variety of cacti, amaryllis, cyclamen, and poinsettia. Parts of all these plants can cause serious illness and even death if ingested. I have plants that are harmless, as well. Nevertheless, most of my environment can injure a child who mistakenly believes that if it looks succulent and colorful, it must be delicious. Preschoolers never wander unescorted through my home. A complete list of poisonous plants is not possible in this text. Some florists, most nurseries, and all poison-control centers can provide the names of poisonous plants. The key to safety for children is to know the names of plants to which they have access, and to prevent access to those plants known to be harmful. Remember: A poison control center cannot help you if you are able to tell them only that your child ate "something green" or "some kind of flower."

HOUSEHOLD CHEMICALS If consumed in small quantities, many household chemicals may not be poisonous or lead to critical illness. You should still *always* call your local poison control center. These household substances may include candles, chalk, crayons, pens, pencils (graphite), dog or cat food, deodorants, dirt, soap, grease, oil, hair spray, hand lotion, hydrogen peroxide, lipstick, petroleum jelly, rouge, shampoo, shaving cream, suntan lotion, birth-control pills, antacids, laxatives, and stool softeners. If it is on this list, some child somewhere has tried to eat it!

- Use child-resistant caps on all medications.
- Throw expired medicine away by flushing it down the toilet.
- Keep all medicine in its original container and do not mix it with other medications.
- Keep all poisons out of a child's reach, keeping in mind that children can be very cagey and very resourceful (children will climb and access high cabinets that are not locked, dig through the underclothes in your dresser, and become enormously curious about areas that are "forbidden").
- Remember that your child is cared for occasionally by others, including grandparents, aunts, uncles, baby-sitters, and friends who may not be as diligent as you are. Do not hesitate to educate them about the dangers of poisoning, and ask them to help keep your child safe by keeping their own medications out of reach.

TREATMENT OF POISONING VICTIMS

Your treatment of a child who is not ill will depend on advice from the poison control center or your doctor. Vomiting should never be induced in children who have consumed acids, alkalis, or hydrocarbons, or if they may develop an altered mental status. Children who are not fully alert, or who may become drowsy, are at great risk of aspirating the material into their lungs. Vomiting may be called for in limited other circumstances. Vomiting can be induced by administration of a medicine called Syrup of Ipecac. This medicine is available at the drug store and should be a part of all first-aid kits. Be careful to track the expiration date on this medicine. Given with plenty of fluids, children will vomit within five to fifteen minutes (I timed it in the ambulance once with a teenager I was treating. It took exactly seven minutes. Make sure you have something handy for them to vomit into!). Another important medicine that belongs in every first-aid kit is activated charcoal. This is also available at the drug store and can also expire if stored unused for too long. The charcoal absorbs the poison in the gastrointestinal system. The Syrup of Ipecac causes vomiting. You should never give Syrup of Ipecac and charcoal together or the child will simply vomit up the charcoal before it can do any good.

Medics carry some medications that may be useful in serious poisoning cases, but their primary job will be to protect a child's airway and transport them to a hospital quickly. They usually carry activated charcoal and Syrup of Ipecac. Naloxone can reverse the effects of narcotic overdose if administered in time. Medics also carry drugs that may be necessary to arrest a seizure, maintain a normal blood pressure, and control the effects of some antihypertension and cardiac medications.

At the hospital the poison will be eliminated from the child's body if possible. Gastric lavage (sometimes called pumping a child's stomach) is only helpful if performed within a short time following ingestion. Bowel irrigation with the use of strong lavage solutions may help for substances not rapidly digested. Antidotes for some poisons exist, but treatment with some antidotes can be almost as dangerous as the effects of the poisons themselves. Sometimes doctors can only provide support for a child and treat any symptoms as they arrive. Since these symptoms can be life threatening, the child must be in a hospital with physicians directing his care.

- If your child develops an altered mental status, begins having trouble breathing, or shows dramatic changes in skin tone and color, call EMS, and remember the ABCs of emergency care.
- Call your local poison control center regardless of your child's condition. This number needs to be posted next to every phone in your home.
- Sometimes poisoning can be treated at home and sometimes not. Even if your child is not yet ill, depending on the nature of the poison, the amount ingested, when the exposure took place, and your child's age and weight, you may need emergency assistance.

INHALANT ABUSE

Inhalant abuse is a bizarre behavior on the part of children who want to "get high." They will inhale vapors and fumes from a wide variety of sources and feel a dizziness similar to a marijuana high or alcohol intoxication. Sometimes they are inhaling poisons that affect the nervous system. Often, they are inhaling gases that prevent them from breathing enough oxygen. If the concentration of poison is excessive or if they are deprived of oxygen too long, they die. In 1996, the National Institute on Drug Abuse (NIDA) estimated that one in five teens had tried inhalants as a means of achieving this dizzy feeling. Children can die the very first time they take part in this activity. Children have been discovered using inhalants in grade school; this is not strictly a teenaged problem. The poisons can cause their hearts to work too hard and can lead to cardiac arrest. Or the substance can cause damage to brain, blood, kidney, liver, and bone marrow. If they become so enamored of this "high" feeling, they may breathe enough fumes to prevent sufficient oxygen flow to brain and heart cells.

Signs and symptoms may include:

- Slurred speech
- Disorientation
- A dizzy, dazed affect
- The appearance of being drunk

It can be difficult to distinguish between signs of inhalant abuse and the use of alcohol or illicit drugs. Inhalant abuse is a form of drug abuse, but without the danger of being arrested for possession of illegal substances. Commonly used inhalants are listed below. These substances are legally purchased and easily obtained, even by young children:

glues/adhesives	gasoline	fabric protectors
nail polish remover	propane gas	whipped cream
marking pens	paint thinners	aerosols
butane lighter fluid	spray paints	air conditioning
household cleaners	typewriter correction	coolants
	fluid	cooking sprays

Look for paint or ink on a child's hands and face. Search for a chemical odor on his clothes or breath. If you suspect your child may be abusing inhalants, enlist your doctor's assistance immediately. Together, you can educate your child about the deadly nature of inhalant abuse and help him to understand that just because these substances are easily accessible does not make them harmless. And you can provide him with the tools he needs to combat peer pressure.

INTENTIONAL OVERDOSE

He was 15 years old. He was awake and alert. He was a strong, healthy young man with no existing illness. He claimed he had taken an overdose of Tylenol. When? Right after he arrived home from school, around 3:00 P.M. It was now 9:00 P.M. and too late to help him vomit the pills back up. How many did he take? Two whole bottles full. He still had the now-empty bottles with him. They each originally contained two hundred tablets, fifty milligrams each. The calculation was simple. He had ingested ten full grams of acetaminophen. Why? I asked gently. The reason was irrelevant to his immediate care, but the question begged. "It's my mom's birthday," he replied icily and returned my gaze with enough anger and hostility to frighten me. I cocked my head to one side and thought of my own son as I looked at him. I reached my hand out and lightly touched his arm.

"Okay," I said. But I had a job to do. "Did you take anything else?"

"No."

"Have you been drinking or smoking anything?"

"NO!" he yelled in my face.

"Were you trying to hurt yourself?" I asked.

His faced scrunched up. "I guess so," he answered.

"Have you ever tried to hurt yourself before?"

"No."

"Do you want to die?"

A long pause ensued. He stared at the ceiling in the ambulance and tears began rolling down his cheeks. "I just wanted to get back at my mom," he said.

Acetaminophen is an analgesic, a painkiller. It is also an antipyretic and can be the best stuff in town to help bring a child's fever down. There are generic forms of acetaminophen and several brand names. The most popular is Tylenol.

In toxic amounts, far less than what my young patient took that afternoon, acetaminophen can cause massive, lethal damage to the liver. A child may not show any signs of illness during the first twenty-four hours after ingestion. Within days, however, they may become critically ill. Even if they survive, so much liver damage can occur that they may be chronically ill for the rest of their lives. Some children who attempt suicide by taking acetaminophen overdoses wind up on transplant lists, with a new liver their only hope for the future. While there are treatment protocols for acetaminophen poisoning, some of these children die.

Children may ingest almost anything in a suicide attempt. They may overdose on common medications like aspirin or prescription medications like Aunt Millie's Valium. Unfortunately, many prescription antidepressants on the market can cause critical illness and even death when taken in toxic amounts. Treatment at the hospital depends on the substance ingested, the amount ingested, and the time the child overdosed. As with accidental poisonings, the focus of treatment will be to minimize absorption of the substance, enhance elimination of the substance, and administrate an appropriate antidote. If you discover your child has overdosed on a medication and you suspect he may have been trying to take his own life, you must protect yourself. Children who are capable of hurting themselves may be capable of harming someone else. Do not hesitate to call for assistance. Protect his airway if he is not alert or if he is already unresponsive. Breathe for him if necessary. If you are able to give breaths, check for a pulse. If you cannot feel a pulse, begin CPR. Make sure help is on the way.

- Poisonings in children can be accidental or intentional. Treatment will involve minimizing exposure to the poison, elimination of the poison from the body and administration of an antidote.
- While waiting for help, protect yourself and remember the ABCs of emergency care: Airway, Breathing, Circulation.

SPECIAL CARE FOR SPECIAL-NEEDS KIDS 15

✚ **You Are Your Child's Greatest Advocate.**

✚ **How to Get to the Right Hospital.**

✚ **Prevention Techniques Must Be Custom Designed for Special Needs Children.**

Because her child had a long seizure history, Mom didn't call for help right away. His seizures had never lasted for more than seven minutes. At the seven-minute mark, she called 911. Unfortunately, she lived in a rural area. By the time I arrived, her son had been actively seizing for over twenty minutes. Mom met me at the door with her four year old in her arms, jerking and shaking violently. Blood from his mouth covered the front of her blouse. She plopped him into my arms. I carried him back to the well-lit ambulance enormously concerned about his airway and told the driver to move. The hospital was still another twenty minutes away. Mom followed me into the vehicle.

The blood was not blocking his airway; she had been diligent about clearing his mouth. He was breathing rapidly, but each breath had good volume and his lungs sounded clear. His color was surprisingly good. I placed him on his left side, administered oxygen through a mask, applied a pulse-oximeter probe to one of his fingers, and took his blood pressure and pulse. I rechecked his airway, which remained open and clear. I attached electrodes necessary to monitor his heart rhythm. I then tied a tourniquet around his arm, drew blood to test his blood sugar level, and started an IV. As I worked Mom remained close, watching everything I was doing but not getting in the way. We traded information calmly and clearly. She had obviously been through this before. He had a long, complex medical history. She knew it all by heart.

I administered diazepam through the IV. This is a strong drug that usually stops a seizure quickly. While the clonic activity stopped (the violent shaking and jerking), the child remained tonic (stiff and rigid). I called the physician at the hospital on the radio and explained what was happening. He ordered additional diazepam. Even as I pushed the additional medication through the IV line the child's seizure returned to a clonic state, even more violent than before. I then glanced at the cardiac monitor and began to perspire. His heart rate was over 250 beats per minute. I could still detect his blood pressure, but it was very low. I called the doctor back and was ordered to continue monitoring the child's airway closely, but to take no additional action until arrival at the hospital, now only minutes away. I climbed to the front of the ambulance and quietly told my driver to run the other cars off the road if he had to. My driver would never do that, but he understood the implication. He leaned on the air horn.

The child continued seizing at the emergency department for an additional twenty minutes. In all, he suffered a seizure state for over an hour. When we arrived, Mom walked in with us and helped us transfer him to the hospital bed. Nobody tried to lead her away or suggest that she wait elsewhere. Throughout the ordeal she remained calm and informative. Her son was given diazepam, lorazepam, phenytoin, and finally phenobarbital before the seizure was arrested. At no time did it become necessary to intubate him, and as soon as the seizure stopped, his heart rate and blood pressure returned to normal ranges. As the rest of us walked away, sighing with relief, I glanced back and watched Mom lean down to kiss her son's face and whisper love into his ear. What a wonderful, extraordinary mom!

A s a paramedic I have cared for many people of all ages with special needs. Some are cared for with heroism and selflessness. Some suffer from horrifying care inadequacies. I have taken them for emergency care from bleak institutions where they rarely have contact with other human beings. I have taken them from the arms of mothers whose entire lives have been dedicated to the child's care and comfort. I have seen children cared for in private homes that looked like hospital facilities, with state-of-the-art equipment and the assistance of professional providers. I have faced the drawn and haggard faces of mothers and caregivers on the verge of physical and emotional breakdowns from a lack of support and assistance and training.

Precious few resources have been dedicated to providing guidance and training for parents of special-needs children in the event of an emergency. Guess what? These children also sometimes become acutely ill or suffer injuries and need EMS. The guidance below is offered, without the benefit of specialized training or volumes of medical research, but from the heart of a paramedic who understands and cares.

There are several basic tenets of emergency medical care for children with special needs that differ from the balance of the pediatric community:

- EMS providers sometimes lack adequate training in caring for children with special needs. **You are the expert**.
- Caregivers for children with special needs should prepare a written emergency care plan with the assistance of the children's doctors that is updated on a regular basis and easily accessible in an emergency.
- Logistics of transport to a hospital can take extra time.
- Hospital choices can be very difficult.
- Injury and illness-prevention techniques require creativity and innovation.
- Your well-being is pivotal.

WHAT DO EMS PROVIDERS KNOW?

An EMS provider may know a great deal about your child's illness and circumstances, based on his level of training and experience. Or he may know nothing. He may be familiar with Down syndrome, but only in terms of altered mental abilities and not the physical challenges these children face. He may know general terms regarding other altered mental abilities in children, but he may never have heard of Rett syndrome, Fragile X syndrome or the different conditions represented by the term *pervasive developmental disorders* (PDDs). He may be familiar with muscular dystrophy, but have no training in differentiating between types like Duchenne's or Becker's. He may never have heard of Guillain-Barré syndrome. He may have heard of cerebral palsy, but will not necessarily know the difference between spasticity that may be normal for your child and signs of a seizure.

My late father was blind. He was always amused by people who thought they needed to raise their voices, assuming that if he was blind he must also be deaf. But prehospital providers will not automatically know that your deaf child lip-reads and does not sign, or signs and cannot read lips. They will not automatically be capable of understanding a child's garbled speech, even when a child has worked hard to learn to speak clearly and you can understand them easily. They may not realize that a child unable to communicate may still hear and understand everything you say. You and those who respond to help you in an emergency must work as a team. As a parent, you must be prepared to give rapid, precise lessons on your child's normal behavior, methods of communication, and how the child responds if something hurts.

YOUR CHILD'S CHAMPION

You must be your child's champion and ultimate advocate. This requires that you become an expert on his illness. You must know more than all but the greatest specialists about his condition. This is only possible with diligence and persistence. Hospital librarians can be very helpful. Find and read every piece of information on your child's condition that you can find. Quiz the doctors about handling emergency situations. "But what if this happens, Doctor? What if that doesn't happen?" Parents can also join support groups and learn from the mistakes and experiences of other parents. If your child has an unusual or rare disease, you must be prepared to teach prehospital providers about appropriate emergency care.

If your child always has an altered mental status or uses an alternative means of communicating, let the EMS providers know immediately. If your child is not normally alert and oriented, you will need to describe your child's normal mental status and then explain what has changed for the medic to understand the significance of your child's current condition. It is important for you to translate your child's messages and signals, if necessary, to help the provider understand the nature of the child's emergency and the history of his present illness. What causes him additional pain? What makes him more comfortable?

At the very least, you must be prepared to give (and, sometimes, even spell) the technical name for your child's condition. You must have a full list of medications that your child takes on a daily basis, including doses and frequency. You must have a complete list of medications that your child is allergic to or cannot take due to drug interactions. If your child suffers from side effects of medications, you must pass this information along as well. If your child's blood sugar level bounces from high to low, if it is usually very low mid-morning and high in the evening, this can be helpful for the providers in both the ambulance and the emergency department to interpret current levels correctly. If your child has seizures but has not responded well to diazepam in the past, tell the medic.

Within the U.S. Department of Health & Human Services (HHS) exists the Maternal and Child Health Bureau (MCHB). Together with the National Highway Traffic Safety Administration (NHTSA), a special program was initiated to address Emergency Medical Services for Children (EMSC). Within that program a task force has been working to identify and address emergency medical needs for special-care children. The Children with Special Health Care Needs task force advocates the use of a standardized form to rapidly communicate important medical data to emergency care providers. While various pilot programs have been initiated in several states, that standardized form is not yet available nationwide.

Someday this standardized form will be available for all children with special health-care needs. Like the medical identification bracelets worn by many diabetics and patients with chronic diseases, and like the "Vials of Life" stored in the refrigerators of many elderly and chronically ill patients, this form will provide immediate information for the paramedics and emergency department staffs regarding a child's condition. Unless and until that standardized form becomes "Standard of Care" for special kids, caregivers, parents, and doctors must work together to make this same information readily available to providers in an emergency. Whether the information is kept on an index card or piece of paper or framed on the wall, anyone caring for your child should have immediate access. At a minimum, this document should include:

- The child's full name and address
- Date of birth
- Guardian's name and address
- Emergency contacts
- Doctors' names and contact information, including pediatrician and any/all specialists treating the child
- List of all major illnesses and disabilities
- Baseline description of the child's physical and mental status
- Baseline vital signs and laboratory studies
- Immunization history
- List of all medications
- Allergies to medications and foods

While not necessary to provide life-saving treatment in an emergency, additional information on this document can save time and reduce frustration later. This additional information includes the child's social security number and insurance data, family religious affiliation, and hints for providers about communicating with your child. The document should be updated regularly or anytime changes occur in the child's condition or treatment plan. While privacy and confidentiality issues are more important in some cases than in others, making this information accessible to day-care providers, school officials, baby-sitters, and extended family members can be critical in an emergency. You must decide when and how this information should be shared with other caregivers.

WHAT WILL DELAY TRANSPORT?

Transport times for special-needs children can be prolonged. Ambulances cannot carry children seated in wheelchairs. There are special vans that can transport your child this way, but they typically do not have emergency lights and sirens and sophisticated communication equipment. If your child does not need lights and sirens and communication equipment, you do not have an emergency and non-emergency transportation can be arranged with a private company. If your child needs to travel by ambulance, they will be transported on a stretcher that locks securely to the floor of the truck. Fragile children may have to be moved very carefully, and it can sometimes take extra time and effort to make them comfortable and not interfere with normal breathing patterns. Prehospital providers may need your guidance in both moving the child safely and securing them comfortably in the ambulance.

Not all ventilatory equipment and supplies are compatible. If your child is dependent on a ventilator or needs intermittent positive pressure breaths, prehospital providers may have to resort to using medical tape to adapt their equipment to meet your child's needs. If your child needs frequent suctioning, your catheters may not fit on the ambulance's machine. Do not become upset. This is another opportunity for you and the prehospital providers to work as a team. You all may need to be creative and flexible. It can be enormously helpful if you request a friendly EMS visit before an emergency occurs, preferably when a respiratory therapist is visiting your child. Respiratory therapists can be magicians when it comes to adaptation of equipment. If the medic presents his equipment, the therapist can compare what he has to what your child needs and adaptive devices can be ordered to prepare for an emergency.

Medics can perform many invasive skills when they are necessary to save a child's life, but they rarely work with adjunctive equipment like feeding tubes and colostomy bags and urinary catheters. You may need to show them how to appropriately clamp off, tie down, and secure some of these devices before they move your child. Many children with complex medical histories have developed a sensitivity, and occasionally even severe allergy, to latex. Many ambulances now carry latex-free supplies, from gloves and oxygen masks to tape and IV catheters. Let them know about your child's allergy or sensitivity. If they do not have latex-free equipment, they can work carefully without gloves. The gloves worn by prehospital providers are used to protect them from their patients, not the other way around.

WHICH HOSPITAL?

When a child has a rare or unusual illness, parents quickly learn where the closest regional pediatric center is located. This is where the pediatric specialists who know the most about their child's illness will probably practice. This is where any caregiver would want the child taken in the event of an emergency or an acute illness. This is probably where the child will land, but not necessarily right away. If your child's life is in danger, he will be taken to a nearby hospital to be stabilized first. Even if your child's life is not immediately threatened, the more complicated a child's condition, the longer his medical history, the less secure the prehospital providers will feel about making sound care decisions during an extended transport. They may involve an emergency physician on the radio early and may have many, many questions for you. They may not feel comfortable taking your child to a distant hospital.

Depending on your child's condition, it is more appropriate to go to the nearest hospital for stabilizing treatment and transport later to a specialized hospital with more highly trained personnel in the ambulance. This can be a pediatric or intensive care nurse and sometimes even a doctor. Sometimes the same ambulance and medic that brought you to the nearby hospital will transport your child to a specialized hospital, but only after the medic has been given more extensive instructions regarding care during transport. You may be very anxious about your child's condition, or about the need for your child to be at that specialized hospital, or for your child to be in the care of that one physician who knows him best. Regardless, it is in your child's best interest to be cared for by providers comfortable with the treatment plan, comfortable with their ability to implement that treatment plan, and who are able to make needed changes to that treatment plan in the event your child's condition changes. You should discuss the logistics of transport in an emergency with your physician before any emergency occurs. You should investigate local EMS capabilities and options for transport before the need arises.

PREVENTING INJURY

IMPROVISE, INNOVATE, AND OVERCOME These are words I have heard frequently from firefighters and those responsible for rescuing people entrapped in crashed cars or collapsed buildings. If they do not happen to have the right power tool, they know to reach for hand tools. If they cannot reach a trapped victim with fancy, high-tech equipment, they will jury-rig crude lever systems or a block and tackle and accomplish the same goal. I believe the phrase originates from a military source. Regardless, like those who risk their lives to rescue us from burning buildings and crashed cars, parents of special-needs children must also be creative to keep their children safe. An injury prevention plan must be custom designed for your child. These techniques depend entirely on the child's individual capabilities.

Try to imagine in as many ways as you can how your child could be hurt. Write them down and devise a method of prevention for each one. Is your child mobile? Even for a child with limited mobility, much of the injury-prevention information in this book may still be applicable. Can he run into the street if left unsupervised? Will a new lock on an old door prevent this? Could he crawl into the pool? Would a new door that only opens away from the pool help? Can he access poisons or medications? Can you eliminate this threat simply by storing these chemicals in a high cabinet or a locked closet? Can he be hurt simply by rolling and falling out of bed? Is he constantly being banged by a bothersome appendage to a wheelchair, walker, or brace?

If a child is confined to a wheelchair, can he still reach electrical outlets, window shade cords, or pots of boiling water on the stove? Can the wheelchair fit through doorways leading to staircases or ledges? Can a child leave your apartment or property without your knowledge? Does he have a means of communicating his name and address if he becomes lost? Does his gentle nature place him at higher risk of walking away with strangers? Does he have a means of calling for help if he begins to choke or become distressed?

All parents of special-needs children must practice fire drills. The more immobile a child is, the more trapped he is in the event of a fire. Call your local fire department and request a friendly visit. You will be amazed at how many innovative suggestions a firefighter will make regarding your child's safety if fire or smoke threaten. And the more they know about your child and his special needs, the more apt they will be to locate and rescue your child if an emergency occurs. You are not alone. There are many people out there with ideas that have not occurred to you yet, with new ideas to replace old ones, and with suggestions you will find helpful.

Children with seizure disorders are at very high risk of injury when they seize, especially if they fall from heights. While seizing, nobody can keep his head above water or protect his own airway. Children with known seizure disorders should learn to shower instead of bathe at a young age. If they are unable to shower, they should not be left unsupervised in the tub. They should never swim alone. There can be a benefit to risk: If they do not try, they never will; if you do not let them, they won't. If children are taught to fear all risk, they may never know exhilaration or joy. But some risks are not worth taking. Children without special needs should not ride ATVs and jump on backyard trampolines unsupervised. Children with seizure disorders should not swim alone. Period.

PREVENTING ILLNESS

The more ways pathogens can enter your child's body, the higher your child's risk of becoming ill. Tube feedings introduce a pathway for pathogens that most children do not have. So do tracheostomy tubes, suction catheters, urinary catheters, and colostomy bags. While you may spend most of your time with your child, medical providers—like doctors, nurses, aides, respiratory therapists, and physical therapists—spend most of their time with other patients, some of whom have infectious illnesses.

The providers themselves are healthy and have strong immune systems; most microorganisms do not even make them ill. They may not even realize that they carry with them on their clothing, lab coats, and hands the very pathogens that can threaten your child's life. Unfortunately, some of the most prevalent microorganisms found in acute and long-term care facilities where these providers work are drug resistant. These include methicillin-resistant *Staphylococcus aureus* (MRSA) and vancomycin-resistant enterococcus (VRE). While the providers who care for your child may not even realize they are infected, these pathogens can represent a nightmare of recurrent illness for your child.

Any and every piece of equipment or device introduced into your child's body should be sterile. Equipment and supplies used frequently around your child should be cleaned regularly with very hot water and antiseptic detergents. Aseptic technique (gloves, alcohol wipes, and sealed, packaged needles) should always be used to gain venous access, whether for IV fluid and medication administration or for simple blood draws. Depending on the nature of your child's condition, medical providers may need to don gowns, masks, and gloves before treating your child. This is more important for nurses, aides, and therapists who encounter patients with infectious illness frequently than it is for neighbors, family, and friends. Surgical orifices, like G-tubes, J-tubes, tracheostomies, and colostomies must be washed and meticulously cleaned regularly. Urinary catheters must be changed regularly and cleaned frequently.

Special care is necessary to prevent exposure if your child has an immunosuppressive illness that makes him vulnerable to infection. Similarly, if your child has a communicable illness, special care must be taken to avoid exposure for you and for others who may care for your child. In the event of an emergency, health-care providers may be unwilling to risk mouth-to-mouth rescue breathing if they believe there is risk of disease transmission. If your child has AIDS, is HIV positive, or suffers from hepatitis or tuberculosis, having a protective mask immediately available for *providers* can save your child's life. As a paramedic, I am far more concerned about caring for a child without special needs who is running a fever of unknown origin than I am of children with known communicable illnesses. If I know what I am facing, I know exactly how to protect myself. Your familiarity with your child's illness and with information regarding disease transmission may make your decision to ventilate your child in an emergency simple. For others who care for your child, this decision may be difficult. Have protective equipment available to make sure that whoever is with your child at the time an emergency occurs feels comfortable providing appropriate treatment.

TAKE CARE OF YOU

Your well-being is the greatest gift you can give to your child. An exhausted, stressed-out caregiver is not the best caregiver. A burned-out, tired mom or dad can cause the whole family additional stress. I have responded to help special-needs children when it was the caregiver I wanted to treat the most. Some ill children receive round-the-clock nursing care covered by insurance. Some children do not qualify for *any* nursing or home care. If your child needs intensive support, they need intensive support. The insurance company should offer an appropriate level of assistance. If they do not, challenge them, repeatedly. Let them know that you need more help. Tell them that if you do not receive at least some assistance, they will soon have two patients instead of one. Explain what your typical day is like and insist that the time demands are unreasonable.

If you are still without enough help and feel unable to cope, reach out to the community around you. Many of us who want to help simply may not know how. Maybe you do not need help providing care for your child, but you would appreciate a neighbor or friend who can pick up groceries or supplies occasionally. Perhaps it would help if someone would run your vacuum, fold your laundry, or cook an occasional meal. Sometimes you may simply want a long, hot bath and the knowledge that someone is sitting near your child's bed who will call you if you're needed.

The work necessary to care for some children with special needs can be overwhelming. The burden can be compounded by isolation. You do not have to be alone. If you feel uncomfortable leaving your child, consider buying a computer. If you can't attend support group meetings, there are Web sites and chat rooms where other parents like yourself have an opportunity to learn and share and vent. Take care of yourself first—and give them a hug from me.

- In order to be your child's champion, you must become an expert on his illness. You must be prepared to teach emergency medical providers about your child's condition.
- Insist that your child's doctor assist you in preparing an emergency care plan.
- Initiating treatment for your child and transporting him to the hospital for continued care may take extra time. You and the emergency medical providers who respond to help must work as a team.

- Injury and illness prevention schemes must be custom designed for your child and may require creativity and imagination.
- Taking care of yourself first is not selfish. Nourishing your own physical and emotional health is a necessary part of providing the best possible care for your child.

EPILOGUE

The same medical command physician I had spoken to on the radio, Dr. William Zajdel, met Alice and I at the door to the trauma center. Dr. Zajdel had been busy on the telephone gathering an appropriate team while we wound our way through traffic. Already with him was a specialist in pediatric emergency medicine, an anesthesiologist, another emergency physician, a respiratory therapist, and a host of critical-care nurses.

The team was as concerned about Alice's condition as I was, and they were prepared for the worst. Had Alice required advanced interventions, including a surgical airway, action could have been immediate and aggressive in order to save her life. As the team assessed Alice, their relief was palpable. Her airway remained open and showed no signs of swelling or obstruction. She remained alert and oriented. She continued to move all of her extremities well. Her initial neurological examination was normal. Alice's X rays and CT scan showed no immediate damage as a result of her accident. She was monitored closely overnight and sent home to her family.

Without question, Alice's true heroes were her mom and dad. Dad *didn't panic or lose control. He made sure Mom was calling for help and carefully lifted his daughter to the ground. He knew to minimize movement of her neck. He knew how to perform a jaw-thrust maneuver to open her airway, and how to perform mouth-to-mouth breathing. He continued holding her head and neck still and continued monitoring her airway even after she began breathing on her own again.*

Mom didn't lose control either. She didn't start screaming or crying. She didn't run around in circles. Once Alice regained consciousness, she realized her daughter was looking at her, watching. She taught her daughter that day how to survive a crisis by providing an example. She used a calm approach, quietly talking to her daughter and explaining what was happening in a manner that did not frighten Alice. Throughout the ordeal, Mom's eyes and her voice asked her daughter to trust, conveyed confidence and compassion, and delivered an ageless and extraordinary power—the love of a mother for her child.

APPENDIX:
RESOURCE GUIDE

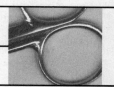

**American Academy of Child &
Adolescent Psychiatry**
P.O. Box 96106
Washington DC 20090
800-333-7636
www.aacap.org

**American Academy of Emergency
Medicine**
611 East Wells Street
Milwaukee, WI 53202
800-884-2236
www.aaem.org

American Academy of Pediatrics
141 N.W. Point Boulevard
Elk Grove Village, IL 60007
847-434-8000
www.aap.org

American Burn Association
625 N. Michigan Avenue
Ste. 1530
Chicago, IL 60611
800-548-2876
www.ameriburn.org

**American College of Emergency
Physicians**
P.O. Box 619911
Dallas, TX 75261
800-798-1822
www.acep.org

American College of Surgeons
633 N. Saint Clare Street
Chicago, IL 60611
312-202-5155
www.facs.org

American Heart Association
7272 Greenville Avenue
Dallas, TX 75231
214-373-6300
www.americanheart.org

American Medical Association
515 N. State Street
Chicago, IL 60610
312-464-5000
www.ama-assn.org

American Public Health Association
Injury Control and Emergency
Health Services Section
4770 Buford Highway N.E.
Atlanta, Georgia
770-488-3112
www.icehs.org

American Red Cross
8111 Gatehouse Road
Falls Church, VA 22042
703-206-6000
www.redcross.org

American Trauma Society
8903 Presidential Parkway
Ste. 512
Upper Marlboro, MD 20772
800-556-7890
www.amtrauma.org

Association of Emergency Physicians
127 Branchaw Boulevard
Lenox, IL 60451
800-449-4237
www.aep.org

Brain Injury Association
105 N. Alfred Street
Alexandria, VA 22314
800-444-6443
www.biausa.org

Brain Trauma Foundation
523 East 72nd Street
New York, NY 10021
212-772-0608
www.braintrauma.org

Citizen CPR Foundation
C/o National Center for Early
Defibrillation
University of Pittsburgh
230 McKee Place, Ste. 911
Pittsburgh, PA 15213
412-647-7932
www.citizencpr.org

Compassionate Friends, The
P.O. Box 3696
Oak Brook, IL 60522
630-990-0010
www.compassionatefriends.org

Emergency Medical Services for Children (EMSC)
National Resource Center
111 Michigan Avenue NW
Washington DC 20010
202-884-4927
www.ems-c.org

Emergency Nurses Association
915 Lee Street
Des Plaines, IL 60016
847-460-4000
www.ena.org

Families USA
1334 G Street NW
Washington DC 20005
202-628-3030
www.familiesusa.org

Food Allergy & Anaphylaxis Network, The
4744 Holly Avenue
Fairfax, VA 22030-5647
703-691-3179
www.foodallergy.org

Health Care Financing Administration
7500 Security Boulevard
Baltimore, MD 21244
410-786-3000
www.cms.hhs.gov

Health Resources and Services Administration
Maternal and Child Health Bureau
U.S. Department of Health and Human Services
EMS for Children Project
5600 Fishers Lane, Room 18A-55
Rockville, MD 20857
www.ems-c.org/   At this site, click on "Topics A to Z"
Choose E
Click on Emergency Medical Services for Children

International Association of Fire Chiefs
4025 Fair Ridge Drive, Suite 300
Fairfax, VA 22033
703-273-0911
www.ichiefs.org

International Association of Fire Fighters
1750 New York Avenue NW
3rd Floor
Washington DC 20006
202-737-8484
www.iaff.org

Joint Commission on Accreditation of Healthcare Organizations
1 Renaissance Boulevard
Oakbrook Terrace, IL 60181
630-792-5000
www.jcaho.org

National Association of Emergency Medical Technicians
408 Monroe Street
Clinton, MS 39056
601-924-7744
www.naemt.org

National Center for Injury Prevention and Control
Centers for Disease Control and Prevention
U.S. Department of Health and Human Services
4770 Buford Highway
Atlanta, GA 30341
www.cdc.gov/ncipc

National Clearinghouse on Child Abuse and Neglect Information
330 C Street SW
Washington DC 20447
703-385-7565
www.calib.com/nccanch

National Emergency Medicine Association
306 West Joppa Road
Baltimore, MD 21204
410-494-0300
www.nemahealth.org

National Fire Protection Association
1 Batterymarch Park
Quincy, MA 02269
www.nfpa.org

National Health Information Center
P.O. Box 1133
Washington DC 20013
800-336-4797
http://www.heath.gov/NHIC/

National Highway Traffic Safety Administration
U.S. Department of Transportation
400 Seventh Street SW
Washington DC 20590
www.nhtsa.dot.gov

National Safe Kids Campaign
1301 Pennsylvania Avenue NW
Suite 1000
Washington DC 20004
www.safekids.org

National Safety Council
1121 Spring Lake Drive
Itasca, IL 60143
www.nsc.org

National Sudden Infant Death Syndrome Resource Center
2070 Chain Bridge Road
Suite 450
Vienna, VA 22182
703-821-8955
www.sidscenter.org

Society of Trauma Nurses
2743 South Veterans Parkway
Springfield, IL 62704
www.traumanursesoc.org

United Network for Organ Sharing
1100 Boulders Parkway, Suite 500
Richmond, VA 23225
www.unos.org

U.S. Consumer Product Safety Commission
4330 East-West Highway
Bethesda, MD 20814
800-638-2772
www.cpsc.gov

U.S. Fire Administration
16825 South Seton Avenue
Emmitsburg, MD 21727
www.usfa.fema.gov

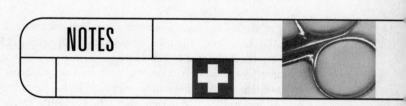

NOTES

PROLOGUE

1. *Accidental Death and Disability: The Neglected Disease of Modern Society*
   National Academy of Sciences National Research Council, 1966.
2. *Injury Facts, 1999 Edition* (Itasca, Ill: National Safety Council, 1999).
3. Ibid.

CHAPTER 1. PREPARING FOR AN EMERGENCY

1. A. K. Shetty et al., "Preparedness of Practicing Pediatricians in Louisiana to Manage Emergencies," *South Med J* 91, no. 8 (August 1998): 745–48.
2. B. W. Heath et al., "Pediatric Office Emergencies and Emergency Preparedness in a Rural State," *Pediatrics* 106, no. 6 (December 2000): 1,391–96.
3. C. O. Davis et al., "Use of EMS for Seriously Ill Children in the Office: A Survey of Primary Care Physicians," *Prehospital Emergency Care* 3, no. 2 (April/June 1999): 102–6.
4. American Academy of Pediatrics Ad Hoc Task Force on the Definition of the Medical Home, "The Medical Home," *Pediatrics* 90, no. 5 (November 1992): 774.

5. G. P. Young et al., "Ambulatory Visits to Hospital Emergency Departments: Patterns and Reasons for Use," *JAMA* 276 (August 14, 1996): 460.

6. Lloyd M. Krieger, "Managed Care Faces Emergency Room Showdown," *Insight on the News* 13, no. 16 (May 5, 1997): 30.

7. Nina Bernstein, "38% Asthma Rate Found in Homeless Children," *New York Times,* May 5, 1999, B1.

8. Chang et al., "Geographic Distribution of Pediatricians in the United States: An Analysis of the Fifty States and Washington, D.C.," *Pediatrics* 100, no. 2 (August 1997): 172.

9. "Emergency Medical Services Agenda for the Future," National Highway Traffic Safety Administration with the Health Resources and Services Administration, Maternal and Child Health Bureau. http://nhtsa.gov

10. Robert Pear, "Many States Slow to Use Children's Insurance Fund," *New York Times,* May 9, 1999, A1.

11. "State Children's Health Insurance Program (SCHIP) Aggregate Enrollment Statistics for the 50 States and the District of Columbia for Federal Fiscal Years (FFY) 2000 and 1999," United States Department of Health and Human Services, Health Care Finance Administration. http://www.hcfa.gov/init/chsatus.htm

CHAPTER 5. COPING WITH TRAUMA

1. *Injury Facts, 1999 Edition* (Itasca, Ill.: National Safety Council, 1999).

2. S. Coffman et al., "Perceptions, Safety Behaviors, and Learning Needs of Parents of Children Brought to an Emergency Department," *Journal of Emergency Nursing* 24, no. 2 (April 1998): 133.

3. S. Shafi et al., "Impact of Bicycle Helmet Safety Legislation on Children Admitted to a Regional Pediatric Trauma Center," *Journal of Pediatric Surgery* 33, no. 2 (February 1998): 317.

4. D. L. Johnson et al., "Send Severely Head-Injured Children to a Pediatric Trauma Center," *Pediatric Neurosurgery* 25, no. 6 (December 1996): 309.

5. J. E. Svenson et al., "Factors Associated with the Higher Traumatic Death Rate Among Rural Children," *Annals of Emergency Medicine* 27, no. 5 (May 1996): 625.

6. B. H. Harris et al., "Hospital Reimbursement for Pediatric Trauma Care," *Journal of Pediatric Surgery* 31, no. 1 (January 1996): 78.

CHAPTER 6. AUTOMOBILE ACCIDENT

1. *Injury Facts, 1998 Edition* (Itasca, Ill: National Safety Council, 1999).
2. D. A. Patrick et al., "Driveway Crush Injuries in Young Children: A Highly Lethal, Devastating, and Potentially Preventable Event," *Journal of Pediatric Surgery* 33, no. 1 (November 1998): 1,712.
3. J. M. Lynch et al., "The Continuing Problem of All-Terrain Vehicle Injuries in Children," *Journal of Pediatric Surgery* 33, no. 2 (February 1998): 329.
4. J. Y. Liu et al., "Teenage Driving Fatalities," *Journal of Pediatric Surgery* 33, no. 7 (July 1998): 1,084–88.

CHAPTER 7. BURNS

1. *Injury Facts, 1998 Edition* (Itasca, Ill: National Safety Council, 1998).
2. M. J. Karter, *Fire Loss in the United States During 1999* (Quincy, Mass.: National Fire Protection Association, 2000).

CHAPTER 8. DROWNING

1. American Academy of Pediatrics Committee on Injury and Poison Prevention, *Injury Prevention and Control for Children and Youth,* 3rd ed. (American Academy of Pediatrics, 1997).

CHAPTER 10. HEAD TRAUMA

1. S. Puranik et al., "Profile of Pediatric Bicycle Injuries," *Southern Medical Journal* 91, no. 11 (November 1998): 1,033.
2. W. C. Boswell et al., "Prevention of Pediatric Mortality from Trauma: Are Current Measures Adequate?" *Southern Medical Journal* 89, no. 2 (February 1996): 218.
3. *Accident Facts, 1998 Edition* (Itasca, Ill: National Safety Council, 1998).
4. E. C. Powell et al., "Bicycle-Related Injuries Among Preschool Children," *Annals of Emergency Medicine* 30, no. 3 (September 1997): 260.
5. J. S. Osberg et al., "Skateboarding: More Dangerous Than Roller Skating or In-Line Skating," *Archives of Pediatric and Adolescent Medicine* 152, no. 10 (October 1998): 985.
6. F. K. Winston et al., "Hidden Spears: Handlebars as Injury Hazards to Children," *Pediatrics* 102, no. 3 (September 1998): 596.
7. J. E. Schunk et al., "The Utility of Head Computed Tomographic Scanning in Pediatric Patients with Normal Neurologic Examination in the Emergency Department," *Pediatric Emergency Care* 12, no. 3 (June 1996): 10–15.

CHAPTER 13. FEVERS AND SEIZURES

1. S. I. Bauchner et al., "Parents, Physicians, and Antibiotic Use," *Pediatrics* 103, no. 2 (February 1999): 395.
2. H. K. Simon et al., "Over-the-Counnter Medications: Do Parents Give What They Intend to Give?" *Archives of Pediatrics & Adolescent Medicine* 151, no. 7 (July 1997): 654–57.

CHAPTER 14. WHEN POISONS GET IN

1. T. L. Litovitz et al., *1996 Annual Report of the American Association of Poison Control Centers Toxic Exposure Surveillance System* 15 (1997): 447–500.

BIBLIOGRAPHY

Aithen, M. E. et al. "Minor Head Injury in Children: Current Management Practices of Pediatricians, Emergency Physicians, and Family Physicians." *Archives of Pediatrics and Adolescent Medicine* 152, no. 12 (December 1998):1,176.

America Academy of Pediatrics Ad Hoc Task Force on the Definition of the Medical Home. "Medical Home." *Pediatrics* 90, no. 5 (November 1992):774.

American Academy of Pediatrics Committee on Adolescence. "The Teenage Driver." *Pediatrics* 98, no. 5 (November 1996):987.

American Academy of Pediatrics Committee on Adolescence. "Suicide and Suicide Attempts in Adolescents and Young Adults." *Pediatrics* 8, no. 2 (February 1988):322.

American Academy of Pediatrics Committee on Child Abuse and Neglect. "Investigation and Review of Unexpected Infant and Child Deaths." *Pediatrics* 104, no. 5 (November 1999):1158.

American Academy of Pediatrics Committee on Environmental Health. "Toxic Effects of Indoor Molds." *Pediatrics* 101, no. 4 (April 1998):712.

American Academy of Pediatrics Committee on Injury and Poison Prevention. "Bicycle Helmets." *Pediatrics* 95, no. 4 (April 1995):609.

American Academy of Pediatrics Committee on Injury and Poison Prevention. "Children and Fireworks." *Pediatrics* 88, no. 3 (September 1991):652.

American Academy of Pediatrics Committee on Injury and Poison Prevention. "Drowning in Infants, Children, and Adolescents." *Pediatrics* 92, no. 2 (August 1993):292.

American Academy of Pediatrics Committee on Injury and Poison Prevention. "Injuries Associated with Infant Walkers." *Pediatrics* 95, no. 5 (May 1995):778.

American Academy of Pediatrics Committee on Injury and Poison Prevention. *Injury Prevention and Control for Children and Youth*. American Academy of Pediatrics, 1997.

American Academy of Pediatrics Committee on Injury and Poison Prevention. "Skateboarding Injuries." *Pediatrics* 95, no. 4 (April 1995):611.

American Academy of Pediatrics Committee on Injury and Poison Prevention and the Committee on Sports Medicine and Fitness. "In-Line Skating Injuries in Children and Adolescents." *Pediatrics* 101, no. 4 (April 1998):720.

American Academy of Pediatrics Committee on Injury and Poison Prevention and the Committee on Sports Medicine and Fitness. "Trampolines at Home, School, and Recreation Centers." *Pediatrics* 103, no. 5 (May 1999):1,053.

American Academy of Pediatrics Committee on Pediatric Medicine. "Guidelines for Pediatric Emergency Care Facilities." *Pediatrics* 96, no. 3 (September 1995):526.

American Academy of Pediatrics Committee on Pediatric Medicine. "The Role of the Pediatrician in Rural EMSC." *Pediatrics* 101, no. 5 (May 1998):941.

American Academy of Pediatrics Committee on Sports Medicine and Fitness. "Horseback Riding and Head Injuries." *Pediatrics* 89, no. 3 (March 1992):512.

American Academy of Pediatrics Committee on Substance Abuse and Committee on Native American Child Health. "Inhalant Abuse." *Pediatrics* 97, no. 3 (March 1996).

American Academy of Pediatrics Task Force on Infant Positioning and SIDS. "Positioning and Sudden Infant Death Syndrome (SIDS). Update." *Pediatrics* 98, no. 6 (December 1996):1,216.

Andazola, J.J. et al. "The Choking Child: What Happens Before the Ambulance Arrives?" *PreHospital Emergency Care* 3, no. 1 (January/March 1999):7.

Anderson, B.D. et al. "Diversion of 911 Poisoning Calls to a Poison Center." *PreHospital Emergency Care* 2, no. 3 (July/September 1998):176.

Arkovitz, M.S. et al. "Pancreatic Trauma in Children: Mechanisms of Injury." *Journal of Trauma* 42, no. 1 (January 1997):49.

Baker, R.C. et al. "After-Hours Telephone Triage and Advice in Private and Nonprivate Pediatric Populations." *Archives of Pediatrics and Adolescent Medicine* 153, no. 3 (March 1999):292.

Bauchner, H. et al. "Parents, Physicians, and Antibiotic Use." *Pediatrics* 103, no. 2 (February 1999):395.

Bauchner, H. et al. "Reducing Inappropriate Oral Antibiotic Use: A Prescription for Change." *Pediatrics* 102, no. 1 (July 1998):142.

Bensard, D.D. et al. "Small Bowel Injury in Children After Blunt Abdominal Trauma: Is Diagnostic Delay Important?" *Journal of Trauma* 41, no. 3 (September 1996):476.

Berman, S. et al. "Otitis Media-Related Antibiotic Prescribing Patterns, Outcomes, and Expenditures in a Pediatric Medicaid Population." *Pediatrics* 100, no. 1 (October 1997):585.

Bernstein, N. "38% Asthma Rate Found in Homeless Children." *The New York Times,* May 9, 1999, A1.

Bhattacharyya, N. et al. "The Childhood Air Gun: Serious Injuries and Surgical Interventions." *Pediatric Emergency Care* 14, no. 3 (June 1998):188.

Bond, S.J. et al. "Nonoperative Management of Blunt Hepatic and Splenic Injury in Children." *Annals of Surgery* 223, no. 3 (March 1996):286.

Boswell, W.C. et al. "Prevention of Pediatric Mortality from Trauma: Are Current Measures Adequate?" *Southern Medical Journal* 89, no. 2 (February 1996):218.

Brenner, R.A. et al. "Deaths Attributable to Injuries in Infants, United States 1983–1991." *Pediatrics* 103, no. 5 (May 1999):968.

Brown, J.L. *Pediatric Telephone Medicine: Principles, Triage and Advice.* 2nd ed. Lippincott-Raven Publishers, 1997.

Cady, G. et al. "2000 200-City Survey." *Journal of Emergency Medical Services* 26, no. 2 (February 2001):24.

Canty, Sr., T.G. et al. "Injuries of the Gastrointenstinal Tract from Blunt Trauma in Children: A 12-Year Experience at a Designated Pediatric Trauma Center." *Journal of Trauma* 46, no. 2 (February 1999):234.

Carraccio, C. L. et al. "Family Member Knowledge of Children's Medical Problems: The Need for Universal Application of an Emergency Data Set." *Pediatrics* 102 (2 Pt 1) (August 1998):367.

Coffman, S. et al. "Perceptions, Safety Behaviors, and Learning Needs of Parents of Children Brought to an Emergency Department." *Journal of Emergency Nursing* 24, no. 2 (April 1998):133.

Cox Jr., C. S. et al. "Pediatric Blunt Abdominal Trauma: Role of Computed Tomography Vascular Blush. *Journal of Pediatric Surgery* 32, no. 8 (August 1997):1,196.

Christakis, D. A. et al. "Is Greater Continuity of Care Associated with Less Emergency Department Utilization?" *Pediatrics* 103, no. 4 (April 1999):738.

DiScala, C. et al. "Injuries to Children with Attention Deficit Hyperactivity Disorder." *Pediatrics* 102, no. 6 (December 1998):1,415.

Farah, M. M. et al. "Firearms in the Home: Parental Perceptions." *Pediatrics* 104, no. 5 (November 1999):1,059–63.

Flores, G. et al. "Access Barriers to Health Care for Latino Children." *Archives of Pediatrics and Adolescent Medicine* (November 1998):1,119.

Friday, G. A. et al. "Profile of Children Requiring Emergency Treatment for Asthma." *Annals of Allergy, Asthma and Immunology* 72, no. 7 (February 1997):221.

Gandhi, R. R. et al. "Laparoscopy in Pediatric Abdominal Trauma." *Journal of the Society of Laparoendoscopic Surgery* 1, no. 4 (October–December 1997):32.

Gervasini, A. A. "Care of the Critically Injured Child: Nonaccidental Injuries." *Critical Care Nursing Quarterly* 20, no. 2 (August 1997):79.

Grant, W. J. et al. "Tracheobronchial Injuries After Blunt Chest Trauma in Children—Hidden Pathology." *Journal of Pediatric Surgery* 23, no. 11 (November 1998):1,707.

Grossman, L. K. et al. "Decreasing Nonurgent Emregency Department Utilization by Medicaid Children." *Pediatrics* 102, no. 1 (July 1998):20.

Gruskin, K. D. et al. "Head Trauma in Children Younger Than 2 Years: Are There Predictors for Complications?" *Archives of Pediatrics and Adolescent Medicine* 153, no. 1 (January 1999):15.

Harris, B. H. et al. "Hospital Reimbursement for Pediatric Trauma Care." *Journal of Pediatric Surgery* 31, no. 1 (January 1996):78.

Hartzog, T. H. et al. "Pediatric Trauma: Enabling Factors, Social Situations, and Outcome." *Academy of Emergency Medicine* 3, no. 3 (March 1996):213.

Heath, B. W. et al. "Pediatric Office Emergencies and Emergency Preparedness in a Small Rural State," *Pediatrics*, December 2000, 106:6, p. 1,391.

Heighton, A. J. "Assault on Columbine." *Journal of Emergency Medical Services* 24, no. 9 (September 1999).

Injury Facts, 1999 Edition. Itasca, Ill. National Safety Council, 1999.

Injury Facts, 1998 Edition. Itasca Ill.: National Safety Council, 1998.

Jerby, B. L. et al. "Blunt Intestinal Injury in Children: The Role of the
Physical Examination." *Journal of Pediatric Surgery* 32, no. 4, (April
1997): 580.

Johnson, D. L. et al. "Send Severely Head-Injured Children to a Pediatric
Trauma Center." *Pediatric Neurosurgery* 25, no. 6 (December 1996):309.

Keller, M. S. et al. "Conservative Management of Pancreatic Trauma in
Children." *Journal of Trauma* 42, no. 6 (June 1997):1,097.

Krieger, L. M. "Managed Care Faces Emergency Room Showdown." *Insight
on the News* 13, no. 6 (May 5, 1997):30.

Kurkchubasche, A. G. et al. "Blunt Intestinal Injury in Children. Diagnostic and Therapeutic Considerations." *Archives of Surgery* 132, no. 6
(June 1997):652.

Lavelle, J. M. et al. "Evaluation of Head Injury in a Pediatric Emergency
Department: Pretrauma and Posttrauma System." *Archives of Pediatrics
and Adolescent Medicine* 152, no. 12 (December 1998):1,220.

Li, G. et al. "Characteristics and Outcomes of Self Inflicted Pediatric
Injuries: The Role of Method of Suicide Attempt." *Injury Prevention*
3, no. 2 (June 1997):115.

Lieu, T. A. et al. "Outpatient Management Practices Associated with
Reduced Risk of Pediatric Asthma Hospitilization and Emergency
Department Visits?" *Pediatrics* 100, no. 3 (September 1997):334.

Liu, J. Y. et al. "Teenage Driving Fatalities." *Journal of Pediatric Surgery* 33,
no. 7 (July 1998):1,084.

Lynch, J. M. et al. "Hemodynamic Significance of Pediatric Femur Fractures." *Journal of Pediatric Surgery* 31, no. 10 (October 1996):1,358.

Lynch, J. M. et al. "The Continuing Problem of All-Terrain Vehicle
Injuries in Children." *Journal of Pediatric Surgery* 33, no. 2 (February
1998):329.

Mangione-Smith, R. et al. "The Relationship Between Perceived Parental
Expectations and Pediatrician Antimicrobial Prescribing Behavior."
Pediatrics 103, no. 4 (April 1999):711.

Marshall, K. W. et al. "Air Bag-Related Deaths and Serious Injuries in
Children: Injury Patterns and Imaging Findings." *American Journal of
Neuroradiology* 19, no. 9 (October 1998):1599.

McConnochie, K. M. et al. "How Commonly Are Children Hospitalized for Asthma Eligible for Care in Alternative Settings?" *Archives of Pediatrics and Adolescent Medicine* 153, no. 1 (January 1999):49.

Miller, K. et al. "Pediatric Hepatic Trauma: Does Clinical Course Support Intensive Care Unit Stay?" *Journal of Pediatric Surgery* 33, no. 10 (October 1998):1459.

Mlcak, R. et al. "Emergency Management of Pediatric Burn Victims." *Pediatric Emergency Care* 14, no. 1 (February 1998):51.

Monaco, J. E. "Commonly Ingested Nontoxic Substances." *Pediatrics for Parents* 18, no. 3 (March 1999):7.

Moss, R. L. et al. "Clinical Judgement is Superior to Diagnostic Tests in the Management of Pediatric Small Bowel Injury." *Journal of Pediatric Surgery* 31, no. 8 (August 1996):1,178.

Accidental Death and Disability: The Neglected Disease of Modern Society. National Academy of Sciences National Research Council, 1966.

Neumark, Y. D. et al. "The Epidemiology of Adolescent Inhalant Drug Involvement," *Archives of Pediatrics and Adolescent Medicine* 152, no. 8 (August 1998):781.

Osberg, J. S. et al. "Skateboarding: More Dangerous Than Roller Skating or In-Line Skating." *Archives of Pediatrics and Adolescent Medicine* 152, no. 10 (October 1998):985.

Oyen, N. et al. "Combined Effects of Sleeping Position and Prenatal Risk Factors in Sudden Infant Death Syndrome: The Nordic Epidemiological SIDS Study." *Pediatrics* 100, no. 4 (October 1997): 613.

Parkinson, G. W. et al. "Anxiety in Parents of Young Febrile Children in a Pediatric Emergency Department: Why Is It Elevated?" *Clinical Pediatrics* 38, no. 4 (April 1999):219.

Patrick, D. A. et al. "Driveway Crush Injuries in Young Children: A Highly Lethal, Devastating, and Potentially Preventable Event." *Journal of Pediatric Surgery* 33, no. 11 (November 1998):1,712.

Pear, R. "Many States Slow to Use Children's Insurance Fund." *The New York Times*, May 9, 1999, A1.

Pearson, G. D. et al. "A Retrospective Review of the Role of Transesophageal Echocardiography in Aortic and Cardiac Trauma in a Level I Pediatric Trauma Center." *Journal of American Society of Echocardiography* 10, no. 9 (November–December 1997):946.

Powell, E. C. et al. "Bicycle-Related Injuries Among Preschool Children." *Annals of Emergency Medicine* 30, no. 3 (September 1997):260.

PreHospital Trauma Life Support Committee of the National Association of Emergency Medical Technicians in cooperation with the Committee on Trauma of the American College of Surgeons. *PHTLS.* Edited by N. E. McSwain et al. 3rd ed. Mosby Year Book, 1994.

Puranik, S. et al. "Profile of Pediatric Bicycle Injuries." *Southern Medical Journal* 91, no. 11 (November 1998):1,033.

Randolph, G. D. et al. "Trends in the Rural-Urban Distribution of General Pediatricians." *Pediatrics* 107, no. 2 (February 2001):E18.

Rivara, F. P. "Pediatric Injury Control in 1999: Where Do We Go from Here?" *Pediatrics* 103, no. 4 (April 1999):883.

Schmitt, B. D. *Pediatric Telephone Advice.* 2nd ed. Lippincott-Raven Publishers, 1999.

Scholer, S. J. et al. "Predictors of Injury Mortality in Early Childhood." *Pediatrics* 100, no. 3 (September 1997):342.

Schunk, J. F. et al. "The Utility of Head Computed Tomographic Scanning in Pediatric Patients with Normal Neurologic Examination in the Emergency Department." *Pediatric Emergency Care* 12, no. 3 (June 1996):160.

Seidel, J. S. et al. *Prehospital Care of Pediatric Emergencies.* 2nd ed. Sudburg, Massachusetts n.p.: Jones and Bartlett Publishers, 1997.

Shafi, S. et al. "Impact of Bicycle Helmet Safety Legislation on Children Admitted to a Regional Pediatric Trauma Center." *Journal of Pediatric Surgery* 33, no. 2 (February 1998):317.

Shepherd, G. and W. Klein-Schwartz. "Accidental and Suicidal Adolescent Poisoning Deaths in the United States, 1979–1994." *Archives of Pediatrics and Adolescent Medicine* 152, no. 12 (December 1998):1,181.

Shetty, A. K. et al. "Preparedness of Practicing Pediatricians in Louisiana to manage Emergencies." *Southern Medical Journal* 91, no. 8 (August 1998):745.

Shorter, N. A. et al. "Childhood Sledding Injuries." *American Journal of Emergency Medicine* 17, no. 12 (January 1999):32.

Shorter, N. A. et al. "Skiing Injuries in Children and Adolescents." *Journal of Trauma* 40, no. 6 (June 1996):997.

Simon, A. J. et al. "Is Continuity of Care Preserved in Children Who Utilize the Pediatric Emergency Department?" *Pediatrics* 95, no. 1 (January 1995):37.

Simon, H. K. et al. "Over-the-Counter Medications: Do Parents Give What They Intend to Give?" *Archives of Pediatrics and Adolescent Medicine* 151, no. 7 (July 1997):654.

Smith, G. A. et al. "The Rockets' Red Glare, the Bombs Bursting in Air: Fireworks-Related Injuries in Children." *Pediatrics* 98, no. 1 (July 1996):1.

Smith, G. A. et al. "Trampoline-Related Injuries to Children," *Archives of Pediatrics and Adolescent Medicine* 152, no. 7 (July 1998):694.

Stoddara, J. J. et al. "General Pediatricians, Pediatric Subspecialists, and Pediatric Primary Care." *Archives of Pediatrics and Adolescent Medicine* 152, no. 8 (August 1998):768.

Strange, G. R., ed. *APLS: The Pediatric Emergency Medicine Course.* 3rd ed. American College of Emergency Physicians and the American Academy of Pediatrics, 1998.

Suominen, P. et al. "Prehospital Care and Survival of Pediatric Patients with Blunt Trauma." *Journal of Pediatric Surgery* 33, no. 9 (September 1998):1,388.

Svenson, J. E. et al. "Factors Associated with the Higher Traumatic Death Rate Among Rural Children." *Annals of Emergency Medicine* 27, no. 5 (May 1996):625.

Thouran, V. H. et al. "Validation of Surgeon-Performed Emergency Abdominal Ultrasonography in Pediatric Trauma Patients." *Journal of Pediatric Surgery* 33, no. 2 (February 1998):322.

Townley, R. *Safe and Sound.* New York, Simon and Schuster, 1985.

Trachiotis, G. D. et al. "Traumatic Thoracic Aortic Rupture in the Pediatric Patient." *Annals of Thoracic Surgery* 63, no. 3 (September 1996):724.

Highlights of the National Health Care Expenditure Projections 1997–2000, U.S. Department of Health and Human Services, Health Care Finance Administration. September 14, 1998.

Emergency Medical Services Agenda for the Future. U.S. Department of Transportation, National Highway Traffic Safety Administration and the U.S. Department of Health and Human Services Public Health Services, Health Resources and Services Administration, Maternal and Child Health Bureau, 1996.

"State Children's Health Insurance Program (SCHIP) Aggregate Enrollment Statistics for the 50 States and the District of Columbia for Federal Fiscal Years (FFY) 2000 and 1999." U.S. Department of Health and Human Services, Health Care Finance Administration. http://www.hcfa.gov/init/chsatus.htm

Van Stuijvenberg, M. et al. "Temperature, Age, and Recurrence of Febrile Seizure." *Archives of Pediatrics and Adolescent Medicine* 152, no. 12 (December 1998):1,170.

Vernon, D. D. et al. "Effect of a Pediatric Trauma Response Team on Emergency Department Treatment Time and Mortality of Pediatric Trauma Victims." *Pediatrics* 103, no. 1 (January 1999):20.

Warman, K. L. et al. "How Does Home Management of Asthma Exacerbations by Parents of Inner-City Children Differ from NHLBI Guideline Recommendations?" *Pediatrics* 103, no. 2 (February 1999):422.

Weinreb, L. et al. "Homeless Children Are More Likely to Have Poor Health and to Use More Medical Services Than Low-Income Housed Children." *Pediatrics* 102, no. 3 (September 1998):554.

Winston, F. K. et al. "Hidden Spears: Handlebars as Injury Hazards to Children." *Pediatrics* 102, no. 3 (September 1998):596.

Young, G. P. et al. "Ambulatory Visits to Hospital Emergency Department: Patterns and Reasons for Use." *The Journal of the American Medical Association* 276, no. 6 (August 14, 1996):460.

Zuckerman, G. B. et al. "Predictors of Death and Neurologic Impairment in Pediatric Submersion Injuries. The Pediatric Risk of Mortality Score." *Archives of Pediatrics and Adolescent Medicine* 152, no. 2 (February 1998):134.

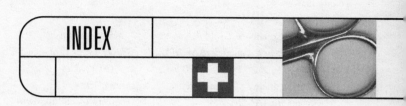

INDEX